ONE STORY, THIRTY STORIES

ONE STORY, THIRTY STORIES

*An Anthology of Contemporary
Afghan American Literature*

♦ ♦ ♦

EDITED BY
ZOHRA SAED AND SAHAR MURADI

The University of Arkansas Press
Fayetteville • 2010

ISBN-10: 1-55728-946-8 (cloth)
ISBN-10: 1-55728-945-X (paper)
ISBN-13: 978-1-55728-946-9 (cloth)
ISBN-13: 978-1-55728-945-2 (paper)

14   13   12   11   10   5   4   3   2   1

Text design by Ellen Beeler

♾The paper used in this publication meets the minimum requirements of the American National Standard for Permanence of Paper for Printed Library Materials Z39.48-1984.

Library of Congress Cataloging-in-Publication Data

One story, thirty stories : an anthology of contemporary Afghan American
    literature / edited by Zohra Saed and Sahar Muradi.
        p. cm.
    Includes index.
    ISBN 978-1-55728-946-9 (cloth : alk. paper) — ISBN 978-1-55728-945-2
    (pbk. : alk. paper)
    1. American literature—Afghan American authors. 2. Afghan Americans—
    Literary collections. I. Saed, Zohra, 1975– II. Muradi, Sahar, 1979–
    PS508.A43O54 2010
    810.8'0891593073—dc22

                                                              2010027659

Contents

Foreword by Mir Tamim Ansary   ix
Introduction   xi

POETRY

SEDIKA MOJADIDI
"Marriage to Azim"   3

MASOOD KAMANDY
"Time Passes in Colorado"   7

DONIA GOBAR
"As I Watch"   9

MARIAM GHANI
"Notes on the Disappeared"   10

NAHID FATTAHI
"Pick Me, Please!"   13

JESSAMYN ANSARY
"age three at grandpa's funeral"   15
"The Invention"   16

QAIS ARSALA
"Horns of the Tiger"   17
"Demystified Calamity"   17
"Placebo"   18

SAHAR MURADI
"Of My Mother"   19
"Exile, or My Father's Elbow"   21

KHALIDA SETHI
"*Astagfurillah* (God Forbid!)"   23

ARIANA DELAWARI

"Oh la Lo" 25

"Cheshme Siah Daree" 26

ZOHRA SAED

"Neptune Avenue" 28

"Family Album" 29

NAHEED ELYASI

"Awaiting My Return" 32

YALDA ASMATEY

"My Thoughts . . . If You Don't Mind" 34

AMAN MOJADIDI

"What Can One Say about Living in Kabul?" 36

WAJMA AHMADY

"What? You Never . . ." 39

FICTION

MIR TAMIM ANSARY

"Dreaming in Dari" 43

WALI SHAAKER

"Identity Card" 50

FARHAD AZAD

"The Broken Window" 54

"An Old Garden" 56

DONIA GOBAR

"Aya" 59

NAHEED ELYASI

"Living on a Prayer" 66

NUSHIN ARBABZADAH

"Like a Rabbit Caught in the Spotlight" 70

WAJMA AHMADY

"My Earliest Memories"   73

ESSAYS

MALIHA ZULFACAR

"Coming to America, 1966"   85

AMAN MOJADIDI

"Home"   93

YASMINE DELAWARI JOHNSON

"The Girl with the Green Eyes"   103

ASADULLA ABUBAKR

"The Irony of Life and the Survival of the American Dream"   106

KHALIDA SETHI

"My Mother"   113

RAMEEN JAVID MOSHREF

"The Odyssey of Coming to America"   116
"Who the Hell is the Foreigner?!"   121

SAHAR MURADI

"The Things They Wait For"   125

NADIA MAIWANDI

"The Enemy"   128

ZOHRA SAED

"A Week Later"   135

FAHIM ANWAR

"Stand-Up Comedy"   140

TAREQ MIRZA

"Journey to Afghanistan, September 2002"   145

ARIANA DELAWARI

"A Penny"   154

HOMIRA NASSERY
"Voting in Afghanistan"   161

HALIMA KAZEM
"Afghan Awakening"   165

WAHEEDA SAMADY
"The Cab Driver's Daughter"   171

BISMILLAH IQBAL
"Hope Street"   174

AFIFA YUSUFI
"Daughter of the Imam: From Kandahar to Queens"   181

MARIAM EBRAT
"The Critic"   190

FARHAD AHAD
"An Afghan American Perspective"   196
"Memories from Kabul's Playing Fields"   197

AWISTA AYUB
"You Proved Me Wrong"   201

BLOGS

MASOOD KAMANDY
"Dispatches from Kabul"   209

GAZELLE SAMIZAY
"Gazelle Speaks"   234

Appendix: Themes Index   249
Chronology of Afghan American History   255
Index of Authors and Titles   263
Contributors   267

Foreword

American literature like America itself is a patchwork of ethnic influences. Today a new voice is joining that multicultural conversation. Afghan Americans are among the newest (and smallest) of America's ethnic communities, just several hundred thousand people distributed across the country in scattered pockets, a community born of a disaster halfway around the planet: in the last decades of the twentieth century, a revolution, an invasion from the north, a civil war, and finally a descent into chaos, utter chaos, which drove millions of refugees out of Afghanistan. Among those millions, a tiny minority had the means and motivation to make it all the way to the United States, and here, bereft of context and connections, cut off from their national history, family memories, and childhood dreams, they struggled to forge a new life as exiles in a strange land.

Out of this immigrant experience, a literature is now emerging. Most English-speaking readers got their first taste of the new voice from Khaled Hosseini's landmark 2003 novel, *The Kite Runner.* But in the wake of Hosseini's dazzling debut, and in the soil he tilled, seedlings have begun to sprout here and there. In 2007, my coeditor, Yalda Asmatey, and I published *Snapshots,* the first anthology of short works by young Afghan American writers. Now, Zohra Saed and Sahar Muradi have compiled this larger and far more comprehensive collection, an admirable achievement.

Every immigrant group in America grapples with similar issues—but similar only in broad outline. This collection reveals what it is that makes the Afghan American experience particular and distinct, what sets it apart. Art wells out of personal experience, and personal experience can never be severed from history. For this generation of Afghan Americans, there is but one definitive historical event, and it's not the long-ago founding of the Afghan kingdom, not the wars of independence from the British, not any of the usual conventional turning points that give a national narrative its shape. No, for Afghan Americans the seminal event of their shared history is happening right now. It is the violence that has been raging since the 1970s and the exile it engendered. The mythic narrative is taking shape in real time, and we're in the middle of its birth.

When Afghan Americans sit down at the keyboard to compose, their thoughts are drawn inevitably to the destruction of the world their parents were born into and to the riddle of identity that confronts them as

Muslim immigrants in the United States. There is no ignoring their disjunction from the society surrounding them nor their need to claim a place in that same society. At the same time there is no escaping the urge to look for roots in an ancestral homeland many remember only dimly or have never seen, a homeland that is even now undergoing a radical transformation, thereby intertwining the quest for identity with the metaphysics of time and change, evanescence and loss.

In short, this is a literature haunted by catastrophe. But those who took the brunt of the catastrophe directly are not the ones giving voice to it. That first generation of Afghan exiles, for the most part, were too busy surviving to shape their experiences into literature. It is largely their children who take up the work, and their experience has not been the same as their parents'. They grew up struggling to navigate the shoals and rapids of life in American high schools and suburbs, at work, on the streets, and in all the various arenas that define American public life, all the while trying to reconcile the worlds inside and outside their homes. But they grew up in the shadow of the catastrophe, and that darkness pervades the works collected in *One Story, Thirty Stories,* even when the writer is exploring a situation that might crop up in anybody's literature—such as the tormented relationship between a girl and her mother, as dramatized by Naheed Elyasi in her disquieting exploration of family dysfunction; or the pathos of dislocation in old age, evoked so delicately by Sahar Muradi in her fragile portrait of her grandparents. Some pieces in this book may have a light tone—and yet, even here, the Afghan American reader (or this one at any rate) can feel the weight of darkness leaning into the light.

Coping with catastrophe is not, of course, the end of literature. Art born out of a particular collective history, however wrenching, comes into its own only when it mulches history into meaning, when it weaves the warp of everyday life—those intimate dramas of love and loss, striving and spiritual effort, familiar to people of every culture—into the woof of great events that constitute a public narrative, a shared myth. By tapping the wellsprings of their own history, the writers represented in *One Story, Thirty Stories* are taking that crucial first step toward absorbing the unique experience of Afghan Americans into the universal themes that inform human experience as a whole.

Mir Tamim Ansary
Author, *West of Kabul, East of New York,*
Destiny Disrupted, and *The Widow's Husband*

Introduction

Thirty years ago, on December 27, 1979, the Afghan Communist president Hafizullah Amin, his family and staff, had their meal laced with sedatives by their Russian chef. This was just hours before Soviet soldiers, disguised as Afghans, raided the palace in Kabul. In forty-three minutes, a war began that would last thirty years.

In 1980, shortly after the Soviet invasion, the United States became involved in supporting the Afghan mujahideen, nationalist guerrilla fighters, with weapons and military training. For American foreign policy during the Cold War, it was integral to become involved in Afghanistan because of its strategic geopolitical location. It also allowed Americans to regain a sense of fighting for a "good war" after the failures of the Vietnam War and the embarrassment of the Iran Hostage Crisis. The decade-long Soviet-Afghan war resulted in an Afghan "victory," draining the Soviet Union financially and leading to its ultimate collapse in 1990, concluding the Cold War.

The binarism of an "evil empire" versus a "free world" ended after the Cold War but was resurrected again, ironically, in Afghanistan. In 1996, the Taliban, an extremist Islamic religious movement, took advantage of a devastated civil infrastructure and seized control of the country. In exchange for financial support, it provided a base in Afghanistan for al-Qaeda, a multinational terrorist network. After the al-Qaeda–orchestrated attacks on the World Trade Center and Pentagon on September 11, 2001, the U.S.-led coalition launched a war in Afghanistan against the Taliban in October. Despite all the images of reconstructed Afghanistan as a success story in nation-building (circa 2003), "Operation Enduring Freedom" has transformed into a full-fledged war that has not ended but only deepened, with a resurgent Taliban. As we write this, thirty thousand American troops are poised to join fifty thousand already in Afghanistan, and the Afghan government is struggling to keep a hold over the country.

What is overtly known about Afghanistan and Afghans is war, destruction, and ruins, with a streak of red poppy fields and blue burqas to color the two-dimensional images of this small and landlocked country. What we offer in this first anthology of Afghan American literature is beyond these stereotypical images. It is now most urgent for us to ask, "What does it mean to be Afghan American at a time of war? How does the Afghan interlace with the American at a time when occupying these two geographic spaces in harmony seems less and less possible?"

This anthology brings to light the longer and deeper relationships between the United States and Afghanistan, the firsthand stories of Afghans who became Americans, and a map of the "Little Afghanistans" within American cities. What mostly defines Afghan American literature and artistic expression is war—surviving, witnessing, escaping, and remembering war—but also our varied arrivals to the United States, creating new homes, stitching new identities, swimming in and out of two cultures. Many Afghan Americans in this anthology came into writing as an act of urgency, even before 9/11. For some, it was a means of accessing mythic origins, handed down by parents in lush colors in contrast to the grays of newsprint on the war, or the stark white walls of ignorant questions from strangers. For others, it was a way of surviving the two streets that intersected at our front doors, leaving us wondering how to be Afghan, how to be American, and ultimately how to create a third space where our contradictions could be our strengths.

For women writers, in particular, this intersection was compounded by the gender differences between cultures. In writing, these voices claimed a space free to reflect. For other writers, where our mother tongue did not come easily, we felt at home in English and yet brought to it a lineage of the "sweetness" of Dari, or Pashto, or Uzbeki, or Hazaragi. The result is a multilingual weave of literature that finds home in its reception, in the inner ears of the listeners/readers who can decipher our new Afghan American "creole." These transplanted writers find, through the act of writing, a way to share and bridge the blank distance between "here" and "there."

To better understand the Afghan American literary tradition, it is important to contextualize our arrival and root-taking in the United States. The Soviet-Afghan war resulted in the greatest influx of Afghan refugees into the United States. In the early 1980s, mostly affluent, educated Afghan families were able to emigrate here. Many used life savings to pay smugglers to get their families out. Doctors, engineers, lawyers, and businessmen in Afghanistan now took jobs in the United States as service workers, taxi drivers, and food vendors. After becoming openly involved in the war in 1986, the United States airlifted Afghans from villages and gave them refugee status. In the diaspora, we came together across class, ethnicity, and rural/urban lines to build communities and renarrate our lives.

The 1980s was a time of adjustment and transformation. Storefront mosques slowly appeared on the streets of New York City and California.

These mosques were not the architectural wonders of our parents' generation; mostly, they were humble rooms in four-story buildings, or the second floors of houses with illustrations of domes and minarets to make up for the lack of ornate design. These mosques were places where Afghans came together for comfort, for company, and to carry on our traditions. In Queens, New York, the housing projects were filled with new Afghan refugees. Their numbers were so large that this area became known affectionately as Deh Afghanan, village of Afghans. This concentration of Afghans helped create a self-sufficient community of Afghan specialty shops, restaurants, and translation offices all along Main Street. Similar neighborhoods bloomed in other parts of the country when adventure, or desperation, or the cultural claustrophobia of immigrant neighborhoods thrust families off to New Jersey, Virginia, California, Colorado, Nebraska, and Texas. We children were raised in communities where a strong work ethic became the cornerstone of our lives, especially if our families owned businesses. Because of this new work-centered consciousness, gender relations changed. Because children became translators for their parents, parent-child relationships, which were very strict in Afghanistan, also changed. Children, especially elder children, grew to feel responsible for their families and for their parents.

We began rebuilding our lives in this new country, but with both ears attuned to what was happening in Afghanistan. Our parents believed our stay in the United States was temporary and that we would return after the war ended. But following the withdrawal of the Soviets from Afghanistan in 1989, this generation of Afghans was disappointed by the subsequent civil war and became resigned to the reality of not being able to return. Not surprisingly, thousands of Afghans became American citizens during the 1990s. Meanwhile, Afghanistan slowly disappeared from the American nightly news.

In the mid-1990s, we as second-generation Afghan Americans began articulating our experiences. Although Afghanistan disappeared from the news, it was every bit as much a part of our lives. Our parents reconstructed Afghanistan in our homes. Families designated "Afghan rooms," replete with rug-covered sitting mats; they hung maps and displayed flags. Afghan newspapers like *Caravan* were circulated at the newly opened grocery stores. Many of our parents' generation were self-proclaimed political experts, and we, the children, breathed this air of politics and memories of homeland. We weaved these moments, these voices, these inherited memories, into our own experiences of America, rural or urban, inner city or suburban, and became a mix.

Another milestone was our entrance into college, where American multiculturalism allowed us a space to build community among our peers in the form of Afghan student clubs and publications. By the summer of 1997, three Afghan American youth magazines were being published: *Afghan Communicator, Afghan Mosaic,* and the online *Lemar-Aftaab.* The young college students who were involved in these magazines were pioneers in the Afghan American community. They went on to build other community organizations, like Society of Afghan American Professionals; more commercial publications, like *Zeba* magazine; and radio stations, television stations, cultural events, and conferences. These were also the first to return and partake in the reconstruction process in Afghanistan after 2002.

Although Afghan American writing existed long before 9/11, it was the media attention to Afghanistan that made our voices and the interactions urgent and necessary and opened up a space for this distinct American experience. It was important to be visible and vocal at a time when vilification of Muslims and of Afghanistan was common in mainstream media. Many of us felt responsible as Afghans and as Americans to show our faces, to speak out, to tell our stories and point to the connections and complexities between American and Afghan cultures. The flourishing of writing in response to and following 9/11 grew from this simultaneous political and personal urgency to give an account of ourselves.

In an email sent just after 9/11, Mir Tamim Ansary wrote: "I am from Afghanistan, and even though I've lived here for thirty-five years, I've never lost track of what was going on there. So I want to tell anyone who will listen how it all looks from where I'm standing." This email caught the world's attention and paved the way for an Afghan American perspective. Ansary's subsequent memoir, *West of Kabul, East of New York: An Afghan American Story* (Farrar, Straus, and Giroux, 2002) was the first book that addressed both the Afghan and American experiences and the places where they converge. But it was through the fiction of Khaled Hosseini's *The Kite Runner* (Riverhead, 2002) that the world saw Afghanistan as we Afghan Americans remembered it. Not only did the international bestseller provide a welcoming entry into our culture for non–Afghan readers, but it also opened up doors for Afghan Americans to fictionalize and share their experiences. The phenomenal reception of this novel made us feel a sense of inclusion. Our stories were being heard and understood where once there was great invisibility.

Literature is paramount in Afghan culture. The American anthropologist Margaret Mills refers to Afghan society as a "literary illiterate" society. Despite having rudimentary or no formal education, an average Afghan can recite poetry from Sadi, Firdausi, or Rumi. The *shahyir* (poet) has a several-centuries-old history in Afghan literature. The list of classic poets is endless and includes greats such as Rudaki and Jalāl ad-Dīn Muhammad Rūmī, who is known in Afghanistan as Jalāl ad-Dīn Balkhī because he was born in the Balkh region. Another notable poet born in the same region was Rabia Balkhi, the first recognized woman poet in Afghanistan, who wrote in the mid-tenth century. A shrine was built for her by the green mosque in Mazar-i-Sharif (Balkh province), where it still remains despite wars, testimony to the perseverance of women's voices in Afghanistan. Another distinguished writer, Khushal Khan Khattak, the famous seventeenth-century Pashto poet, wrote his lyrics with all the flair and flavor of a warrior.

The poet is essential to preserving Afghan cultural memory. Poetry is an egalitarian tradition. It is beyond gender restriction. It is beyond class. Poetry is memorized in schools and in kitchens. Poetry games (*shayr jangi*, poetry battles) are encouraged. One of the most popular television shows for teens and children in present-day Afghanistan is a game show were teens recite poems based on a letter that the moderator selects. These poems are either poems memorized from the literary greats or poems they compose on the spot. The life of poetry extends beyond the esoteric corners that have been given to this literary craft in the United States. In Afghanistan, poetry remains the dominant form of literary expression.

We named this anthology *One Story, Thirty Stories* from the poetic line that begins Afghan fairy tales: *Afsanah, seesanah . . .* This is to acknowledge the significance that storytelling has had in our lives, its impact on our memories as Afghan Americans. *Qisakhani* (storytelling) is a time-honored tradition, a skill every Afghan is trained in whether the stories are fairy tales, religious lessons, family legends, or, as Soraya's father says in Khaled Hosseini's *The Kite Runner,* "neighborhood gossip." The *nawisenda,* the fiction writer, belongs to a relatively new kind of literary profession that gained respectability after modernist fiction was translated for Afghans in the 1930s by the intellectual visionary Mahmud Tarzi. Translations of modernist writers like James Joyce inspired a new genre of Afghan literature, the novel, whose adherents hoped to cut ties with the *qisa* (stories) and build a narrative style that was based more on the psychology of the characters rather than on the fantastical adventures in fairy tales.

The careful path that Tarzi had laid for a new literary form was lost on a generation raised (and many born) abroad, many who could not read in the indigenous language, and many who did not have access to these texts. The new genre, the Afghan American literary genre, returned to the *qisa* and braided these rich oral stories into individuals' own life histories. Suddenly fairy tales of journeys provided a way for Afghan Americans to tell their own stories of migration and survival.

Despite this long history, however, it is the essay, not poetry and not fiction, that is represented in the greatest numbers in this anthology. Perhaps it is necessary for those who have survived to write personal essays, testimonials, to remember what we lost in order to build on what we have salvaged and what we have found in our new homes in the United States. Blogs also fall within this nonfiction prose category, and in the blogs we have chosen, we see evidence of hesitations, investigations, and renovations of identity as Afghan American. Perhaps it is not surprising that in order to mark our migration from there to here, we lean back to the poetry and myths of our grandparents, who, whether they were from villages or cities, set to memory entire libraries of Afghan literature. It is in the space between storytellers and story-listeners that Afghan American literature is born.

For many Afghans who came to the United States, their stay here was meant to be temporary. There is a sense of wanting to return, and of feeling responsible for those left behind. The sense of helplessness of Afghan Americans during the Taliban years is now being expressed again, as if writing must be for the mythic homeland and as if being Afghan American requires a commitment to bringing peace to Afghanistan. This survivor's guilt, this sense of responsibility for Afghans, has not been shed by many Afghan Americans. It is a unique case, perhaps comparable to that of Palestinian Americans, people who have survived being erased from history and from lands. The endlessness of war, the near impossibility of peace, has taken its toll on the kind of work they feel they "should" produce.

So much of the Afghan American experience of the last three decades has been shaped by war. The quarter century of conflict uprooted our parents and "disappeared" our relatives. It split the earth between those who stayed and those who left, between those who fought for the home they knew and those who fought for a new home. For many Afghan Americans, it was a war we missed, but also one we inherited. The writers in *One Story, Thirty Stories* navigate us through the jagged landscape of the Soviet invasion, the civil war, and the current American presence.

In the essay "Home," Aman Mojadidi places us on the ground along-side mujahid fighters after the Soviet war has ended. Through the eyes of a young Afghan American man, we experience a homecoming without a home. Mojadidi confronts the destruction, while waging his own internal battles. His pacifism collides against a desire for retribution, juxtaposed alongside his own guilt and sense of privilege. In the end, the idea of "home" remains elusive and still out of his reach.

Implicit in the theme of war is the idea of loss. The inability to comprehend the immense deprivation resulting from war echoes throughout the pieces. How do we regain what has been lost? How do we survive? These are the kinds of questions posed in the poem "Of My Mother," by Sahar Muradi, where serene photographs of the mother belie the tragedy of her forced eviction from her country: "*Madar jaan,* how do these pictures stay intact? How do you contain everything that you carry?"

Nowhere, perhaps, is that balancing act more taxing than in the stories centered on September 11, 2001. In "A Week Later," Zohra Saed journeys through New York City, which she is convinced is "going to crack beneath [her] like an egg." As she traverses the spaces between death threats and flag-waving zealots, armed only with her poetry and a double-barreled wound, she asks, "God should bless America, but in these days of simplifications and Us vs. Them, do I have the right to claim America as my own in order to bless? And what about Afghanistan? Do I have the right to bless Afghanistan without being pointed out as a traitor? Can I put both these flags on my car and not worry about vandalism?"

Similarly, in "The Enemy," Nadia Maiwandi wonders how "the girl with all the rock albums and the annoying Valley Girl vernacular" could be considered "the enemy." Sharing this theme of war are two songs by the Afghan American performer Ariana Delawari. In these songs, Delawari creates cover songs of familiar Afghan pop ditties and nursery rhymes, dressing them in a new language that evokes images of war and hardship. Miriam Ebrat's piece, "The Critic," offers us the life of a young Afghan American actress who is chosen to be part of the Hollywood film *Charlie Wilson's War.* This Afghan American muses about the position of Afghan refugees now "acting" as refugees. How does one authentically perform as an Afghan and as a refugee?

When asked during an interview what came to mind when he thought of exile, the Kashmiri poet Agha Shahid Ali answered, "The ability to inhabit several circumstances and several historical and national backgrounds simultaneously." This is written clearly on the posture of the Afghan exile. We at once physically inhabit the house of "now" while mentally residing in the room of "what if." As such, we occupy no distinct space but hang suspended, somewhere between the poles of memory.

Exile, and its concomitant physical and psychological strain, affects much of this anthology. Following the Soviet invasion of Afghanistan, Afghans made up one of the largest refugee populations in the world for two decades. Here we reflect on what might have been, on our mothers' hard-worn hands, on our fathers' aborted goals, and on our grandparents' itinerant lives. Either we write the story of our own lives in exile in the United States, or we grapple with understanding the struggles of our families who are everlastingly torn between countries.

The recurring question of "what if" threads through both Yasmine Delawari Johnson's "Girl with the Green Eyes" and Sedika Mojadidi's "Marriage to Azim." Delawari Johnson juxtaposes her own life with that of Sharbat Gul, the "girl with the green eyes," the young Afghan girl made famous by her picture, which graced the cover of *National Geographic*. Of the same age as Sharbat Gul, Delawari Johnson compares her own comfortable Southern California upbringing, replete with sleepovers and carpools, to that of Sharbat Gul, stricken with war, poverty, and displacement, and asks, "Why her and not me?" Similarly, in "Marriage to Azim," the writer and filmmaker Sedika Mojadidi imagines a different fate for her male cousin Azim, one where he survives the war and marries her. "What if" then becomes a loaded question, heavy with a sense of injustice, of culpability, and also of remorse.

A number of the stories look at parent-child relationships. In "My Mother," Khalida Sethi expertly weaves a series of fragmented pieces around her relationship with her mother, emphasizing her sense of shame and embarrassment and her recognition of her mother's strength and survival. Other pieces draw on the exilic temperament of the father. In "The Cab Driver's Daughter," by Waheeda Samady, and "Exile, or My Father's Elbow," by Sahar Muradi, the father is portrayed as a man perpetually looking backward, trying to recover his losses. In Samady's essay, a backyard garden symbolizes both a retreat from the harsh life of being a taxi driver and an attempt to re-create the paradise of the homeland. In Muradi's prose poem, it is not that the father simply recalls the past, but that he constantly compares it to the present and is continually disappointed. Meanwhile, Muradi's "The Things They Wait For" tells the story of Afghan grandparents being volleyed back and forth between their children's homes and coming to terms with their own sense of placelessness and perpetual waiting.

Not all the stories that deal with exile focus on disappointment or shame. For example, Zohra Saed's poem "Neptune Avenue" celebrates the solidarity of a gang of children born in Afghanistan and raised in many cities before settling in Brooklyn: "Ahh! The power of ten children with their own language . . . [who] own the block through the force of [their] play." And in "Coming to America, 1966," the pioneer female Afghan student Maliha Zulfacar retraces her journey across the United States with a sense of humor and quiet triumph.

If it is remembrance that keeps a story alive, then the role of memory and language is critical to the exilic temperament. When a person is forcibly or voluntarily separated from his or her home, language becomes the place of refuge. As American poet Gary Snyder says, "My language is my home." This could be read literally, as in the sanctuary of the mother tongue and its significance to the émigré adrift in a foreign country. But language presents its own challenges, especially as that mother tongue becomes underused or the new tongue habitual. Rather, language represents a kind of shelter and cover, as the speaker of the poem "Neptune Avenue" identifies: "Our language is the roof we carry over our heads."

"I'm sorry. I don't know the words in Dari," says Tareq Mirza to the two Afghan professors he is trying to assist, in his essay on returning to Kabul in 2002. The experience of forgetting, or being without language, repeats itself throughout many of the pieces in this collection. In the almost thirty years spent apart, the language once shared has become fuzzy—a distant voice for some of us, a lack of communication in words and sometimes in gestures.

"I had left the United States feeling as if I was no longer an American. Now I was leaving Kabul feeling as if I was not an Afghan either." In 2003 the photographer Masood Kamandy returned to Afghanistan to rebuild the Photography Department at Kabul University, and in his blog, *Dispatches from Kabul,* he chronicles his life in Afghanistan, visiting the grave of the late Ahmad Shah Masood and forging his newfound friendships in Kabul. When his father returns to visit Kabul, Kamandy writes, "My father's watch is still set to Colorado's time. / He arrived one week ago and explained that he never changes his watch." Kamandy analyzes his father's response to returning after thirty-six years: "In his room, I saw him practicing his handwriting, / copying the first poem in Rumi's *Mathnawi,* about a flute. / He wrote that its sound is the pain of its loneliness, having been separated from the wood it was made from."

In a more celebratory essay, Homira Nassery captures the optimism of

Afghanistan in the reconstruction years and during the first presidential election in 2004:

> I look at the list of candidates, so professionally prepared, that ballot, and I put a big X in my selection box, then add a happy face, then circle the picture too, just in case someone doesn't get it. . . . To no one in particular, I say, "Here's one for peace and justice." I want to go outside, celebrate, let out a war cry, and give highfives to everyone. Yeeeee-haaaaa! How fabulously cool is this moment?

Also on an optimistic note, Halima Kazem's article muses on the friendship that blooms among the women at the office she works at in Kabul after she takes on the position of an impromptu yoga instructor: "Determined to help them experience a bit of yoga, I closed all the curtains and locked both entrances. 'Now you have nothing to worry about,' I said. The women immediately took off their headscarves and jackets, revealing brightly colored tanks and T-shirts." The women find the yoga posturing familiar, like the movements in Islamic prayer.

Aman Mojadidi has a more critical view of the Kabul to which he returned to aid in humanitarian projects after 2002. His position as an Afghan American gives him a critical lens with which to read the situation in Kabul: "Another whiskey please! And then off to save the impoverished, the ones who can't save themselves. But do they really need saving?"

Afghan American literature is surprisingly different from other examples of Asian American literature. Best-selling female authors have spearheaded Iranian American literature, with which it shares some experiences and a related language. While the Afghan American publishing scene has featured largely male writers, there are more Afghan American women writers than a few years ago. Many of these women have developed their own narrative style, distinguished by its fragmented, poetic prose that sometimes borrows from Afghan folkore. This fragmented poetic narrative by Afghan American women writers suggests an ambiguity that denotes, or by the act of writing *asserts,* a claim to being unrestricted and undefined. Many of the women use this space to reflect on the limitations and contradictions of being an Afghan American female, with common themes including shame, guilt, and modesty. Not all of the women's writings are in this form, however. The writings of Naheed Elyasi and Wajma Ahmady, and the poetry of Khalida Sethi, go beyond this aesthetic of rumination and indirectness to raw declarations of womanhood. Yet all the women poets pose powerful and critical questions and in this questioning breathe new space in which to build an Afghan feminist consciousness.

As part of our memory-making as Afghans in the United States, so much of the stories are inspired by photographs. In our hasty departures from our country, our families brought minimal belongings with them, especially photographs. We had so few concrete images of what life was like that the few photos we did have became part of the myth of Afghanistan, of homeland, of a time that could not be caught and a time that was radically distant from the images of Afghanistan we saw in the papers. These photographs made the stories vivid and tangible. We couldn't look at a photo without marking the layers of loss. More than the photo, it was everything implicit in the photo that became part of our writings. We can understand why so many of the writings here begin with family photos. Sahar Muradi's "Of My Mother" begins with a photograph of Muradi's mother. Zohra Saed's "Family Album" is about a series of lost photos in the migrations. Again, Yasmine Delawari Johnson's "Girl with the Green Eyes" is addressed to the *National Geographic* cover of the Afghan girl in a refugee camp, a photograph by Steve McCurry.

Family is another theme in this anthology. For Afghans, there is no separation between self and family. This is in deep contrast to the American concept of Emersonian self-reliance, which is what leads to friction between the children raised here and their parents. This conflict is central to many of the works in this collection. In the self-making process, the narrator or the protagonist acknowledges the parents' sacrifices and labor but struggles to create a space to meet their own expectations. In Fahim Anwar's essay, he becomes the engineer his parents want, but also creates a space for himself and continues his dream of stand-up comedy. Wajma Ahmady's short story acknowledges the long history of sacrifice a doctor-father made to raise his family. While recognizing this, the protagonist also struggles to become an independent woman without getting married, which is essential to her self-making as a writer. Either conflicts with the family bring the family together, or the children become resentful of their parents' sacrifice.

Whether in the "here" or the "there," the themes in this collection identify the constant shifts in who we are as Afghan Americans, how we name ourselves, the perpetual "reconstructing" we are engaged with all the time. The beauty of these stories lies in this grappling, this questioning and wondering, this piecing together, this taking apart, and in the looking backward and forward.

In Judith Butler's *Precarious Life,* her thoughtful exposition on post-9/11 America, she writes that when we see "the face"—the human, vulnerable face—a greater understanding of our own fragility and precariousness is grasped. Returning to "face" Afghanistan as a literary exercise enables us to comprehend and relate to one another. These writers have faced conditions of catastrophe and yet create from this anew: a new constellation of stories and experiences that radiate out and find each other, reflect each other. This collection solidifies the place of Afghan Americans on the American literary landscape. Afghan and American are part of the same fractured light of this constellation.

Zohra Saed & Sahar Muradi
New York City, January 2010

POETRY

♦ ♦ ♦

SEDIKA MOJADIDI

Sedika Mojadidi's prose poem is a dream of the one who has survived war. "What if" she had married the cousin she had been promised to as a young girl? Mojadidi's cousin Azim was killed while living as a refugee in Peshawar. Mojadidi was a teenager growing up in Florida when she received the news. Gendered spaces and expectations for young women are at the fringes of this elegy to Mojadidi's cousin Azim.

Marriage to Azim

THE KITE

The fields in Qarghah where we live are submerged in sheets of ice and light. I am seven years old with thick black braids standing on a roof with you. You, my cousin, are thirteen, I think. I stand shivering, my teeth chattering, in blue plastic slippers and white socks. There are no winters in Florida. I've never seen kite flying on roofs in January before. This day is the only time.

Looking up to this sky, remote and piercing, I can't seem to remember the orange clouds in Florida that I left behind. If I never see Florida again, it will be too soon. What is there, anyway, but rows of shopping malls and gas stations and perfect dead green lawns; heat that chokes in the small apartment I shared with my parents and sisters. I am invisible there. There is never a day there that is mine like this one on the roof with you.

The year is 1972. My parents give up the temporary life we have in Florida to come back home. In the first few days, I am lost in a wash of unfamiliar noises, dust that covers me, words spoken that I do not understand, and weeping relatives who say they know me. I miss television and cereal and the sound of English. But we are going to live here forever, and soon it takes no time for the scent of Florida to disappear.

My uncle's angular house and sprawling gardens in Qarghah, where we live, become a warm cocoon of no school and borders where I chase paper boats in streams, where strangers who smell of green tea embrace me and call me *little one.* In this first winter in Kabul, I taste snow. I taste corn roasted and warm *naan* peeled fresh from a tandoor. My name is not peculiar. Relatives say it with an ease that begins to tickle. I begin to speak only Farsi, drinking in the raw words forming in my mouth. I am of a place where the ground beneath my feet is my mother; the quiet joy of these days—a small shaft of glass cutting into my heart.

Somebody is screaming in the distance—a boy in brown pants is frantically letting his kite string loose, struggling to keep his string from getting cut. Suddenly your kite whistles up—trapped in a pool of ether. We watch it scratch across the sky singing in a shrill voice, a siren's call warning us not to go too far over the roof's edge.

You are dancing back and forth, hands delicately holding a thread you feed upward and pull down, up down, up down, again and again. There are other symphonies of boys playing, like you—clenched and buoyant, on flat roofs near us. But there is only you, Azim. Did we exchange words? Did you say something important to me? I see your mouth moving mutely and I remember. I hug my icy shoulders and think of the coat that, in my thrill, I left behind in the house. I think of asking our servant girl to fetch it for me.

There are a few more quiet scenes of you at this age. I can see you silently and hurriedly doing your prayers at dusk. I can't remember you ever arguing with anyone. You were too old to play with me, but at dinner, I see you quickly shoving spoonfuls of *pilau* in your mouth. Your face down, eyes lowered in a quietness that drapes you, fills you, gives you a look of sheepishness even as you grow older. You never raise your voice, you never seem to mind your place in the family. You will always do what your father told you.

At seven, I am still young enough to be allowed on a roof alone with my boy cousin; if we'd stayed long enough for me to grow older here, I would have been asked to leave. If we were teenagers, the sight of you and me alone together would have been forbidden. I would be kept like all the other women, at home—to stay closer to God. How could I love a cousin who was like both my brother and my first crush? I do. And it consumes me once I turn fifteen. Then, I would have gladly indentured myself to find Qarghah again.

I remember the sun reaching the middle of the sky. I see you wipe your hands on gray pantaloons, pulling your sweater down. Your head is shaved. Your lanky body—an extension of the thin string laced between your fingers.

I see the road to Kabul in front of us, a stretch of blinding white chiseled through mammoth hills. This is the same road we will take a year later when we have to leave. The same road you and everyone else in the house will take when they escape. The same road they will take our cousins on when they disappear into Pul-e-Charke prison. I see the road shade into spring, summer, fall and another winter, the cycles of seasons that will not include you or me, we will have gone. By then a host of new foreigners in tanks and woolen uniforms will descend onto the road and reach into the heart of this house for what remains behind. Later, the Taliban will squat in our beloved white-slabbed rooms, bringing with them blackened windows and greasy pots, turning our living room into a barn for their goats. More soldiers and bodies will fall across the fields, across the streets, across my beloved Qarghah. And with them they will all make this house their own for a while. Our world was so obscure and insulated. Why would anyone want it?

Your kite almost cuts the boy's string, almost. When I am fifteen without ever asking me, our fathers promise us to each other. Who is the girl I might have been if you'd lived long enough?

My lips, I think, are blue, but still I will not leave. Quickly, your kite swerves its crowned head and then wraps itself around the yellow kite you've decided to take. You spent hours making this one. At night, I watched you through the door. On this morning, you rush out of the house to stake your modest claim on the cosmos. I trail behind. As I climb the ladder to the roof, the first thing I see is your kite gliding unfettered in a sky sprinkled with specks of colored paper, a translucent ruby spinning upward, like a rocket with no end in sight. You never drop your gaze, not even once, to see me.

I was the second or third choice when your father asked my father. I was the American cousin they decided to save from herself.

Somehow, you maneuver the kite to nose-dive into a boy's yellow masterpiece swimming circles above our heads. There is the sound of wind whipping through our clothes, the crackling of paper and air and me turned to you in adoration. Silent, cold, and ecstatic that you've allowed me to accompany you this winter day and watch you fly your prize. In the fading sun of my eyes, your young body remains etched for me in this pose: arms pulled toward the future, hips braced, legs bent— fingers cautiously teasing the string. Your face unfastened and intent on its focus: a crimson kite lifted in microscopic glory begging and pleading for this day not to end. But in the frame of this cut-out I keep, the edges are a vacuum—what is outside has not yet come. You are still my Azim shifting in and out of feedback—reaching up for all of us who cannot. We are the only ones suspended on this roof.

MASOOD KAMANDY

*Writing on his blog, chronicling his trip back to Kabul, Masood
Kamandy connects his photos of the family home with this poignant
poem of homecoming and the meaning of time. There are exiles
of place, and then there are exiles of time. In this poem,
his father is an exile of both place and time.*

Time Passes in Colorado

My father's watch is still set to Colorado's time.
He arrived one week ago and explains that he never changes his watch.

I imagine him looking down, and seeing a blue sky
full of clouds in Fort Collins. Or maybe
it's a picture of my mother in a frame made from peacock feathers.

Looking up, he sees a dark sky that pours down on Afghanistan
after years of drought. Buildings are racing toward the heavens
and behind them he sees an image in the passing
angry clouds of himself as a young man.

It's been thirty-six years since he last set foot on this soil.

In his room, I saw him practicing his handwriting,
copying the first poem in Rumi's *Masnawi*, about a flute.
He wrote that its sound is the pain of its loneliness,
having been separated from the wood it was made from.

"They got married, and left the next day," all of my relatives explain to me.

It's a story I feel like I've never heard.

One woman cried,

"You all left and we stayed here alone.
Why did you leave us?"

I saw the house he grew up in.
Distant relatives greeted us joyously at the burgundy gate,
where "KAMNDY" was etched.

The perimeter walls were still there,
but on the inside, the walls of his house had long fallen.
All that remained were its fingerprints in the mud brick walls,
and a wood stove in the center of the plot,
perhaps there to warm the absence.

Beside the house was a small shrine,
and my father went in to say a prayer.

Outside it started to rain.
As I heard the drops falling around us,
I began to count until I felt a raindrop wet my forehead.

Fifteen seconds,
It felt like such a long time.

DONIA GOBAR

Donia Gobar's poem is sister to the poem "Dead Are My People," in which Khalil Gibran laments his helplessness as a poet who would be more useful to the starving Lebanese (during World War I) if he were an "ear of corn." As an Afghan American engaged and emotionally involved with the situation back in Afghanistan, Gobar has written a poem that expresses the overwhelming feeling of futility in the face of these images of war. The poet is witness and in this role of witness documents abstractly the shreds of a collective experience.

As I Watch

Presenter's PowerPoint scans, spans
as moments un-peel time
and the words,
bold and blank,
bleed
slipping in ribbons of
silence
around dark bodies in gray places,
tongue-tied brick walls,
faces, gazes . . .
around foggy features
and thousand-tongue frozen gestures.
As blank words scream in soft silence
as faded wounds
bleed
in dark silence
through the valleys of the past
through the allies of the cast . . .
As I watch
oh, as I watch in darkness

MARIAM GHANI

Index of the Disappeared is an ongoing, collaborative, community-based inquiry into the human costs of public policy; the erasures and absences created in real lives by the secrecy and suppression of documents and data; and the role played by language—not just as spoken by but as spoken about and around communities—in defining (and potentially redefining) the rights, struggles, and public perceptions of immigrants in the United States. It has developed over a period of several years in several different forms: a video (How Do You See the Disappeared?); a Web project (How Do You See the Disappeared? A Warm Database); an offshoot/nested project including video, prints, and postcards (Points of Proof, see below); a series of critical texts and artists' text projects published in various on- and off-line venues; a series of imagined portraits; a 'zine (Index of the Disappeared: Catalogue #.100) with contributions from other artists working with parallel ideas; and, finally, an installation in the form of a library, Index of the Disappeared, which archives all the previous forms of the project, collects all the documents about and interventions in the immigration debate that we have accumulated over the years, adds a series of books that connects those primary documents to broader ideas and issues circulating in contemporary society and culture, and also serves as a site for the writing and archiving of additional alternative histories. The following is text composed and collected in 2004–8 for this project, Index of the Disappeared, a collaboration with Chitra Ganesh.

Notes on the Disappeared (04–08)

1.

A case of mistaken identity:
wrong place, wrong time,

wrong name, wrong face.
That grove of pomegranate trees
not an orchard after all but a reliquary.

2.

Extraordinary renditions
for ordinary men.
Their only protection
what they carried in their pockets:
a white coin for the black day,
a blue bead for the evil eye.

3.

Traps built by the language of law
for all with foreign tongues.
Your name held against you
like a loaded gun.

4.

Men without countries: canaries in mines.
The walls of indefinite detention
bricked in around them for good luck.

5.

This is no time for compromise.
We are all presumed threats
until proven otherwise.

6.

The second time was my first mistake;
torturers are not born but made.

7.

A letter so secret,
once read its existence could never
be spoken of again.
The trick: recognizing the envelope.

8.

Measure the erasure
that meets our dissent.
We must not forget that
compliance is consent.

9.

Your silence
will not protect you
when the border moves.
There's no place like home.
There's no place like home.
There's no place like home.

NAHID FATTAHI

Nahid Fattahi heard stories of laborers in Herat, who stand on the corner of a street for hours in hopes of being picked up for construction work. There are some days when they are lucky and work for some hundred afghanis, but there are endless days that these men go home with nothing, ashamed of their empty pockets and hands.
Fattahi wrote this poem in honor of these men.

Pick Me, Please!

He can't go back home.
She said there is nothing to cook.
The kids are hungry don't forget food.
He stood on the corner with a hundred other men.
With every car that passed by, they all jumped.

Pick me, please!
    No me!
I'm stronger, why not me?
    I'm old but experienced, pick me!

Sweat on their faces, lips dried with thirst,
Old shirts with holes in them, dirty collars
Secondhand shoes without laces on,
Trousers muddy and hair gray from dust.
They all looked the same.

    Let me go and work today,

He said to the man next to him.
    My kids are hungry, and my wife is sick
    Let me go and make the one hundred afghanis
    Tomorrow will be your turn, I promise.

Don't talk about hunger to me!
Don't tell me your wife is sick!
I lost my daughter to hunger!
My son's feet are bleeding!
He has no shoes.
He walked barefoot,
Answered the other man.

With every car that passed by, they all jumped.

Pick me, please!
    No me! I'm stronger, why not me?
I'm old but experienced, pick me!

They pushed and pulled one another.
Two hundred hands were trying to reach the car.
Two hundred eyes were gazing at the car.
One hundred mouths were shouting:

Pick me, please!

JESSAMYN ANSARY

Jessamyn Ansary has been writing poetry since before she was able to commit the words to paper. As a child she would wake her parents up in the middle of the night, asking them to transcribe her latest lines. Although she never became fluent in Farsi, she heard it spoken often growing up. She became fascinated with the way words sound, even if absent any apparent logical meaning. She believes that the rhythm and the sound of words can often convey an emotional truth that plain statements do not express, which is what she hopes to accomplish in her poems. Ansary is third-generation Afghan American.

age three at grandpa's funeral

Mom bought me donut holes in a white bag,
and left me on the porch. She went inside.
Donut holes were new to me, desire a vague
sugar ache—I hesitated, then untied

the bag—but suddenly a dog—big, loud,
ran up—barked, pawed—and then my lovely sweets
were in his devil's mouth, and he—pleased, proud—
galloped away. I learned that joy was fleeting,

fragile—so I screamed and cried. Mom rushed
to me, comforted me, brushed back my loss
with kisses, rubbed noses, and gave me cold crushed
roses, into the open earth, to toss.

Then closed her father's eyes. Then buried him.
Children and parents—what things we do for them.

The Invention

What words communicate this heat? the writer asks—
what tone of voice? what lost
inflection? In his studio, the painter
warms his knuckles on his tea, desperately
smearing tempera on paper, a red streak
in a white sky.

Sometimes I run down hills so steep, my skin
falls faster than my bones. Imagining
you are falling through the air next to me,
once more whispering—
I am in too deep, too deep,
and still I will tell you that I do not understand.
My cat chirps rapturously at a goldfinch
through the window, turns back
to look at me, as if to say—
soon we will feast!
Meanwhile the finch has flown away.
It's the green of your eyes, blinking silently
at me in the cold morning, the green
earth smirking
at her brilliant invention—
how much
is lost
after translation.

QAIS ARSALA

*Qais Arsala's poetry captures the exilic Afghan experience. The
longing for homeland is evident in these poems. Arsala
shares his memories of Afghanistan in an effort to rebuild
the collective memory of Afghans' post-Soviet war.*

The Horns of the Tiger

Straitjacket memories
Of those morphine-flavored nights . . .

These tears of blood can almost sedate the scarred and maimed souls
Desperate cries from the voiceless, forgotten children
Are befallen upon deaf ears of blind savages who are disguised as
    Liberators

Shrapnel hurricane turns a sage into a madman
And a madman into a prophet
I try to close my eyes to imagine a time when the delicate *showperaks*
    outnumbered the polished Russian rockets

I try to imagine those days of innocent kids playing *tushla* and *danda*
    kilak and chasing the *gowzanboors* off the streets of Kabul

I try to reach for the untouchable
To scream for what cannot be . . .

Demystified Calamity

Oh how have I lost
the seeds of innocence
these sacred leaves falling and aching for another way knowing
when to triage the serum of truth.

Cursed is the smile within which lies dormant the mutation of a tear.
Truth is a virus perched upon that branch of angst.
What is the Barometer of chance
that the collapse of frozen embers will set you free?

Placebo

Fractured mosaic
stare at last to lament for nothing more,
love beckons us to harness the odor of guilt
Nourishing spears of destiny dismantle any illusions of
The beloved

everything is chaos
Turmoil abound
history of insignificant embraces
to the music of deafening silence

Death is now
to these tired eyes
I wasted time not breaking down these walls
But the truths themselves
Oh they beckon and wail
I'm a slave of my own mind

Anger seems insignificant in the vastness of life
Liquefied Dust singing eulogies of me
Ode to the demons inside tormenting and taunting my ascension
out of this cage of straitjacket-flavored nights.

SAHAR MURADI

*Sahar Muradi's poetry deals with the family, and through this
storytelling, we enter an understanding of the experience of Afghans in
America. The running theme in the following two poems is loss—its
unspeakableness, its consequences. Exile is sometimes a physical
manifestation, such as in the second poem, where feet are allergic to
the new land they are shuffled around in. Homeland is a hologram,
found in old textbooks and in her father's dreaming eyes.*

Of My Mother

Madar jaan, your face. Your face is more than language knows. I cannot
explain your face. A handful of family photographs, from the last twenty
years in America. And your face is the only challenge. Who but the
mother has a face more than language?

Madar jaan, how do these pictures stay intact? How do you contain
everything that you carry? How do you remain on these thin gelatin
sheets with the feat of a dancer stuck on a page?

Did your mother sense in the dark of her belly how hard you'd live?
Could she predict all your losses? Did she guess the pressure of her last
embrace before we boarded the bus for Pakistan? Or the redness of your
brothers' red eyes? Or the last flashes of your country through a dirty
window?

Did she expect the three hundred days between the night of my father's
escape and the morning of our departure? Or the number of weeks the
black Beetle parked outside our house?

Or the number of knocks on our door each night before Shabnam
answered that *padar* was away on business? Did she see the last flashes of
your country through a dirty window?

Madar jaan, did she see how wide my father would open the windows and condemn the *kalashnikovs* on the streets? Did she see the black ringlets of his name on the list of who would be snatched to hell? Did she see your nephew snatched? Did she see the last flashes of your country through a dirty window?

Did she guess the price you'd sell our house for at the last minute? Or everything you'd leave inside it?

Did she see your students ask you where you were going? Or when you would be back? Or the last flashes of your country through a dirty window?

Madar jaan, the last flashes of your country—!

On the bus sucking sugarcane. You give us sugarcane stalks to keep busy with, to keep our mouths shut with. If we speak, the soldiers who stop the bus will know we aren't border people. So you silence us with these sweet, sticky plants and keep us dirty. Two weeks, no baths, and wrapped in three layers. It's how we can pass. Border people have nothing, so we carry nothing. The hurt in Jawad's hands from the absence of his slingshot; he wonders if there'll be blackbirds where we're going. Shabnam tries to keep her feet still; there is a little itch, a tiny tickle in them, where the pedals of her tricycle fit. How long would it take to reach Pakistan on a tricycle? I think of my little bag, my *khalta-gac,* the pillowcase that I keep all my treasures in—apple seeds and lost buttons and little webs of lint. Your mother says she will keep it safe, for when we come back from the trip, with new treasures. But you, you have so many more things than we do, so your missing is so much bigger. It takes up all the room on our seat. It splits the vinyl, fogs the windows, and spreads to either end of the bus. It's already hard to be comfortable, with the rocks under the tires and the dust in our eyes and our lips sealed tight around the cane, but now your missing is coming off your face like steam, and none of us can breathe.

◆ ◆ ◆

Madar jaan, your face is more than one. It is not a single face. Someone once told me that I have so many different faces, and that makes me beautiful, that the measure of beauty is the ability to change expressions completely. After Kabul, you never kept the same face.

The three photographs we have from Afghanistan. The first, your portrait as a teenager, in black and white profile, your blouse of daisies, your hair in waves, the cool beauty of your face, eyes softly open, halfway dreaming.

The second, you newly married, sitting on a porch beside my father's grandmother and his great-aunt, in your pink bellbottoms and a brown and tan sweater that you designed yourself and that my father knitted in his factory (you said he finally got it right after four tries), with your long hair reddened at its ends and lazy smiling eyes.

The third, at a party with you in the center surrounded by your two daughters and your son. Shabnam, on your right, at five years and in a green gingham dress, mouth in a wide-open laugh and hands apart as if she'd just clapped them; me, at three, standing up on a platform between you and Shabnam, wearing a red gingham dress and a smile made of mischief, in my hands something small and blue; Jawad on your left at twelve in a red shirt with tan outline, in his right hand a cup and the cup at his lips, hiding his mouth. You are at the center in a dark skirt and white T-shirt on which is printed a black and white photograph of my father. In your hands, a plate of cake and a spoon between your fingers. Your hair is tied back, your face glowing a light pink makeup, and your eyes, your eyes are homes to tender things.

Exile, or My Father's Elbow

Every day Bob walks into the café and asks my father, *hey, Ali, how's that elbow?*

My father stands behind the register, his elbow propped up on the counter, his head in his hand, and looks out the window.

Bob laughs, *don't work that elbow too hard now!*

He loves the water, where there is a lake, a pond, he stands for hours, silent, lost in it.

It is lunchtime and my mother is making sandwiches a dozen a minute, and chatting with customers over her shoulder and whispering in Dari to my father—who ordered what, extra bacon, on a sub roll, large or small salad—and my father, not hearing, making wrong calculations, the window at his side, my father will disappear.

Sometimes it is the water, and sometimes it is the freezer, the trunk of the car, the television, a closet. But it is worse with a bowl of pomegranates, a plate of watermelon, a dish of dates, when he does not simply go back, but he compares.

Bob says, *but, Ali, it's just a parking lot.*

In Flagstaff, Arizona, on a family trip, on the side of the road outside a fish restaurant, where the river cut through the rocks and we knelt among them and ate *chabli kabobs,* he said, *this is Paghman.*

During dinner, between spoonfuls of *qorma challow,* he tells us about the white snaking pattern in the mountains of Mazar-i-Sharif said to be the spirit of Hazrat Ali, about Zohake Mahran, "King of Two Snakes," and his pair of reptiles which he wore like scarves around his neck and fed human brains to every day, and about the Koh-i-Nor diamond, the size of a sunflower, looted from India, inherited by king after king, and, when the British arrived, hidden for years within a wall in Jalalabad.

Bob asks, *between you and me, who works harder you think, your wife or your elbow?*

In his first phone calls to us at college, he asked us to look up old atlases in the libraries, to send him copies of the ancient maps of Persia and Baluchistan, of countries that no longer exist.

My mother will say, *instead of memorizing all those dates and places and stories, why don't you learn the prices?*

Every night he goes online, elbow on the desk, hand at his lips, glasses dripping down his nose, and reads the latest news.

You will wear down the skin, Bob teases.

KHALIDA SETHI

Khalida Sethi's poetry challenges gender expectations within Afghan families. The narrator of the poem is living in two worlds. One place that is aware—hyperaware—of the sexualized body and another, the mother's world, that attempts to neutralize the body of desire.

Astagfurillah (God Forbid!)

With you I change pronouns and de-sex my words.
Tongue rattles words come strained even my nerves protest the
    changing of "love, relationship, lust" into "friend, friendship, like."
Because with you,
amma, aunt, mother,
I can't imagine living honesty and virtue at the same time.
These things are not things in an Afghan girl's hands.
These words are sins in an Afghan girl's mouth.

We listen crazy, happy, to American Music.
Your index finger thumping fast on the steering wheel.
"you spin me right round baby" sing, sister, sing.
But love and seduction are feelings foreign to a heart purified in
    Wudu.★
Thank God we are too pure and clean for anything but approved
    arrangements.
My skirt rebels above my knees and I am reminded with a harsh slap to
    the thigh that my chastity is your honor.
My Chastity Is Your Honor.
There is, it seems (doesn't it?), so much power in the thin layer of skin
    between my legs.
That little bit of woman
scares

★ *Wudu* means "ablutions."

inspires whole laws and customs.
Our thinnest, smallest flesh demands *such* attention.
Imagine the demands of my whole person.
Imagine what our whole bodies could do.

ARIANA DELAWARI

Ariana Delawari revises an Afghan nursery rhyme and gives it a feminist twist. She writes: "'Oh La Lo' is a nursery rhyme that my grandmother used to sing to me when I was a baby. I wanted to cover the song somehow, and when I sat down to cover it, I started thinking of the song from the perspective of a mother or a grandmother in Afghanistan. So the first three verses are sung to a little girl. The last two verses are sung to the world at large.'"

Oh la Lo

oh la lo la lo la lo
derakhte seb en zard aloo
zard aloo ra ou borda
dukhtar'e khow borda

little girl go to sleep,
mama's got a mouth to feed
shots ring through the town,
the echoes of his need to lead

little girl don't you wake,
mama's got some blues to shake
they killed your daddy on that day,
when they covered your mama with the shame shame

little girl someday when you wake
you're gonna change their ways,
little girl someday you show your face,
unveil your grace

the bastard child of modern day
carries all the blame away

in far-off lands they're tucked away
while ego's hand holds onto fame

airbrush all my lines away
mama's livin hard today
grace your billboard with my face
the marquee reads "the bastard child of modern day"

oh la lo la lo la lo, oh la lo la lo la lo

*In this revisioning of a song for a girl with black eyes by Afghanistan's
Elvis, Ahmad Zahir, Delawari interweaves both cultures' She writes:
"'Cheshme Siah Daree' was my favorite song to sing and dance to as a
kid. When I wanted to cover it, I realized that the meaning of the song
had changed so much. What had originally been about someone
having dark or mysterious eyes had changed to eyes that had seen war
and suffering. And the part of the song about taking someone to their
home came to mean something very different in a land of refugees.
So I took the original chorus and wrote my own verses.'"
Both of these songs are featured on a CD Delawari
released with her band, Lion of Panjsheer.*

Cheshme Siah Daree

*Cheshme siah daree korbanet showam man
khana kouja daree memanet showam man
Cheshme siah daree korbanet showam man
khana kouja daree memanet showam man*

your eyes they cannot hide the pain you hold inside
oh those eyes, they look a lot like mine
oh take me to your home, the one you cannot find,
the rubble stands alone among the landmines

Cheshme siah daree korbanet showam man
khana kouja daree memanet showam man
Cheshme siah daree korbanet showam man
khana kouja daree memanet showam man

oh even though the lines of time you cannot hide
I see your faith and I am filled with pride
oh won't you show me all those things that you have seen
and maybe we can show the rest how it has been

Cheshme siah daree korbanet showam man
khana kouja daree memanet showam man
Cheshme siah daree korbanet showam man
khana kouja daree memanet showam man

oh you hold a thousand years, the truth of what's to come
so far but oh so simple, this could be the one
and I knew when I saw those faces I would be the one to trace it
a map to gather all the tribes to live as one

Cheshme siah daree korbanet showam man
khana kouja daree memanet showam man
Cheshme siah daree korbanet showam man
khana kouja daree memanet showam man

ZOHRA SAED

Zohra Saed's playful poem about a polyphonic childhood in a swarm of cousins introduces the perspective of the child refugee. Conscious of the multiple languages acquired in the trip from Afghanistan to America, but not yet fully conscious of the reasons for this constant moving, the child sees Neptune Avenue as more than a place in Brighton Beach, Brooklyn. The next selection of poems is from a series based on family photos that were lost. Saed preserves these lost images in her words and, in the process, chronicles war through the very intimate moments these photos capture.

Neptune Avenue

On the streets of Brighton Beach,
    when we swing from fire escapes and jump on the hoods of cars,
we own the block through the force of our play
    and the clicking and clacking of our tongues.

Ah! The power of ten children with their own language! It is enough.
We are our own gang. Self-sufficient when we are not bound to school,
we exist happily on fragmented languages. The bread crumb of slang
from the many streets we grew up in: Kabul, Mazar, Jalalabad, Riyadh,
Jeddah, and Brooklyn. Our language is the roof we carry over our
heads—even when we are separated into different classes at school.

If only mothers would let us be!

We'd rather stretch our weekends and wrap it across the belly of the
year. We'd rather dangle out every day on the fire escapes of the second-
floor mosque, spill the Khutba onto the sweating concrete by opening
the windows wide. Then jump onto the sidewalk, align our velvet prayer
mats next to parked cars and play Imam and Ummah as passerbys gawk
at the magic of our "flying carpets" and at one five-year-old brother

serious faced, hand over ear,
       singing out the call to prayer with a sugar-sweet throat.

We quit school! We quit suspecting lunch-ladies of slipping in slivers of swine while we aren't looking!

We are willing to live within the bubble of cousins praying or gossiping in wild tongue flips as neighbor children stare in awe. When their mouths ache from the strain of our language, we blow kisses at them.

We have won another battle of the streets, but still our mothers want us to clean our rooms and fathers demand our report cards!

What choice had we? In the day, our mothers are the sun and at night our fathers. To mark the celestial transition, mothers set in the kitchen an hour before fathers come home. They hide behind the steam of cooking while we children stand in line with colorful plastic combs in hand—waiting our turn by the only mirror we can reach on our own. Later, we visit them to approve us and prepare our welcome for fathers.

    Our tough skins are for the block and for the neighbors.

At home, we are forever courting our parents with neatly combed hair, sweet voices, trimmed nails and memorized prayers.

We are the constellation.
    We shine each time they smile at us.

Family Album

PREFACE

Kabul, 1974
Mountains are mothers
here in a land as large as a hug,
same size as a melon, without the nourishment.

KHYBER PASS, 1984

Lost uncle
18 was your talisman
until the Communists came

Only the muted yellows and browns of the '80s
bear witness.
A Beatles tape in your back pocket
does not save you.

PESHAWAR, 1984

The orange Japanese thermos, a gift for him on his last Riyadh visit,
is visible at the top right hand of the photo, close to where his head is
    resting.

Gray beard, pale blue Kameez, full stomach still robust,
face lit despite death, he is stretched out on the floor.

My youngest aunt reads the Quran over his head.
Her face   a curl of pain.

In the midst of grief,
who can bear to snap a photo?

Migration, the scatterings that war creates, makes us tourists of death.

BROOKLYN, 1986

My hair is curled again
and I stand in a velvet frilly frock at Coney Island
while girls whirl around me in neon bathing suits.

I am always overdressed in photos she sends back.

MEDINA, 1979

Mosque is mother too, beneath her arch the dust is Zohra, age four, eyes
darkened with Kohl, named after a star and existing as one of the ivory
columns.

Grandfather leans against the pale blue Honda, lifts me to the sky,
Reach!
Reach!
I am his telephone line to God.

EPILOGUE

Brooklyn, 2009
Twenty-eight years rooted here in one brick spot of Brooklyn
as if in penance for grandfathers who are defined by the stretch of
    footprints—
the marks of their lives stitched mostly on dry earth and stone
while mine is neatly confined to a small neighborhood
with shish kebab shops on each block
and where even the fish from the bay have heads like sheep.

NAHEED ELYASI

*Naheed Elyasi's poem is about the struggles of Afghan American
women. On the one hand, she counters the racism that she finds in her
new home, and on the other, she speaks out against the sexism within
her community. In this tracing of her journey from there to here, she
realizes that she is lost and that the return she is hoping for is
her own sense of self as an independent woman.*

Awaiting My Return

Twenty-five years have passed since I left my home.
Twenty-five years since I belonged somewhere.

A nigger, a chink, a terrorist.
Being rich,
being dirt poor.

I don't fit in with my own people.
I am too American, they say.
Too wild, a bad girl,
my sexuality oozes.
I have my own mind.
I question.

I don't fit in with Americans.
I am exotic. I am foreign.
It's in my face, my voice,
my accent, my wild untamed black hair.

I don't know who I am. Who I should be?
Twenty-five years of being a chameleon.

I don't want others to define me.
They want to possess me.
Take my soul, my identity.

I cry out.
You will not break me.
I will not be your nigger.
I will not be your chink,
a terrorist, or exotic feast for the white man.

I will be me.
Confused,
lost, searching.

A part of me died in that journey.
The void has only gotten deeper.

I've often thought of going back.
Fear keeps me paralyzed.

What if my void becomes more vast and endless?
These thoughts run amuck.
Keeping me paralyzed,
awaiting my return to myself.

YALDA ASMATEY

Yalda Asmatey, coeditor of the first collection of work by Afghan American writers in California, writes this poem as inspiration for those who are struggling to find a place for themselves. She offers not only her thoughts on the topic of faith and perseverance but encouragement to continue building one's life despite challenges.

My Thoughts . . . If You Don't Mind

You are strong.
Stronger than you know.
It's about you.
Not them. Not
that country. Not
those people. Not
even the books you read. Not
even the degrees you work for.

It's about you.

This physical body that
occupies a space in time, and it's the soul—
the very substance that gets us to wake up in the morning
and takes us into a deep sleep at night.

You are not to give up in any way. And it's okay,
the battle that rages inside of you. It's okay.
It's because you are human. Believe me, I
know. I know exactly how this feels. I wear shoes every day,
fortunately, but I tell you what—
physically I wear them, but
symbolically my one foot is here in California walking the streets of
Berkeley and Walnut Creek, while the other—the other has run away

with my heart to that place I call home and it's there—walking,
running, pacing itself with the belief that change can happen starting
from within. So at some point, the two feet, the two shoes, the one
    heart—
they will come together in the way they are supposed to.
But you must believe.

AMAN MOJADIDI

Aman Mojadidi has been working in Afghanistan for several years now in the nonprofit sector. This prose poem documents the conflicting emotions and realities of being an Afghan American in Kabul. Meant to capture Kabul in a specific time, this prose poem is a time capsule, one that is honest about the political situation and Mojadidi's own ambivalent identity.

What Can One Say about Living in Kabul?

Kabul, Afghanistan 2006

Where things go "boom" in the night while children dream of fallen kites and parents lie awake thinking of what they will feed them tomorrow. Where youthful love resembles a Bollywood film and frustration simmers beneath the unturned skin of unemployed men passing you on the street. Where militaries and militants play their war games, each thinking they know what's best for everyone else; while most everyone else just wants the fighting to stop. To stop hearing bombs explode in the not distant enough distance and seeing men with guns roaming around playing fiddle on their AK-47s. Children on Chicken Street fighting over who gets to sell you matches, while adults try to dig deep into your pockets selling you "all handmade, very old" tapestries and fur coats you'd be too embarrassed to ever actually wear in Kabul . . . or at least you should be. And what about the day-streets where everyone seems to live?

Men sitting around
　　walking around
　　　　looking around
　　　　　　looking at you.

But when driving at midnight, most all have disappeared into the night, while a few appear in the headlights—out of the dark and into the dark they seek out their homes amid the settling dust. Where weekends can be had by the lake just outside of town and mornings can still be magical; nestled beneath the bright sun, above the shimmering lake, and between snow-covered mountains. These are the happier days! Yes, the happier days when one can appreciate being in such a land. And there's also the "moneyer" side of things . . . dinners for dollars, lots of them. Among expats and foreigners and music and alcohol, we forget about the world outside . . . at least for a while. "But is that so wrong?" I ask myself as images of pasty-faced colonialists slowly fade into my head saying, "Of course it isn't!" Another whiskey please! And then off to save the impoverished, the ones who can't save themselves. But do they really need saving? Like coins we set aside as "ours," only to be spent later when the world has lost interest and turned its sights on new vulnerables, or old vulnerables that now seem vulnerable again.

And the question that never grows old:
"Where are you from?"

And the difficulty I have in trying to explain how I don't know. How nowhere feels like home. And how it's not really about where I'm from, but where I'm going. Not far enough . . . from my own fear, my own uncertainty in all that makes up this fragile life. And here on the street, the butcher keeps butchering, and the soldier keeps soldiering, and the fruit seller keeps fruit selling, and the beggar keeps begging, and the, well, you get the point. Or do you? Does anyone really know what's going on here? Where the price of paradise is strapped to one's chest and paid with the push of a button? Where militaries come and go bringing freedom in a bullet and Burger King behind barbed wire? Where teachers in cardboard schools with collapsing roofs get trained once and forgotten and keep beating students with a stick when they don't answer quickly enough? Where health clinics lack basic medication because it's all ended up in the streets of the bazaar for sale on the open market? But Afghanistan is an open market, full of opportunity, full of potential—the potential to exploit. To put profits before people and to pay the minimum because people will do it for that price. And you can say they have a choice, but then never ask yourself, "Do they?" And what about those IEDs? Incomplete Educational Directives? Wait, no, that's not what anyone wants to talk about. It's the Improvised Explosive Devices we're all worried about.

Improvised, making it up as they go, a cell phone, a teddy bear, an oil can. Did you know that a bag of rice could kill you? So among such things, how does something resembling love grow in one's heart? Where the soil is no longer fertile, unable to nurture those emotional roots so that what grows may properly bear fruit? But who wants to hear me speak about love? I don't. So let's talk about other things like . . . how 'bout them L.A. Lakers? But Qarghah Lake is low again so we fear drought. Come on, snows of Paghman, fall! And more importantly, melt! So there is water once again and we can start to fear floods. And now the cold is settled in. Into my skin, into my bones, and into my dreams where death made special appearances lately, impersonating my mother. Staring into yellow-green eyes, I'm told it could mean I saved her. Taken the life in my dreams so the dreams in her life could survive and death stays away. And I want to believe her. I want to believe in her. But she's restless, and unsure of the answers to questions that guide her hair through the fingers of her left hand. And then another night begins to fall, putting the day's dust to rest and pushing people off the street and into their cold, dark homes so . . .

What can one say about living in Kabul?

WAJMA AHMADY

*Wajma Ahmady captures both the joy of family life, a transplanted
Afghan family, and the shame of not having her American friend
understand or appreciate the delicious messiness of home.*

What? You Never . . .

*"Everywhere I go, it's me and me. Half of me living my life, the other
half watching me live it."*

—SANDRA CISNEROS

*"About the truth, if you give it to a person, then he has power over you.
And if someone gives it to you, then they have made themselves your
slave. It's a strong magic. You can never take it back."*

—CHAQ UXMAL PALOQUIN

It was after a weekend trip home. My friend came with me, an extra
half off on a companion Amtrak ticket. On the way back, she touched
her jeans and socks and said to herself, but loud enough for me to hear,
"How did they get so dirty?"

And I said, "Maybe it was when we were playing with my cousins at
the park?"

But then she said, "No, I was really careful. I think it was at your
grandmother's house. The kitchen floor was really dirty."

I looked at her and wanted to say, "What? You never lived in a house
where you started cleaning right after the last person finished eating, but
the minute you're done washing the floor you see that it's dirty all over
again just like it had been before and instead of crying, you laugh, you
laugh so hard because now everyone is in the kitchen laughing with
you and all the while you hear their voices like sweet hushes, theirs in

yours, and yours in theirs, and you know that you wouldn't give anything up for this, kneeling on the kitchen floor with the wet, wet rag and your heart filled with their voices?

What? You never slept on a *tushak* on the floor in one room with twenty people who whispered and talked and told stories and jokes into the dawn of the day even though you said you would sleep when the lights were out?

What? You never ate cross-legged on the floor, food laid out on the *dist-er-khan,* sharing food on the same plate with your cousins and aunts and uncles and neices and nephews, digging your hands into *bolonee* and *kaab-e-lee* and *sabzee,* and just when the last piece of *naan* is gone, your *beebeejan* walks in with a big, big platter saying, "Eat, eat, it's good for you!" and everyone wastes no time except for the Amerikaii who sits there politely and waits her turn?

What? You've never seen a grandfather throw the hollow chicken bones on the *dist-er-khan* and gurgle from the bottom of his throat and hear him spit loudly in the bathroom? That's nothing! In Mazar, they'll do it right in front of you on the street and clean their teeth with *naswaq* sitting there trying to sell you something in the bazaar!

What? You never . . .

Instead, shame crossed my face. I looked down and said, "Ya, it was dirty."

FICTION

♦♦♦

MIR TAMIM ANSARY

From Dreaming in Dari, an unpublished novel: Abdullah is the product of a brief liason between an Afghan man and an American hippie traveling through Afghanistan in the late '60s. His American mother abandoned him when he was four, returning to America, where she died. His Afghan father sent him to America alone in 1980, to live with his American relatives, because the Soviets had just invaded. Now Abdullah—known in America as Abel—is thirty-three years old. He's culturally American and back in Afghanistan for a (post-Taliban) visit. He goes with his cousin Zainab to visit the tomb of his ancestor Sheikh Alaudin, a mystic poet who lived in the eighteenth century.]

Dreaming in Dari

CHAPTER 30

A noise disturbed Abel. He folded up the letter and pushed it back into the pillow. The men were coming back from *namaz*. Samad beckoned to him. "Abdullah-jan. it is time for *zyarat* now, if you're ready."

Abel considered announcing that he had changed his mind. He had what he had come for, his father's letter. Besides, his heart was churning badly, and he needed to process what he'd read. Yet he felt a strange duty to the man who was buried here, a strange reluctance to show him any disrespect.

He followed the group up a pounded dirt walkway and into the mausoleum itself. An intricate floral design was painted on the walls with red, brown and yellow lines. He was led to a large room, open at the top to the sky. In the middle of the room was the sheikh's grave. Grass was growing on the mound of dirt, no doubt nourished directly by rainfall. A latticework of wood surrounded the mound. A few plaques worked into the lattice had words carved into them, no doubt quotations from the poetry of his ancestor Sheikh Alaudin. As they entered, a group of men looked about at them curiously. Atish Gul bounded over and settled into the group like hot water mingling into tea. He said something in a low voice, and Abdullah caught that it was genealogical: he was telling the group that this was the grandson of the grandson of the grandson of the sheikh, a direct genetic descendant of the famous man. The whole group gazed respectfully at Abdullah, a respect he certainly had not earned. He felt burdened by a gaze that placed on him obligations he could not possibly fulfill. An old man crouching beside the door tried to struggle to his feet. Abdullah settled the fellow back down and leaned over to kiss his cheeks, even though he had no idea who the man was. Zainab murmured a name and explained how this man and Abel were related, but it was too complicated for Abdullah to understand right then.

"Um, yes, yes . . . of course . . ." he murmured. Already, he felt deep waters rising above his head. The old man yanked his hand to make him sit down. As soon as he was settled the old fellow cackled cheerfully, "You are like my very own son." He had exactly one tooth, a long incisor in the middle of his enormous grin. His wrinkled skin had the tough yet softened look of ancient leather. "Bless you, my boy, for coming back," he declared. "I have kept watch over your land for you. I have all your deeds and titles at home, don't worry. You and your seed will never lose the sacred soil within sight of the Sheikh Sahib's tomb while I have strength in these biceps. You know about the Amir of Kashmir, of course."

Abdullah shook his head, glancing around at the appointments and furnishings. This room with its many windows, its shade, its grass-covered grave, and its bird nests clinging to every corner and cranny felt permeated by life. The birds twittered and chirped and cooed. A music of bird song intertwined with all the other noises, softly beautifying them. He still felt alienated but also calm.

Old One-Tooth clutched at his arm to make him pay attention to the story he wanted to recount. "The Amir of Kashmir displeased Ahmad Shah Baba, so the emperor ordered that metal stakes be poked right into his eyeballs. At the exact moment that the amir was blinded, the sheikh was performing his ablutions. The water he lifted to his face turned to blood. At once, he said, 'My devoted acolyte, the Amir of Kashmir has suffered harm.' He sent a messenger to his devotee. He told the amir to come to him. So the amir's attendants brought the man to this place, his eyes all bound up with bandages. The amir wailed to the sheikh: 'Look, what has been done to me!' The sheikh said, 'You are faultless. The punishment imposed upon you was unjust. Believe in me and unwrap your bandages.' The amir unwrapped his bandages and *wai!* He could see! His eyes were unblemished and free from pain. He fell at the feet of the sheikh and tried to bestow kisses upon him. Sheikh Sahib said, 'As I have done a kindness to you, go now and you do kindness to others.' But the amir would not forget his gratitude. After the sheikh died, may-God-bestow-peace-on-him-and-his-descendants, that amir spent his treasure and sweat to build this sanctuary over the sheikh's tomb. The acolytes have been coming to this place from hundreds of miles around, ever since it was built, every year, just as you have come, and all others who have come seeking to know God's love."

"Uh huh." Abdullah looked around, hoping his embarrassment didn't show. This tale of the sheikh would make an interesting story to tell to his friends at the institute when he got back. Alice Stokes had an interest in folklore; this would be right up her alley.

The group of acolytes in the alcove by the window had a book open. "Come," they said. "Descendent of the sheikh, read with us. Read with us."

But of course, he couldn't read with them. He squirmed in place, trying to think of an excuse. He was reminded of Prophet Muhammad in the cave when the angel came to him and said, "Read!" and Muhammad had to admit shamefacedly that he couldn't, he was illiterate.

Then Zainab came to his aid, but in the worst possible way. "Abdullah-jan wants to pray first. Go ahead, Abdullah. Say some prayers next to his blessed grave." Without a pause, she added, however, "I will pray too. We can pray side by side."

Grateful to her for offering a model, he moved next to the grave. She knelt down and opened her hands, holding them palms up before her as if to receive water poured from a jug. So this was not official *namaz:* she was just going to meditate.

Well, he could do that. He knelt beside her and copied her pose. He had his back to the acolytes, so they could not see his face. Zainab closed her eyes, and her lips began to move. Say, this wasn't bad: whatever she was saying, she was doing it silently. Perhaps he would not have to perform *namaz* after all. Perhaps he had only to kneel here with his hands raised and spend a few minutes in silence moving his lips.

He could be saying anything—no one would know. But then he thought, as a gesture of respect, he ought to say words from the Quran. Whatever fragments came to mind. The Fatiha, for example. That was a bit of Quran he remembered. Praise be to God, ruler of all creation. His lips moved soundlessly. And after he completed that verse, he remembered another one, the shortest verse in the Quran, the easy one—he still knew it by heart. *Qul Hwalahu Ahad. Allah hu Samad.* God is one! He shares divinity with none! And then his thoughts began to wander. *Hello hello hello how low* Kurt Cobain? What was he doing in Abel's head? Get out, Kurt, you're dead . . . but then it was Fiona Apple's throaty snarl *Please forgive me for my distance . . . the pain is evident in my existence* he had to bring himself back. His butt was stiff. Shares divinity with none. Stay focused. *lum yalid wa lum yoolud.* He was not begat, he begat no one. So strange to be here, Mr. Ancestor. His forearms were feeling the strain of holding up his hands. How long would he have to stay in his pose? Man-oh-man, Grandfather, you really put a guy through the wringer, he thought. Or should I say great, great, great—how many greats away are you anyway? *Please forgive me for my distance.* How long ago did you live, dude? I'm your direct descendant, you know. Genetically I'm just as close to you as any of these other mugs in the room. Closer, actually, by Afghan count—son of the son of the son of the son, etc. And yet I couldn't be further away from you in the cultural universe. My life and yours. A universe apart—a cosmos—more than that. The word is lacking. My life has traveled so fuckin' far away from yours in just those four generations or five, or whatever. *Limitless undying love which shines around me like a million suns . . . the* Beatles are underrated, he thought . . . *calls me on and on across the universe* strange that the world is big enough to accommodate such a distance. In your day, Ancestor, India was inconceivably far away. You astonished people by going there and back. Hmm, now how do I know that? Must have heard it the other night at Agha Lala's. Oh shit, I forgot. Got to keep reciting Quran. Uh oh, shouldn't say "shit" and "Quran" in the same sentence. Or say "shit" in your tomb. Fuck, what's wrong with me? Focus, focus. Hocus pocus. Man, my hands are about to drop off. *Alhamdu'lillahi rabul alamin.*

The words rang in his head as if he had chanted them in that special melodic way that the Quran is supposed to be chanted by those who have the skill of Quranic chanting. *Qiraut.* Much the same as what cantors do. What's wrong with these Muslims and Jews, they're almost exactly the same, why do they keep fighting? Long-ago trouble, unable to forgive. Something's broken there. *Let go the hatred in your heart, the almighty is closer to you than your jugular . . .* The words wailed musically in his head. Wait a minute, how could they be in Farsi, how was he saying the Quran in Farsi? And so musically! Oh wait—that was not inside his head. Wow, going crazy. The acolytes were chanting melodically, singing, you might as well call it. *Loving heart, adore the pagan idol without fear. Passion's pilgrim, nothing but the rapture here* . . . Must be the guy's poetry. Never knew they were going to sing it just like it *was* the Quran. He let his lips keep moving in his conversation with the man whose body had once been buried here, although nothing could be possibly be left of him now except bones. Or do bones dissolve into the earth too? Have your bones dissolved, Grandpa? I feel more comfortable calling you Grandpa. And that's quite okay, you can use "Grandpa" if you like. What was your world like? I wonder. Were you like Atish Gul? Or did you mystify people who knew you and make them feel ashamed? I don't think you did. This Atish Gul is a cool guy; if he's anything like you were, I might have liked you, Grandpa. You could like me still. Your father is dead but you still love him. Death does not end love. You love your mother too. Look inside yourself, Abdullah-jan, all the love you ever felt is still inside. Hate decays if you let it, but Love never dies. You love her too, there was no fault. Everything unfolds as God has planned it, you don't have to be afraid, your soul is safe with me.

It was the devotees singing his verse. Your soul is safe with me. That's what it was, he could hear it quite loudly out there. *Please forgive me for my distance.* What had happened to his hands? *Shame is manifest in my resistance* he couldn't feel them anymore *to your love, to your love* they must have gotten numb, maybe they fell off, hee hee. Oh, sorry Gramps, I forgot I was in your tomb, supposed to be solemn. Who told you that? I love a good song, a hearty laugh, a tasty meal. Didn't you know that? Did you think I separated myself from God's creation? How is that the way to God? You have to love what Allah created if you love Allah.

"Make the pilgrimage to Holy Mecca, everywhere you'll see . . . The image of the friend you love who loveth also thee . . ."

But I can't love her, you see. She loveth thee. I can't, she did that thing, you know. They all said she was bad. They cherished you, you hid from them, you made them sad. I couldn't help it, Grandpa. I was mad. There is no I or me or you or him or her or them or us or we. Separation is the opposite of love but you are love. Be with love, there's nothing but.

"The Buddhists have a temple. Enter it and see . . . it's colored with the love . . . of the one who loveth thee—"

Abel heard himself wondering what was happening. He heard this as if it were someone else's voice calling to him from another room. He wondered how come he could understand the poetry his ancestor's acolytes were passionately singing behind him. He wondered how come he was talking to himself as if he were two people. The answer was spoken by a voice that was closer to him than his ear, closer to him than his consciousness, and it said, "Not alone. No one is alone in the capital of rapture."

And his ancestor's acolytes continued to sing: "Don't hold yourself apart. Nothing holds apart from you . . . for, sweetness, you are love and only love is true."

Abdullah stopped wondering what was happening. He let go of his thoughts and they went drifting out of reach. He felt his parents and all his kinfolk at the family compound and everyone at the institute, and his poor befuddled grandparents, and Katy and shadow legions of others, floating all around him like wraiths, and he was a wraith who could not find the edge between him and them, and in this state, he tasted grief in himself and in everyone else, oceanic grief, and then he sensed something bigger, something much more frightening, millions of other shadows, billions, all of them composed almost entirely of grief, and in his fright he tried to shrink, knowing that he could not experience the grief of all the world and survive. Have mercy on me, Grandpa, I'm too little to contain that much sorrow, I'll die. There's no death if you let go. Death is separation, him from thee from me from she from them from we, but there is no separation in reality, there's only seamless unity. Let go of longing, be with love, you're safe with me. He let it go, the wall crumbled, the anxious barrier dissolved, he let himself and all the others flow together like water with tea, and then he knew: there was nothing out there but everlasting love, binding every atom to every atom in a concatenation of trillions that added up to one. Just one.

Perhaps he blinked. He must have blinked. That must have been what woke him out of his reverie. Out of his prayer, he thought—no other word would do. His hands were still out there. Zainab was no longer kneeling next to him. The acolytes were still singing his ancestor's poetry. He wiped his face, because it was wet with tears he didn't remember shedding. He saw one of the acolytes nudging another and nodding in his direction. Even though he was twenty feet away from them and the words were spoken in a low voice, Abdullah heard what he said: "Sheikh-baba is with him. He is being visited."

Abel tensed up. He'd have to pretend he believed that kind of nonsense. But then he let go of his worry. He had no quarrel with the description, really. Certainly some other voice had sounded inside his head, and not in a bad way. In fact, he felt purified and ready for the world, his senses on alert—with no shields up. He didn't recognize this feeling. All his life, alert included readiness to defend. Alert meant mustered to repel intrusion. Now, for the first time, alert meant ready to let the world in.

He dropped his hands at last and stood up. His knees felt steady. He walked to the circle of his ancestor's devotees and sat down among them. He didn't melt into the group as Atish Gul had done. He was different. Different was okay, though. Different was not separate from. He looked around and saw human being after human being returning his gaze, each one some small soul like himself, battling big odds and struggling to stay afloat. They were all comfortable with one another. The old man with the reedy voice who had been singing offered him the book. "Will you sing a few?"

Abel smiled and shook his head. "I don't know how to read Dari very well."

"Shall I sing some more, then?"

"Please." Abdullah settled back and time passed and the light slowly changed. Zainab had left the room directly after the prayers, but eventually she came back, her basket empty. She had given away all the candies. "We should start back to the city," she said.

WALI SHAAKER

*Set in the Afghan refugee camps in Peshawar, this touching story
reveals the humiliation Afghans suffered in the camps. The young man
of the story has an opportunity to escape from this. Yet Pakistani
bureaucracy is overwhelmingly resistant to allowing him to leave
the camps. Wali Shaaker, a widely published poet and short
story writer, publishes primarily in Dari and is now
working on his first English-language novel.*

Identity Card

"Now that I am here in Pakistan, what should I do next?" I asked myself while I was listening to Ahmad Zahir's song "Tanhaa Shodam Tanhaa," in a small room that I had to share with four other young Afghan men. I remembered what my parents had advised me to do before I left for Pakistan.

"Listen, son," said my father while sitting on his bed with books scattered all around him. "Wherever you go, we want you to finish your school. We want you to become somebody. When you return, we want you to serve your country and family."

I thought to myself, "Well, if I am to go to school and one day go back and serve my country, first I need to get that final signature on my refugee identification card that I have been working on for the past month and half."

Within a few minutes, I was out the door, heading for the refugee identification card office. When I got off the bus, I saw an Afghan man sitting on the sidewalk trying desperately to keep a flock of flies away from a couple of fruit baskets that he had prepared for sale. As I asked him for directions to the refugee office, I realized it was about a twenty-minute walk away on a dusty road along a creek.

It was past two p.m., and the weather was unbearably hot. My shirt was almost entirely wet with sweat as I walked quickly to get to the office. I wanted to wash my head and face using the water of the little creek running alongside the road as if it were racing me. I noticed that a herd of oxen were having a great time playing right in the middle of the creek. So I changed my mind and kept walking on.

As I was getting closer to the office, I saw a long line of at least one hundred Afghan refugee men waiting for their turn to get into the office building. I thought I would never be able to get into the office if I stood at the end of the line. After a brief inquiry of the soldier who was guarding the entrance, I discovered that this line was for those who wished to receive food stamps. There was also a relatively smaller number of people waiting to enter the ID card office. They were hiding from the burning rays of the sun under the shadow of a wall across the street. So I walked over and joined the crowd. I must mention that "slow" is an understatement for describing the way the lines were moving forward.

After a few minutes I noticed an old man, maybe in his late sixties, who seemed worried and restless. He was about six feet tall, and fit. He had quite a bit of pitch-black *surma* around his eyes. Like the winter snow, a long white beard covered his kind-looking face, somehow adding dignity and charisma to his look.

Every few minutes he would get up, cross the street, and talk to a young man who was waiting at almost the end of the line. Then the young man would point toward us, and it appeared to me that he would ask him to return to where he was waiting for their turn to come.

I sat leaning against the wall, looking at the young men across the street and asking myself all kinds of questions: "Where in Afghanistan are these people from?" I had not seen many like them in Kabul.

They all seemed tired and worried, covered head to toe with dust under the hot sun of Peshawar that poured arrowheads of fire at them. They wore patched, old clothes. Most of them were staring at the ground as if they had lost something very precious and were searching to find it.

They all must have families awaiting them in a tent on the outskirts of Peshawar, waiting for them to bring food, and medicine. Wouldn't they want to finish school like I did? Wouldn't their parents want them to be educated? What about the old man? Maybe he had a sick child or grandchild at home waiting for him to bring some medicine and food. Maybe he was hungry himself. Maybe he had lost a loved one in the war? Maybe . . . ? Maybe . . . ?

I kept asking myself these questions even though I felt as if I already knew what the answers were. The people across the street sitting in the shadow with me didn't do much better either. With pale faces and glazed eyes, they were silently waiting for their turn to approach. Meanwhile, the old man kept crossing the street only to be sent back to the shaded area. He reminded me of my *kaukau* (uncle), and his behavior reminded me of a restless bird in a cage that my uncle used to keep in Afghanistan.

Finally, after a couple of hours, it was my turn to enter the ID card office. Five clerks were sitting all around it. From the smell of the atmosphere, I realized that chewing tobacco and cigarettes were among two of the most heavily consumed commodities in that office. The topic of discussion must have been hot, because none of the clerks really noticed my presence for a few extremely long minutes. I slowly approached one of the desks and handed the clerk my ID card to be stamped. He examined it closely from behind the thick lenses of his glasses atop the middle of his nose bridge.

To tell the truth, I was a little nervous: "What if he doesn't stamp it? How am I going to live in this country?"

"Ten rupees!" he announced. I didn't know exactly what he meant by that.

"Pardon me?" I inquired.

"Ten rupees!" he repeated.

Thinking that he was only joking with me, I smiled! But he didn't reciprocate. There were a few moments of silence between us, during which I kept asking myself, "Am I dreaming, or did I hear him wrong?" And I can almost bet that he was searching for a simple phrase to make me understand that he wanted money!

Eventually, with a straight face and a stern tone of voice, he said, "It will cost you ten rupees to get the stamp on your card. Do you want it or not? If you don't, then don't waste my time. I have a lot to do today."

I quickly glanced at the other clerks sitting around the room, who were desperately trying to ignore our conversation. At this moment, I had to make a decision. So I reached to my pocket and took ten rupees out and slowly placed them on his desk. Even though the ceiling fan was revolving like a helicopter blade, all of a sudden, double the amount of sweat started pouring off my forehead than when I was walking in the sun a few hours ago. He stamped the card and slid it toward me.

Although I didn't want to, without looking at the man, I murmured, "Thank you!" and walked out of the office, feeling the heavy weight of guilt and embarrassment on my shoulders.

As soon as I stepped out of the building, I heard two people arguing. I looked up and there he was—the old white-bearded man. He was arguing with the young soldier responsible for guarding the entrance to the building and keeping the waiting line in order. I went closer to find out exactly what he was unhappy about.

The old man's complaint was that the line was too long and that he had to take some food home for his daughter and grandchildren.

"My grandchild is sick at the camp, and I have to take him medicine and be with him. He can't wait any longer. For God's sake, please let us go ahead of these people," he begged.

The young soldier, who seemed to be losing his patience, was refusing to budge. Suddenly I saw the young boy running toward the old man to calm him down. But it was too late. The young guard had lost his patience. He pushed the old Afghan man away, and slapped him very hard. I doubt if there was anyone in that line who didn't hear it. In fact, I am convinced that everyone heard it, and even the waiting men across the street.

I was standing very close to the old man, right behind him. Immediately, he turned his face from the crowd. But his eyes met with mine. In a split second, tears overflowed his eyes, ran down his kind-looking face mixed with *surma* like a creek, and disappeared under his snow-white beard.

I wanted to tell him, "It is okay, *kaukau*. One day this misery in our lives will end and we all will go back home. Just be patient and pray to God to help us get our freedom from the Communists."

But I couldn't—I couldn't say even a word. My throat was filled with sorrow. The old man's face was wet. He was looking up at the sky, as if he was speaking to God. I turned around, and as soon as I took the first step toward the dusty road, my eyes overflowed with tears as well. I tried not to cry, but couldn't help it.

The sun was about to set, and the sky was getting ready for a long and dark night to approach. Soon to disappear, a variety of colors filled the sky—red, blue, violet-gold, and gray. I noticed the herd of oxen still roaming in the creek. Suddenly, I stopped, took my new ID card out of my pocket, and stared at it for a few seconds.

I looked at my face in the picture that was fixed on the corner of the card. It was almost entirely stamped. I tore my card in half and then I tore it again and again. I scattered the pieces in the water, and they slowly disappeared from my sight, dancing on the creek's running water. Then I sat there and cried some more.

While I was crying, I thought I heard my father's voice: "Don't be a coward. Is this how tough you are?" I agreed with him. I had to be strong if I was to survive. I stopped crying and wiped my tears.

FARHAD AZAD

*In these two vignettes about the effects of war on patriarchal figures,
Farhad Azad captures the powerlessness that Afghan fathers
experienced in the face of extremism and the beauty of the small
gardens that were lost to decades of war and destruction.*

The Broken Window

The window was dusty from the outside. The rain hadn't washed it for
months. Dirt caked the broken glass. The wind blew harshly through the
cracks in the glass, making a ghostly sound. The noise awoke the boy, and
he opened his drowsy eyes. He got up from his cold bed on the bare, hard
ground. He then gingerly walked over to the window and touched it.

He looked outside at the apple tree swaying in solitude. Each branch
of the tree moved, and each leaf stretched further than the other. The
cream-colored dirt rose from the ground and flew high into the air. The
open sky was covered with gray and stormy clouds.

The rain was on its way, but there was no thunder or lighting. The boy
glanced at the rolling hills of Faryab. He knew the dry hills needed the
rain so that they could be as green as they were in the spring. The apple
tree needed rain too so it would bear more fruit next year. It hadn't rained
all summer, and now autumn had arrived. The boy wanted spring. He
couldn't remember spring.

The boy spent the drawn-out days by the broken window. When he
ventured outside, he would walk by himself to the bare hills near his
ruined, empty village, where his dilapidated mud-walled house was the
only building standing. He listened to the yellow birds that nested in the
branches of the apple tree. He sometimes took his book of poems and
read. Going outside was rare. He preferred to stay inside and watch the
hills and the apple tree from his broken window.

Through the crack of the broken glass he could see the apple tree as
if it were under water. He could see the hills in different designs and
shapes. He liked that. He would stare through the cracks of the window

for hours. He was never bored. Solitude followed the boy everywhere. Only the broken window, the dry hills, and the single apple tree kept him company.

One drop of rain hit the window. It streaked down and left a trail of mud. The boy's eyes followed the tiny drop. It reached the bottom of the window and disappeared. Another drop fell and then another and another until the window became wet. Soon, the rain quickly washed away the dirt. This made the boy happy. He tried to smile but couldn't.

As it rained harder, the boy heard the creaking sound of the wooden door opening. The boy's father, a tall man with a grayish beard, wearing a chapan, hurriedly came inside. He was dripping wet. He smelled of rain. He sat on the wooden stool and laid the wet rugs that he carried on his shoulders on the floor. He took off his muddy boots and let out a lengthy sigh.

He didn't notice the boy standing by the window. The son knew that his father had not sold their rugs at the bazaar today. For weeks they had sold their household items for food. The old man kept his gray eyes to the ground. Water trickled from his hair onto his face.

He craved something warm. With a painful moan he stood up and went to the stove to start a fire with the little branches that were left. Once they were ablaze, he warmed his hands and then placed an iron teapot onto the rusty stove. He pulled the wooden stool by the fire and sat there, closing his fatigued eyes.

The boy watched his father from the window. He turned around and watched the rain and his father's reflection from the broken glass of the window. The small fire began to warm the little room. The wood cracked inside the stove as the teapot came to a boil.

The man got up, put some tea into the hot pot, and waited for it to settle in the water. He took out a bruised apple from his pocket and placed it next to the stove. He sat by the wall and filled his teacup. He took a sip, closed his eyes, laid his head against the hard mud wall, and fell into a deep sleep.

The boy was hungry. He went to the stove, found the apple, and picked it up. In his corner by the window, he ate it slowly. It was the only thing that he had eaten in days. His skinny hands held the apple as he bit into it.

After finishing his apple he opened his book of poems and read for a while. The thunder and rain shook the house. The rain came down harder. It didn't matter to the boy, for he had fallen asleep.

The wind hollowed through the cracks of the broken window, waking the boy. His father was still asleep. The fire in the stove had died out. He got up and looked out the broken window. It was night. The storm had passed. The sky was clear and dark, without stars.

An Old Garden

Twenty years have passed, but I still remember that summer afternoon in Kabul . . .

The old, wooden door was open. I walked into my grandfather's garden. The entrance walkway was laid with light ivory mountain stone. The garden was a large square yard divided into four sections. A huge pomegranate tree was in the middle. On each side of the pomegranate tree was a small clear pool of water surrounded by clay flowerpots that contained maroon-colored geraniums. One side of the four sections had yellow, red, and white rosebushes. On the other side of the garden, there were a cherry tree and an apple tree which was filled with yellow apples. At the opposite corner was a small vineyard which included white, scarlet, and purple grapes. And in the last corner was a bright flowerbed packed with snapdragons, carnations, black-eyed Susans, purple cornflowers, dellailas, and daylilies. Like a little boy in a candy store, I was mesmerized by the distinct colors.

I heard footsteps. My grandfather, a tall man with broad shoulders and a gray mustache, wearing his black pajamas, entered the garden.

He smiled at me and said in his deep voice, "Salaam, salaam, where have you been?"

I smiled back and told him, "I have been at school."

He replied, "You havebeen at school for weeks without a break?"

I answered, "No, sir. I was rather busy with schoolwork."

He looked at me and said, "Too busy to see your old grandfather?"

I put my head down, and knew he was right. I hadn't seen him in weeks. When I was a little boy, I would spend my days in his garden, but now I had been so busy with school. My family had moved to the Wazir Akbar Khan district in Kabul; it was far away from my grandfather's house in the old city, and we didn't get a chance to visit him regularly.

He looked at me again with his dark green eyes, laid his hand on my shoulder, and said, "I understand. Let's have some tea."

I sat down on a red Mazari rug under the pomegranate tree. I looked up and saw a tiny bird's nest. My grandfather never picked the pomegranates. He cherished the blossoms in the spring, he used the shade in the summer heat, and he ate the fruit in late summer when it fell to the ground or sometimes in the pool of water.

My grandfather's father was a rug merchant. As a young man, my grandfather took his father's trade, and traveled with him to many parts of Afghanistan, but mostly to the cities of Mazar Sharif, Kandahar, and Herat. Like his father, he had a keen interest in gardens. His father had a house on the outskirts of Kabul which had four different gardens. At the age of twenty, my grandfather married and moved into the city and started his business of selling rugs and furniture. In 1934, at the age of twenty-three, he bought the old two-story house.

His passion for gardens never lessened. He would spend hours in his garden. He only hired professional gardeners to put in new trees or cross-breed flowers. On his trips to different cities he collected distinct plants and trees. The pomegranate tree in the yard was a gift from a friend in Kandahar. The white seedless grapes came from a small vineyard in the town of Karzi in the province of Herat. He brought back daylily bulbs from the city of Herat. The purple grapes that grew wild on the walls came from Chahrkar, and the yellow apple tree came from a village near the city of Maimana, and the cherry tree from Paghman. The ivory stone that covered the walkway by the door and the clear water pools came from a mountain close to the city of Ghazni. Altogether, his garden was a composition of small pieces of Afghanistan.

My relatives had moved to the new parts of Kabul, but my grandfather refused to move. He loved his garden too much to give it up. He even named it Baagh-e Ziba (The Garden of Beauty). After my grandmother passed away ten years ago, my grandfather grieved, but it was his garden that kept him going. Now he lived by himself in the old house and with his beloved garden.

He came back with the tea and some candy. We drank tea and relaxed under the tree. He asked how my mom and dad were. I told him that they were always arguing and never stopped. My grandfather looked melancholy and told me not to worry. He went on to say that my mom—his daughter—and my dad were never meant to be together. He told me that it was all a mistake. He then looked at me with teary eyes and said, "This world leaves us in despair and pain, but it is the beauty that we must look upon to survive."

The "beauty" that he talked about was his garden. I knew that his life was not always joyful. He had rough times, but it was the garden he loved that made him endure the pitfalls of life.

We sipped some more tea, and I heard someone playing the rubab next door. He smiled and said that the new next-door neighbors where from Logar and one of their sons played the rubab. I heard the trick strings of the rubab being plucked. I closed my eyes and let the music flow within me.

I heard my grandfather whisper to himself, "Oh this garden of mine, how kind you have been to this old heart . . ."

DONIA GOBAR

This award-winning short story is set in Kabul during the Communist invasion. The son of a late revolutionary, the young protagonist of this story lives in close quarters with his mother. The discrepancy between classes is quite significant in this story. For a moment, the poor young man shares an experience with a wealthy young Kabuli woman. But he returns to the hard labor, loss, and fear of the new Communist government. The class discrepancies are not erased, even in the new regime; only a heightened sense of fear encompasses the city. Donia Gobar is a physician whose poems and stories have been published widely in diaspora publications as well as American publications.

Aya

The faint light of a candle trembled in the bareness of what was their home. Dusky shadows quivered over the narrow drugget, clean-swept mud floor, rusty stove, rolled-up old blankets beside the wall, few cracked dishes upon a shelf, and the only window, with some of its panes covered by old newspapers. The young man watched Aya's old hands while she carefully poured tea into their cups. His mind's eye traveled through the hundreds of hills and valleys on her kind face, to the time when winter had not come to stay on her dark hair.

Gently her voice broke the silence. "You look tired. Why don't you rest a bit? Later you can go to the national fete, Jushn-e Melee. Tonight is the last night, you know . . ."

"National Fete . . ." he murmured, his eyelids getting heavy. Pacing on the edge between sleep and wakefulness, he remembered.

They used to go together to the Meadows, where every year, poor or rich, people celebrated their nation's independence from the "superpower of the time."

His father used to tell him how years ago ordinary people had refused to become subservient to a foreign power and had defeated the invader three times. Then how this current dark period had started, and how the

Black List had reached all those wonderful nameless heroes one by one, in shadowy nights, never to be seen or heard from again. How the brutal governments had deprived people of education, wealth, and freedom of thought, to ensure their own stability and to satisfy their secret allies' political interests; how the religion had been twisted, turned, and deformed to serve the purposes of the government, decade after decade; and still, how the isolated, tough seeds of freedom, in shabby clothes and mud houses, had kept growing . . . those self-taught scholars, invisible to the big world outside.

He remembered that wintry night, when his father had gone to one of his secret meetings, and supper was getting cold. It was years ago. His father did not come back that evening, or ever again . . .

"Now with the Red Flags, they don't like it if people won't show up," said Aya, sipping her tea slowly and continuing, "You might even get to meet the right kind of workers, the comrades."

Sarcasm poured bitterness into his short, light laughter. His eyes still closed, he listened to the wondering voice of his mother saying, "Today I asked them, in the Big House, what dictatorship of proletariat means, and the youngest son told me it means a government by the workers for the workers."

"Wolves in sheep clothing, that is what it means," he murmured. His mother looked swiftly toward him with worry, and rushed to continue: " I told them how hard you work, then the party guests arrived, and I think they didn't hear me, and I had to get back to work. I will talk to them tomorrow." She lowered her voice, almost to a whisper: "I heard them talking about the ones who are showing betrayal by refusing to join the social events. 'Those are enemies of the people, and they should be pun-ished for being traitors,' they said."

He put his empty cup down on the floor beside him and stretched his legs, thoughtfully rubbing his forehead. "Later, on his way out, the Comrade himself asked me if we had gone to the celebration," said Aya, and she sounded alarmed. Then forced hope slipped beside her words as she continued: "I think it's real nice of him letting me still work for them in the house, not anymore young and strong as I used to be. They could have hired a real worker, you know. They could have taken this shack from us, you know." He sneered quietly, and she tried again to convince him, her voice trailing off between the desperate persuasion and thoughts of the vivid past, empty present, and unknown future. "Look, my son! Don't be stubborn like your father . . . as if he had to speak for everyone else. So there, we lost our home and were left all alone. But he was such a good man . . . He used to dream of making sure that every child could go to school. That someday you may become a doctor and help others. Dreamer he was, and he got himself killed."

She sighed, feeling a sharp pain in her chest again. She hurried on: "Listen! You have got to go out tonight. I am fine. The pills that you got for me are good. I took one today, and the pain stopped. Remember? You always loved to go there to Chumman. Now it is the same. Just the color of flag has changed. I would have gone too, but it's a long way for me to walk. I have some patching and mending to do anyway. I'll get supper ready. The soup is still warm, I think." She stood up and slowly moved toward the oven, her back in a curve, bent forward. "This dear old body was once so quick and upright . . ." he thought sadly before drifting into sleep, his head leaning against the wall, slightly turned to one side.

Aya checked the soup. It was still warm. She went to the shelf and took some dishes. She set the low table and placed the glass containing a bunch of wild-grown lavender next to the candles. Suddenly, her face felt ice cold. Sweat drops appeared on her forehead. The pain cut its way sharply from the left side of her chest to her left arm. She could hardly breathe. Her hazel eyes widened in horror. With her right hand, she took out of her pocket the small red capsule, and after biting it open, placed it under her tongue. The unbearable congestion of sudden rushing blood inside her head made her gasp for air. For a short moment she thought that her head would explode. Then slowly the pain left her, drained of strength. The candle was burning low. The enlarged shadow of the mother moved slowly on the wall. She came to her son, and watched him quietly. His handsome face, deeply tanned by long summer days, was covered with dust. Without making a sound, she sat down next to the blanket and leaned back, thinking . . .

"Every thing for the workers," the comrade boy had said, and she had felt like an outsider, guilty for not being the right kind of worker. She was thinking. Had not she worked all the time . . . in the time of kings and in the time of the revolution? No, her son must not end up like her. What must he do to become the right kind of worker? Those who called themselves comrades . . . what kind of work did they do? She kept wondering. Her son's friend had worked all his life. Such an honest and nice young man he was . . . and so full of humor, always making her laugh whenever he came to visit.

One day he had been dragged away by the police. It had been raining that day, lightly. A few potatoes and a bunch of green onions scattered on the sidewalk were left behind. No one saw him again. Poor soul, he did talk too much for his own good, Aya decided. No! Her son was going to be just fine. He would not talk too much, and he would not go to meetings, and he would become the right kind of worker, the comrade kind. Tonight he had a chance. May be he would get to know someone nice . . . Maybe they would notice him. He would be safe then. She would make him go there tonight. He would go for her sake, to make his old mother happy. Yes, he was going to be safe . . .

Through the feverish alleys in the quiet of the summer night, leaving the shack and Aya behind, the tall shadow moved on. Now, away from the construction site where he carried bricks day after day, and away from home where he felt helpless for not being able to change the hard life of his mother, he was alone by himself . . . covered by night and caught in the whirlpool of thoughts . . .

Smiling, Aya had blessed him before closing the creaking door behind him, saying that she would keep the candle burning. A tender feeling warmed his heart. She always waited up for him . . . as long as he could remember. He was a kid when Aya had started to work as a maid in one of those large houses, after his father had disappeared and they had lost their house. Tagging along with his mother, he had run errands around the house. In exchange they got their meals and could stay in the shack. He had been teased and ridiculed by the children of the rich household, and had envied them for going to and coming from school, their cheeks flushed with excitement. He had been watching and feeling out of place and out of time, peeking through an invisible window at another world, a dream world . . .

Childhood had passed him by. Physical work made him strong and brought them leftover food at the back doors of the town's busy motels. Aya, older and weaker, continued to work in the big house to keep the shack. In his mind, still, he dreamt his father's dream. His young heart raced for love and justice. His burning dark eyes told stories of the world of ruins, bricks, and the soundproof labyrinth of the life that they were caught in.

He left the last narrow road. Then, one by one the city lights appeared. He could walk faster on the paved streets. Now he could see the meadow, jeweled with thousands and thousands of lights, and he could hear the festive sounds shutting the doors to the solitary night beyond. He crossed the bridge over the City River and passed the narrow lane to the green meadow. For a mere second the little boy, his hands tucked in the safety of his parents' warm hands, stepped in the large shoes, while scents of ripe melon, steaming snacks and kabobs, kids' chatter, and sounds of laughter and music filled the air in the chumman. His foot hit a rock and the little boy vanished in time.

Fireworks poured bursting stars in gold, purple, green, and crimson. Way ahead, the many decorated camps resembled the miniature palaces of fairy tales. The area was surrounded with flags in the color of blood. Shiny cars were jamming the road to the campsite, dropping off or picking up the ones from the "other worlds." Aimlessly, he walked away from the bright side.

Carefully he inched his way among the ordinary ones, gathered in small family groups sitting around on old blankets. His wondering gaze paused over a small kid's face turned up toward the sky, her mouth full of juicy melon, her juice-dripping fingers still holding another piece close to her mouth. A far-away feeling clasped his heart. He moved on, passing through unfinished phrases and giggles, feeling strangely alone . . . among all these people.

In the nearest camp someone was playing an accordion and singing his mind's words through the verses written by a poet his father had known. His mother used to hum the song, when she was healthier. What happened to that poet? he wondered. A crowd was blocking the view. He stood under a tree, unnoticed in its dark shade, and listened . . .

> Life will come to an end anyway
> Slavery is not needed.
> If slavery be the bargain,
> Then life is not needed.
> If the sky pours rain of pearls
> Upon you with insult,
> Tell the sky, "Leave,
> Rain is not needed."

He left the shade and walked to an empty space and lay down on his back. The grass was damp and cool against his thin shirt and warm skin. He watched the millions of sparkling stars far above. What are people doing just now on the other side of the earth? he wondered with a strange sense of seclusion. Sounds of music, crowd, fireworks, and cars faded behind the glass borders of wild hopes, tender memories, and the already lost "dream world" of his that years ago, sitting on this grass, he had looked forward to. He thought about his Aya. What had happened to her hopes? How hard she was trying to make believe . . . for his sake, believing that he would be safe. How desperately she was trying. His eyes felt the burning, painful sensation of dry tears. He blinked several times, pressing his eyelids together, and then kept his eyes shut. The earth under the grass was hard and matched the muscles of his back. Silently he stayed there. How long? A fallen leaf in the dark whirlpool of life . . .

Nearing whispers of soft steps, a strangely sweet and wild perfume, the gentle rustle of a skirt and its sweeping downy touch on his hair, a thud . . . all as a passing wonderful breeze traversed his solitary world. Before fading away the voice of a woman wavered in a simple phrase—"Oh, I dropped my purse"—and shattered the invisible border. He opened his eyes and leaned on his elbow, turning toward the sound. Floating softly in the night, coming closer and closer to him, was an angel in white. Waves of dark hair bouncing away from the beautiful face of the woman and curling on her almost bare shoulders. Now she was gracefully bending down, so near to him. His heart began throbbing and he lowered his gaze. The small sparkling purse next to his elbow stared mockingly back at him. His ragged hand reached down for the lost treasure and timidly held it up for the delicate hand of the woman, her fresh breath almost touching his, her bright eyes joyous and bold, looking through him. Her fingers softly brushed against his. A strange vibration burned its way to his pounding heart and softened the stab in pleasure.

"Thank you," she murmured quietly, and then she was gone. Her quick and smooth steps took her over to her waiting friends. They circled around her, as if they were listening eagerly to what she was saying. Suddenly in a burst of laughter they turned and looked at him, and then rushed away into their world . . .

The pleasing echo of a voice died in the emptiness of an angry soul. The surrounding sounds became unbearable in the solitude. The bright lights hurt his blurred vision. The far-away starry sky poured its quivering dark blue shadows over him. Somewhere, in some valley of his being, a silent scream started and was joined by many more. All through the mysterious world of his ego, it overflowed, coming to a halt behind his well-shaped lips. A painful lump tightened his throat. His eyes felt like burning coals. When he stood, his wide shoulders seemed to droop slightly. The hushed grass under his leaving heavy feet whispered quietly with the summer breeze. The empty streets echoed the dull sound of the worn-out shoes racing with the night. The alleys, dark and forlorn, shut the doors to sounds of joy and bright colors, and the tall handsome shadow crept in. Dusty roads did not give away the secret of passing shadow, and kept silently puffing to themselves . . .

The shack was dark. He stopped, then walked faster. The screams vanished and fear spread its dark wings. In his mind, denial strived against the lash of forbidden worries and he hauled himself forward. The door was slightly ajar. "Aya?" The word came out of his mouth as a broken whisper. His tongue felt dry and bitter. He said again, "Aya?" and gently pushed the door open. It caught on something. He slid in and bent on his knees. Hesitating and fearful, his hand reached out and touched the curved back, thin shoulders, wintry hair, and the beloved, dear face—so cold, so horribly cold . . .

He called her name, at first soft and pleading, and then the screams returned, from each cell of his body and each hollow of his soul, bursting into sobs. "Aya . . . Aya . . . Aya . . ."

Outside, a stray dog shrieked out of sleep and walked away into darkness . . .

NAHEED ELYASI

*In this exploration of the sometimes dark relationship between mother
and daughter, Naheed Elyasi reveals the abuse in families. An
overbearing mother is close to devastating her teenage daughter, who
is at the cusp of womanhood. However, the daughter, despite
her own fears and insecurities, finds a way, perhaps
the only way, to communicate with her mother.*

Living on a Prayer

"Salam, my daughter," she says as she steps inside my bedroom.

I stop breathing. *Maybe if I don't make any moves, she will leave me alone.*
"Salam," I respond.

*What does she want? Is she going to tell me to do something? Or did she go
through my stuff again, and find a note a friend passed on to me? Did she have a
bad day? Is she happy that I did well on my test? Please God, make her turn
around and leave.*

My mother slowly walks toward my twin bed as if she is trying to see
right through me. Her piercing glare constantly on me. My head sinks
and my eyes follow her feet as they move toward me, each step sinking
into the tan carpet as she gets closer and closer.

I am sitting on the edge of my bed, the radio playing Bon Jovi's "Living
on a Prayer." My world ceases. I stop hearing the music and the only thing
that exists for me in my small bedroom is my mother, my tormentor, coming toward me. She sits directly across from me, very close, to where her
knee is touching mine. She doesn't say anything and looks around at my
walls disapprovingly. She doesn't like the Guns N' Roses banner I printed
out at school and hung on my wall. She thinks it is too American.

She looks down at the pink-and-magenta-flowered comforter that she
so carefully and lovingly made for my bed and turns her nose up.

"Your bed stinks," she says. "I am tired of you wetting your bed every
night. Layla, it's embarrassing that at your age, at thirteen years old, you

pee every night. I am tired of washing your sheets and this room is always smelly. I'm tired of you."

I stare at her, feeling ashamed. I don't know what to say.

Please God, just make her leave. Does she think I wet my bed every night on purpose? Does she really think that I like to go to school smelling like urine? What does she want from me?

"How was school?" she asks me in an unusually calm way. Then she smiles knowingly, as if she is my friend and we're both in on some secret —just between us girls.

"It was good," is all I can muster. My heart starts to race.

"That all you have to say? Good?" My mother asks.

I don't know what to say. Nothing I do or say in these moments is ever right and you are never happy.

I can feel her getting angry. The usual far and distant look comes over her eyes, as if a part of her is leaving. I know she thinks I am being disrespectful, but I am not: she scares me, and I don't know what she wants from me.

"Why you stare stupid at me? You can't talk?" she asks sharply and more loudly.

"What do you want me to say?" I respond meekly.

"Truth," her voice getting louder.

"The truth about what? I don't know what you want," I say quietly. I look at the pink flowers.

"How was school? You pass note to friend? Boy look at you? You secretly make up your face?" She is yelling now.

God forbid I show any signs of turning into a woman.

I fall silent. She has left and the dark anger has taken over.

"You are bad. No manners. Bad Muslim daughter. I wish I killed you as baby," she screams.

She reaches for me, grabbing my shoulders, and starts shaking me. "How was school?" she screams.

Oh God, please stop,

I can't find my voice. I see her head coming at me, her mouth open. Her hands are tightly holding my left arm. Her head is attached to my arm. I move my arm and her head follows. I feel something painful and piercing on my arm. She is biting me, and everything is in slow motion.

Pain shoots throughout my arm and I realize that her teeth are penetrating the soft fleshy skin of my upper arm. The pain vibrates throughout my whole body. My mother's head shakes back and forth like that of a wild animal killing prey by the neck.

My own mother . . . . . . how can she hurt me in this way?

From somewhere I find my voice. "Stop," I scream. "Stop, let go." I push her away and pull my arm back, but she presses harder with her teeth, with all her anger and rage. Her head follows my arm. The pain gets worse.

"Stop." Tears are flowing from my eyes. I start to sob.

After endless minutes of searing pain, my mother lets go and stares at me calmly, as if to show me her power.

"Now you know to not talk back and be disobedient daughter," she says in a steely cold voice.

I never talk back. I simply want you to leave.

My mother stares at me for what feels like hours, then slowly gets up and backs away to the door while still looking at me. She opens the door to leave and I am finally able to breathe again.

Through tear-filled eyes, I look down at my arm, the white tender fleshy part. There is an imprint of every tooth in my mother's mouth.

How can someone have such a big mouth?

Within a few hours, the red marks on my arm turn blue and purple with indentations and ridges.

These became regular punishments I received from my mother, and the marks would last for weeks. There were times I would have several wild bite marks on different parts of my body—almost always in some soft fleshy part where the pain was unbearable. She was really smart in that way and knew where it would hurt the most.

I wanted something bad to happen to me, so she could be sorry for all the injustice that she inflicted on me and then she would suffer the rest of her life. To me this was the best kind of agony and punishment for her—slow and torturous—just like the feelings of inadequacy and pain she regularly inflicted on me.

Something in me went black and I wanted to destroy her. Crying, I slowly got off my bed and walked out of my room and across the hallway into her bedroom. I think she was in the kitchen preparing dinner. I had to find something that she loved and was precious to her and make her feel the loss of it. It was the only revenge I could have.

There was something else operating me, and slowly my hand twisted the knob of her closet to the left. My hand pulled the door open and my feet took a step back; my eyes stared into the closet.

There. Toward the back on a green plastic hanger was her black skirt. One of her few and favorite pieces that she had brought through our perilous two-week journey through the mountains of Afghanistan, through the one year of hot hell living in Pakistan, and now here it rested, in her closet in North Carolina. It was a nice black crepe with six pleats on the left side.

My arms were not my own, they reached into her small closet and grabbed the skirt. I looked down at my hands as the fingers grabbed the black fabric and started to shred it to pieces.

NUSHIN ARBABZADAH

*In this almost dizzying question-and-answer session between two
Afghan friends, one who left and grew up abroad in the United States
and one who remained in Afghanistan, the tension between Afghan
and Afghan American is explored. Topics from gender expectations
to the current war are explored in this playful, sometimes bantering
exchange between friends who remain in conversation despite
the distance they sense between them.*

Like a Rabbit Caught in the Spotlight

You said, "America, is that where it happened to you?" I lied to you, and
said, "No, that was NOT where IT happened." You said, "I know about
America. Their girls are loose. Afghan girls go to America and become
bad." I said, "How so?" You said, "They go dancing. They meet boys. They
become *faased,* polluted." You said, "Toobah," and pulled at your red
shawl. I said nothing. You said, "I know it happened there, in AMERICA."
I said nothing. You said, "Remember when we were children and used to
play on the carpet?" I said "Yes," and lit a cigarette.

"You always wanted to be America and I had no choice but to be the
Soviet Union. We bombed each other," you laughed. "Like this," and you
flew an imaginary plane, "wooosh," and dropped imaginary bombs,
"BOOOM." You made the sound of exploding bombs. "And the carpet
was Afghanistan," I said. You said, "Is that where you learned to smoke
cigarettes? In AMERICA?" I said nothing. "Tell me about the girls," you
said. I said, "I'll tell you about the landscape. About Utah, where a disobedient people were turned into stones." You said, "That's boring." I said,
"I'll tell you about the bears. They have places named after bears. The
Smokey Bear, for example." You said, "Bears are boring. Tell me about the
girls. Are they beautiful?" I said nothing. You said, "Remember when they
forced us to stage a rally outside the American embassy in Kabul?" I said,
"And there was no electricity and the microphone wouldn't work. And
then that guy from the embassy came out with a generator." I looked at
my cigarette.

You said, "And he made the generator work, and the microphone was switched on." I said, "And we shouted, 'Long live America!'" You laughed. I said, "I was so scared that day." You said, "Really? I didn't notice."

I lit another cigarette and ignored your disapproving look. You said, "Those were the days." I said, "We were children." You said, "We shouted 'Long live America!'" I said, "They are not a bad people." You looked at me. "They are not a bad people," I repeated. You said, "I know why you are saying this." I said nothing. You said, "Tell me about the girls in America." I said, "Which ones?" You said, "The ones you knew." I said, "They were girls." You said, "You are not answering my question." I said, "I don't know what you mean." You said, "You know exactly what I mean." I said, "Do you remember what else happened that day outside the embassy?" You said, "They forced us to shout 'Death to America!'" I said, "And we shouted, 'Death to America!' I shouted, 'Death to America.' I was scared." You said, "That was then, but now is now." I said, "But they are the same people. The same Americans." You said, "They were friends then; they are not anymore." I said, "What are they now?" You said, "They are the enemy now." I said, "I know why you are saying this, but you are wrong." You said, "You have lost your *ghairat,* your sense of honor. I know WHY." I said nothing. You sulked. I said, "Don't be like that." You said, "Like what?" I said, "You know what," and stared at my cigarette.

You said, "If you know it, then why don't you tell me?" I said, "Tell you about what?" You said, "Did it happen over there, in America?" I said nothing. You said, "I know it happened there. Who was she?" I said, "Do you really want to know?" You thought for a while. I smoked for a while. You poured yourself another cup of tea. You said, "Do you remember how our teacher used to mispronounce 'Peace Corps'?" I said, "He used to say, 'piss corps.'" We laughed. You said, "He used to say when Americans go to the bathroom, they pee perfume." We laughed. You said, "Those were the days." I said, "We were children then, but we understood everything." You said, "I didn't understand." I said, "That's because you are a woman." You said, "Stop teasing me, or I'll slap you." I said, "See, without Americans you wouldn't be that bold." You said, "Excuse me?" I said, "They have encouraged women's rights, no? They encourage women to apply for jobs, no?" You said, "I go to work, but not because of them." I said, "But without them, there would be the Taliban and you wouldn't be allowed to work." You said, "I hate the Taliban." I said, "Without Americans, they will come back." You said, "No, they won't come back. We will fight them." I said, "I won't fight them. I would be scared." You said, "I know why. You lost your *ghairat.*" I said, "I'll stay home and let you fight them. They won't fight you, though, because you are a woman." You said, "They beat women back then." I said, "Yes," and lit another cigarette.

You said, "They will beat you. They will say that you were a spy." I said, "They will." You said, "This is boring. Tell me more about America!" I said, "Imagine a white rabbit caught in the spotlight." You said, "Yes?" I said, "That's how it feels when you arrive in America." You said, "What do you mean?" I said, "That you freeze, become immobile, like a rabbit caught in the spotlight." You said, "Toobah," and shook your head. I said, "Trust me, that's what would happen to you if you went to America." You said, "No, it wouldn't." I said, "How do you know?" You said, "Because I am a woman, and I haven't lost my *ghairat.*" I said nothing. "Piss corps," I said. "Piss corps," you laughed. "And they pee perfume when they go to the toilet," you said. "And their women have not a single hair on their body," I said. "And the streets are empty because everyone is working," you said. "Apart from early in the morning when everyone walks to work in New York, men and women," I said. "And they can spot an ant from space," I said. "But they can't spot a Talib," you said. "That's different," I said. "How different?" you said. "A Talib looks like everyone else," I said. "That's boring," you said. "Tell me about the girls in America. What are they like?" you said. "They are different," I said. "How different?" you asked. "I knew you would say just that," I said. "You are avoiding my question," you said. "They are just different," I said. "But HOW different?" you asked. "I don't know," I said. "Yes, you know," you said. And then you sulked. I said, "They are not all the same. Some are kind, some are not." You said, "Kind, how kind?" I said, "Just that, kind." You said, "Are they beautiful?" I said, "Which ones?" You said, "What do you mean which ones?" I said, "Afghans in America or Americans in America?" You said, "Both." I said, "Yes." You said, "Yes, what?" I said, "Yes, they are beautiful." You said nothing. I said, "Come on!" You said nothing. I said, "See, that's why I didn't want to answer your question." You laughed. I said, "I knew this would happen if I answered the question."

I lit another cigarette. You poured yourself another cup of tea. You looked at me straight in the eyes. We laughed. You said, "Who was she?" I said, "I'll tell you another time."

WAJMA AHMADY

*In this fictional telling of one young Afghan woman's growth, from
Afghanistan during the Soviet invasion to the streets of California,
Wajma Ahmady deftly encompasses the experience of Afghan
American women. The inventory of losses the young protagonist has
survived is carefully noted. Ahmady captures the struggles that Afghan
American women face as they negotiate a space for themselves that is
on the fringes of traditions and also part of their new lives in America.
Neither here nor there, the young woman in this story takes a stand
for herself and begins the project of feminist self-making.*

My Earliest Memories

My earliest memories are vague, fragmented recollections of specific
events, yet clearly definite about the emotions involved. I felt securely
loved and comforted. Even when the course of events occurring in the
environment around me turned into a whirlpool of confusion, I felt no
sense of direct danger.

PAKA

Occasionally, my maternal uncle, Wahid, would pick me up from the daycare center in Kabul, Afghanistan. He had a small chair on the back of his
bicycle, where he placed me, before riding home. A great sense of excitement engulfed me when I saw him. We rode past open market bazaars
where they sold an assortment of delicacies as well as novelty items: fresh
naan (bread), *bolanee* (appetizer), and *rut* (sweet bread). The invigorating
scents rushed into my nostrils and made me aware of the items being
sold. On one of these days, he was riding past an open bazaar when I saw
a *paka* (fan) stand. There was one fan in particular that caught my attention: a semicircle-shaped mirror fan with bright colors and a magnificent
parwana (butterfly) painted on it. I cried until he stopped the bike. After a
while, he realized that I wanted the *paka*. All of a sudden, I was surrounded

by about five members of my family. They were talking about which fan to buy for me. Finally, I chose the one I wanted, and my maternal aunt bought it for me.

My family went to great lengths to make me happy. My emotional and material well-being was abundantly taken care of in Afghanistan. But even after our standard of living fell when we moved to the States, I never felt deprived. I was aware that I couldn't have particular objects, toys that I saw other kids play with. Yet I never felt a yearning or longing for these things.

MY FIRST ENCOUNTER WITH JAIL

My uncle who picked me up from daycare in Afghanistan came illegally to the States some years after we had arrived. He was placed in a jail with other illegal immigrants who came for a variety of reasons: better economic chances, political and religious freedom from persecution, fleeing a war. The location where he was placed looked like a warehouse from the outside. The windows were tinted a dark grayish hue that made it impossible to look inside. But from the inside, it looked like it could've been any apartment community in Los Angeles: there were children running around, men sitting and playing cards, conversing in their native tongues. The apartment doors of the third-story building faced a courtyard area, where visitors met the inmates. I remember this courtyard filled with the voices of children giggling and talking. My uncle shared a room with two other men; I wasn't allowed to enter the room but wondered how it looked. Did he share a bunk bed with his roommate, like my younger brother and I did? Did he have posters or pictures on the walls? It was a foreign idea for me to think that my uncle was living among strangers.

I heard an eclectic variety of dialects there: Cantonese Chinese, Mexican and El Salvadorian Spanish, Russian, Armenian, Afghan and Iranian Farsi. I recognized divergent dialects within a language by an early age; the sounds in my environment made me very aware and perceptive. The only decisively cold objects in the complex were the massive steel doors and the INS officers. I was nine at the time and had an idea of my uncle's situation. My mother had told me that we were going to a jail but it was a different type of jail: most of these people hadn't done anything bad, but had broken a small rule, and they had to stay there for a little while. My uncle embraced me when we met him inside the complex. He tried to appear excited, yet I could see he was exhausted and fatigued. He had lost weight; he looked different from the once plump, light-hearted Wahid I remembered. He later received his visa and rejoined our family in Los Angeles.

OUR MUZDOOR

I was born in a modest-sized house in Mazar-e-Sharif, Afghanistan, a small city characterized by its rugged unpaved roads and diverse ethnic composition. I spent the first four years of my life in Afghanistan, where I lived with my parents, older sister, and younger brother. By Afghan standards, our two-story home was a large one, for an upper-middle-class family. In the backyard, freshly sun-dried clothes lingered in the air, carefully hung there after being washed by our *muzdoor* (nanny/maid). My best friend and second cousin, Parwana, and I would spend countless hours in this yard: running, laughing, playing tag, competing to gain the most attention from our *muzdoor* (she worked for both of our families). I was jealous of the relationship she and Parwana had; I thought that the *muzdoor* favored her. The *muzdoor* was relatively old, in her late forties to early fifties. She wore *pehran-e-tombon* (a type of dress worn with pants) and a long, transparent white *chadar* (head veil). The *chadar* fell midway from her head down her back, where she gathered it around her long braid. Walking low, hunchbacked, it seemed as if she had a back problem. I watched her as she washed clothes, banging the pieces of clothing against the wide metal pan. I remember feeling her insignificance and pain; I knew that she was looked upon as inferior to us. I sensed it even in the way my parents treated her; she was not one of us. She was called the clothes-washer, but she was much more than that to me. She was my companion when I had no one to play with; she provided comfort when my mother wasn't around. The veins on her hands emerged as pulps of blue color along her dark, dirt-stained hands. These were continually occupied, either by clothes washing or by holding our hands, Parwana on one side and me on the other. She had warm, healing hands, and I held onto them, feeling like I knew a secret no one else did.

Years later, the memory of her came vividly as I was looking at a painting in a small art gallery in La Jolla; it was an oil painting of a woman's hands, cupped together holding peas. The piece was called *An Offering*. I thought about the *muzdoor* (Parwana and her family had eventually been accepted into England as refugees, and I sporadically kept in touch with her). I hoped she had made it out safely. But I realized the reality of her situation. She was a *muzdoor:* the only way she could've left was if a rich family decided to take her with them when they fled. Otherwise, she was among the other innocent victims of the war.

AWSANAS IN THE NIGHT

I remember spending nights at my grandma's house. My mother and father worked in another city, and I often stayed with my grandmother. By this time, the Communists had gradually taken over Kabul and had begun bombing raids. Images . . . the sky obscure and dark, men in uniform floating down to the ground in parachutes, carrying guns . . . monstrous tanks crossing the street. Powerful piercing pain vibrated in my eardrums. I tried to block out the sounds by tightly pressing pillows over my ears, but the pain focused internally. I fell asleep to the sweet smell of my grandmother narrating lyrical *awsanas* (a story in the form of a riddle) in her comforting, familiar voice.

As I am walking across the University of California, San Diego, campus, I feel an indefinite sense of fear as the military airplanes hover above me. It's silly, I think, that I still cringe at the sound of a military airplane.

NOT TOO YOUNG TO REMEMBER

My grandmother's house was a small, one-story flat, composed of clay, alongside a riverbank. She had an expansive yard with a diverse assortment of animals: chickens, goats, sheep, and rabbits. The fertile soil allowed several crops to grow: wheat, scallions, melons, turnips, and eggplants. My grandmother's love always encompassed me; I felt warmth and love there. There were so many inciting smells: the fruits and vegetables, the fresh milk from the goats, the flowers, my grandmother's cooking. It was here that I said goodbye to my grandmother and other family members when we were leaving. We hoped they would join us later. They remained because they didn't want to leave yet; it was my mother's idea for us to leave. My father was among the group of people who thought that matters would calm down. They thought that the Communists would be unsuccessful in taking over. Unfortunately, that was not what happened, because the Communists received support from powerful, influential Afghans. I remember feeling deep pain because I didn't want to leave my grandmother. I said goodbye to them, not quite understanding what was happening.

FLEEING

My last memories of Afghanistan come from our flight from the war. We left in a delivery truck (which usually delivered supplies across the border), filled with people just like us, fortunate enough to find a way to leave. The back of the truck was packed with men, my father being one of them. The only thing covering them was a big cloth that was placed between them and some food supplies. The women and children were in the front. At one defining moment, a Soviet tank was crossing in front of the truck. The driver told us to duck under the seats. My mother breathed these words into my ear. I felt my heart beat quickly at the sound of my mother's voice. I slightly peed in my pants. A Soviet soldier walked up to our truck and exchanged some words with our truck driver. Then he let us pass. It was only years later that I learned that the reason the Soviet soldier let us pass was because the driver bribed him with cigarettes. Most of these Soviet soldiers were in their late teens to early twenties; they felt as ambivalent about the war as the young Afghans did. Many times, you could easily bribe them with hashish, cigarettes, or Afghan sweets. My father told me that one easy place for the Afghan mujahideen (freedom fighters) to ambush Soviet soldiers was at the melon fields; there, they would find the soldiers indulging in sweet melon. "There is nothing like Afghan melon in the world," my dad said. We proceeded on our path and crossed the border into Pakistan. We stopped along the way, somewhere in the early dawn of the morning, to pray. Even though we had crossed into the safety zone, I was very frightened.

THE WOODS

I grew up in Erftstadt-Liblar, Germany, during my early school years. We lived in a refugee camp in a small town one hour from the city of Cologne, Germany. The refugee camp consisted of apartment complexes. Our complex was a couple of blocks away from a woodland area, a famous region that tourists and German residents would flock to year-round. The woodland area was immense: it took more than a day to get through the whole region, which was covered by towering, green trees and stubby, short bushes. The bushes were filled with juicy, colorful berries of all varieties. As I walked through the woods, I would pick blueberries, blackberries, and boysenberries. I devoured the berries. There was a mesmerizing blue-colored lake. I remember the sensation of the vibrant, cool rush of water that sent goosebumps over my body. I was very young then and could not swim and didn't go in very deep.

During the winter, the area was immersed in a blanket of snow. The snow was an ivory, milky color; the texture of the snow was smooth and fluffy. I would immerse myself in the snow. My siblings and I went sledding through the woods. Someone would be maneuvering the sled while the rest of us held on, manipulating the sled to dodge the trees.

ERFTSTADT-LIBLAR

The small town in Germany had narrow, cobblestone streets. One could smell the delicious fragrance of the stores along the way. The bakery had a fresh, sweet smell coming from the many delicacies, including freshly baked bread, pastries, crepes, and cookies. The dairy shop had a different but tasteful smell. It smelled of farm-fresh milk and aged cheese. You could really appreciate the sense of tasting and smelling in Germany because it was a country that savored freshness. In the spring, there were extensive fields of strawberries that were in season. You could go to these fields and spend hours just picking and tasting the strawberries.

The town was small, and everybody knew one another. The people there were sincere, hard-working, and altruistic. Since we were refugees from Afghanistan, the town church supported us, providing us with a place to stay, food, clothing, toys, and some extra money. We participated in different German traditions. One of the traditions was that on the first day of school, the children received a cone-shaped box filled with various presents. The handkerchief was the most important gift. Each handkerchief was individually designed for you to keep throughout your school years.

THE MUDHOUSE

We moved to Highland Park, California, when I turned seven years old. We lived in an apartment on a small street. This time, we lived in an inner city, not a small town. The street contained mostly apartment complexes and a couple of old houses. One in particular was very old. It was made out of mud, and its windows were void of glass. One day my siblings and I smelled smoke. We rushed to find the mud house on fire. I remember feeling a great sense of pain as I stood and watched the house burn. I knew immediately that the inhabitants of the home would be homeless. The house and its inhabitants were just as much a part of our neighborhood as the other homes and apartments. The cause of the fire was unknown; someone attributed it to arson.

HIGHLAND PARK, CALIFORNIA

There are many places I remember in Highland Park: the public library, the public park and pool, and the elementary school. The library was large and broad, containing books from every realm. On the walls of the library, there was a mural representing the Latino community. The library had a comfortable, homelike atmosphere. It was not extravagant, but it was functional and served its purpose. The public park was a recreational area for my siblings and me. It contained a playground, basketball courts, and other sports facilities. It had odd, often repulsive odors. It smelled of urine and vomit. It smelled of a place overused and not watched over. There were many people living in the park: homeless people, alcoholics, and others. But you would rarely see them, because they did not want to be seen. Nevertheless, it was our home just as much as it was theirs.

The public pool was immense. Even with its tremendous size, however, it could not support the number of the kids in the city. It was always overcrowded, filled to the maximum with children who yearned to have a good time. You could hear children screaming, laughing, and talking. There were lifeguards on the towers above, watching.

The elementary school was a middle-sized school. It was a one-story brown brick building. The playground was small but practical. The classrooms were good-sized and efficient. The teachers were exemplary, investing more time than they had. It was a comfortable, nurturing environment that fostered learning.

The aunt who bought me the *paka* (fan) wasn't as lucky as my uncle. When the rest of my family left Afghanistan, she did not flee with them. Her husband and mother-in-law (who had a powerful influence on their decisions) did not want to leave, so she remained. She, Masuda, and my mom's other sister, Farida, were married to brothers and had the same mother-in-law. They were the only immediate family we had who still lived in Afghanistan. Last week, they received their visas to enter the States on the basis that our family would financially support them, with no aid from the government. The U.S. rarely accepts immigrants on refugee status since the Soviets left Afghanistan in 1989. Everyone in my family has agreed to pitch in money from their paychecks, contributing to a bank account that we set aside for them; it is a responsibility that they have all assumed and agreed upon. There are a total of fifteen people coming: both of my aunts and their children, ranging in age from three to eighteen. They have lived in Afghanistan all their lives, throughout the Soviet-Afghan war and the Civil War; they have not stepped foot in another country, except for Pakistan, where they have lived for a year with my grandfather.

They will be coming in two weeks from Pakistan; I am deathly afraid. I don't know what to say to them in my broken Farsi or how to behave.

I remember all the flowery pink cards they sent me, their names carefully yet jaggedly written in English. I attempted many times to write a letter, but I couldn't write a word after *salam* (hello). How could I, a privileged American, pretend to know what their life is like? How could I pretend to have anything in common with them? The truth is I am scared of being judged by them. What will they think of me, a young Afghan woman, living away from home? All these questions come into my mind as I think about our first encounter. Even though we come from the same culture and family, we have lived in opposite worlds. Their living quarters were a one-room home with a dirt floor and no running water. I know that they have endured periods of near starvation. My female cousins had to face the fear of being kidnapped and/or raped as they walked to school. My younger cousins had to be cautious not to step into land mines as they played games in the open fields. My male cousins lived with the daily fear during the war that they would be kidnapped and forced to fight their own people by the Communist soldiers, or that they would be recruited by the Taliban in more recent times. The paradox is that they look up to me because I am an American.

◆ ◆ ◆

Roya, sooner or later you have to do it, I told myself, picking up the phone receiver for the third consecutive time. This time I didn't put it back down. You have the plane ticket to New York; everything is set. I looked at the ticket: March 22, 1999. Just be adamant when you're speaking to him. Besides, how are you ever going to explain your plans to study abroad in Spain or to join the Peace Corps if you can't be brave enough to tell them that you're going to New York City for spring break? You have to break them in slowly. A feeling of permeating fear prevailed as I dialed the digits of my father's work in Los Angeles. My stomach turned in knots while my heart pulsated rapidly.

"Sierra Medical Clinic," answered the operator.

"Hi. Can I please speak to Dr. Younisi?" I asked. "It's his daughter."

"Roya-gul," he said in a warm tone, addressing me affectionately by my Afghan nickname (*gul* means flower). Small talk lasted for some time.

"Dad, do you remember my friend Gabi who lived with me for a quarter last year?"

"Yes, I remember," my dad said enthusiastically. I had told him how she was my savior when I first arrived at UCSD as a transfer student. She was the only person whom I got along with among my roommates.

"I've been thinking of visiting her for some time, and I've decided to see her during spring break."

"Where does she live?" he asked, sounding a bit concerned.

"In New York."

"What?" I heard him lightly chuckle in his sarcastic tone, the way he reacted when he began to get angry. "That is not a good idea."

"I bought the ticket." Silence replaced our conversation for a minute, which seemed like an interminable amount of time.

"Then why are you calling me? You have obviously made up your mind. You're not calling me to ask me if you can go. If you had, we would have discussed this with your mom and decided if this was a good idea or not. Have you talked to your mother?"

I knew well that the decision would not have included my opinion; I also knew how my mother would feel about this trip. I had told her once that I wanted to study in Spain, and she reacted in the way she normally did when she felt ambivalent. She erupted into a myriad of emotions and talked incessantly to persuade me to alter my decision. "You can wait till you get married, and then you can travel with him," she had said. But my near future plans did not include marriage. I began to dial the digits of our home phone number.

I thought of a quote by Lillian Hellman: "If you're willing to endure the punishment, you are halfway through the battle." That quote always entered my mind like a mantra in situations like this: situations in which I challenged traditional definitions of what an Afghan woman could do. Traveling alone was clearly not a part of that definition. When I was growing up, especially in my adolescent years, I was always confused by what the definition even was. I could go to college because that was what women from upper-middle-class, educated families did before getting married. Within this parameter, I could only do things explicitly required, not supplementary, to my education. A college education was not intended to encourage acquiring characteristics such as individuality and independence; nor was its main purpose to promote a career path. Obtaining an education was an affirmation that you were marriageable for a "proper" family.

My parents' ideas about these cultural conventions juxtaposed contradictory emotions. They wanted to stimulate my goals and aspirations, yet they were constantly pulled by obligations cultivated by their cultural upbringing. They realized that a career is pivotal to attaining respect and success in American society, yet they also wanted me to obtain respect in the culture. The objective was to finish school as soon as possible, but I obviously did not follow that plan, experimenting with many majors (undeclared) before I chose writing. I knew early on in high school that I didn't want to follow that path; I had personal goals, distinct from my parents', that I wanted to achieve. I was set on choosing a career that placed importance on independence and personal control, like politics or law, although I didn't have a passionate interest in either of these. I saw writing as mediation, a tool to help me deal with my culture: I could write about the culture and not feel constrained. I am not sure whether I want to continue writing as a career, but it has helped me to consciously break free of these barriers.

ESSAYS

♦ ♦ ♦

MALIHA ZULFACAR

Maliha Zulfacar is currently the Afghan ambassador to Germany.
Zulfacar's story of coming to the United States is especially significant,
since she was the second Afghan woman to study abroad here.
Honest, sensitive, and humorous, this essay reveals the emotions of a
young woman in a foreign place trying to construct her identity as an
Afghan in America, and later as an Afghan woman creating a space
for herself within the hierarchies of Afghan society.

Coming to America, 1966

When my mother kissed me goodbye, I remember her whispering in my ear, "You will come back with a diploma or you will shame us both." To leave for abroad, mainly to Europe and the United States in those days, was the ultimate desire of all Afghans graduating from high school. Theoretically, the students with the highest grades from high school, or the applicants with the highest examination scores, were granted the best scholarships. But this was all in theory. To continue higher education in Afghanistan was something for the middle and lower urban class. However, the opportunity to attend universities in the West was based largely on the right connections.

Privileged children received scholarships to prestigious universities in the United States, and as a second choice to European universities. Middle- and lower-class candidates most often attended universities in the Soviet bloc countries or in neighboring countries such as India and Iran.

In the 1960s, I was living in Shari-Nau, which was considered one of the wealthiest neighborhoods in Kabul. In those days I was totally oblivious to issues beyond family, friends, and school. As much as I was amused at the idea of leaving for the United States, I became uncertain and bewildered when the time came to leave home, friends, and the familiar environment. I was absolutely naive about what was awaiting me. All I knew was that I was going to the States, a place where everyone wanted to go, a place where everyone smiled and was perpetually happy, and a place that was going to be all fun, just like the movies. My vision of the American lifestyle was based on *Gone with the Wind* and *Better Gardening*. In those days, regardless of how well one lived in Afghanistan, the general perception was that life was going to be even better in the States.

On my way to the U.S., I stopped in Germany to visit my brother and uncle. I stayed with my brother for a week. I already felt pressured to go farther away. So I was put on a plane to go meet my other older brother, in London. When I landed, my brother wasn't there to meet me. I simply asked someone at the airport to take me to my brother's address. This is how naive I was. The person drove me to my brother's address. My brother didn't seem apologetic or very excited to see me. I remember him questioning me about my "major." Initially, I didn't have a clue what the term "major" meant. Since I had passed the college entrance examination to attend engineering school at Kabul University, I wanted to study architecture. He then explained to me that the school I was attending was a liberal arts school and that I couldn't study architecture. He then told me bluntly that since I like people and I talked so much, I should major in sociology. I didn't have a clue what sociology was. He wrote "sociology" in Dari on a piece of paper.

I arrived in Pittsburgh, Pennsylvania, to attend my orientation at Chatham College for six weeks. Things in America were strange. When greeting, people didn't stand up or hug each other, and the most memorable thing my counselor told us was not to walk around holding the hands of other girls. In the States, girls only held the hands of boys. This sounded positively immoral to me!

I attended Western College, an all-women's institution in Oxford, Ohio. This was one of the conditions that had made it possible for me to leave the country. I was their first Afghan student. The college policy stated that all international students must room with Americans. My roommate that first year was named Patricia Pinkowski, from Chicago.

I hated being so far away from home. I felt stupid not being able to explain myself well in English. I didn't understand the lectures. I was a good student in Afghanistan; here I felt alienated. I began receiving poor grades, which intensified my depression. I wanted to leave, but didn't know how. Back then, it wasn't possible to make telephone calls, send faxes or emails. My only connection to my home and family was through postal mail service, which took three to four weeks.

I worked as a waitress twelve hours a week in the student cafeteria as part of my scholarship. It was a difficult and demeaning job. What made the job even more unbearable was the exposure to waste. At a table with eight students, there were four half-gallon cartons of milk. Even if one cupful was taken from the milk, the entire carton had to be poured out. Once all the food was cleared off the table, the leftover food was thrown in a big waste basket for pigs. This exposure to waste and waiting on tables were both unpleasant and uncomfortable.

Trying to adjust to the States had a dramatic effect on my body. It delayed my menstrual cycle for five months. I was bloated. I explained my dilemma to my roommate, who then immediately reported my situation to the foreign student advisor. The immediate suspicion was pregnancy, and I was asked if I had a boyfriend. I was extremely humiliated by this question. Naive as I was, I didn't see the connection with my menstrual delays. The foreign student advisor immediately drove me personally to a medical doctor, who gave me some injections and packages of medicine. I was advised to take the medicine every night for three months, starting immediately. Then one evening one of the girls from the hall asked me if I was having sex. Furious, I asked her how I could have sex, not being married. I took her comment as an offensive attack on my morality. I remember crying from humiliation. She then apologized and explained to me that the medication I was taking was birth-control pills and that they were taken by girls who were having sex. The following day I went straight to the foreign student advisor's office and asked her to make arrangements for me to leave the country. I was angry, and I didn't want to stay any longer in that school or this country. She gradually calmed me down and explained the medical reason for the pills—to regulate my menstrual period. I was so ashamed of having that medicine on my dresser that for the coming weeks I swallowed it in hiding, until finally I quit taking it. The lifelong side effect of this experience was the development of terrible acne and loss of hair. The scars of acne added even more to my depression and my adjustment to being there.

The weekends were the hardest. On Friday evenings most of the international students would get together and cook, dance, and hang around together. During the first months, our American roommates would ask us to join them in town to go to bars. Most of us found the bars crowded, smelly, noisy, and full of smoke. We instead decided to stay on campus and chat, listen to music, and dance together. What felt strange to us was the depression of our roommates at not having "dates" to go on. For many of us, the concept of dating was new, and it seemed odd to be so dependent on boys.

The summer was arriving. We were told that the campus would shut down and that we would need to find jobs elsewhere. Although each international student had a host family, in my case it was a bit complicated. I had a host family in Cincinnati, Ohio, which was about a half-hour drive from campus. My family lived in an enormous house, which I was surprised to discover was not filled with children and relatives. When I asked my host mother about her children, I barely understood that they were away at college. Later that evening, I asked about her husband, and she replied that he did not come home very often. After a fantastic dinner with apple pie for dessert, we sat around watching TV. As the night passed, the lady started laughing more and more. Well, I must have missed all the jokes. The following day she was kind enough to drive me around the city and have lunch out at a local restaurant. That night her husband arrived, and the conversation was not very friendly. He didn't eat with us and went straight upstairs. The lady again became funnier and funnier as the evening went on. On the third day, the husband asked me if I wanted to join him for a plane ride. I am sure I was confused about the possibility of a private plane. So I must have accepted the offer, and off I went to take a flight in a private plane. After we returned from the ride, we found the lady on the floor of the living room. I still didn't know what was going on. The next day I was driven back to campus by the husband. Apparently, the wife was an alcoholic, and the husband was living with a girlfriend outside the home. This led the foreign student office to locate me another host family.

The following summer, I wanted to find a job in Colorado. I had heard so often that Colorado resembled Afghanistan. So I applied for jobs through the local Chamber of Commerce. I found a waitressing job at Mesa Verde National Park. First of all, I was very disappointed by the place. Mesa Verde National Park didn't look anything like Afghanistan. I was later told I had come to the wrong part of the state! Anyway, I was there. Almost all the summer kitchen staff were college students, and accommodations were part of the employment deal. During the first week I was told about the native/indigenous communities outside the park. I asked about the possibility of living among them. Arrangements were made, and soon I found myself living with a tribe of Native Americans. It was definitely a learning experience! I was impressed with the unfamiliar way of life of the indigenous community, yet I was confused at not being invited to join them for dinner and special occasions. In those days, not much was exposed in the media about minorities in the United

States. For the first time, I learned about "American Indians" in one of my anthropology classes. Thus, the opportunity to live among them was very appealing to me. My curiosity increased even more when one day I asked one of the women for soap for my shower, and when I returned the soap, the woman refused to take it back. I felt a bit ashamed and thought that I should have purchased a new one, that what I had done was rude. When I then gave her a new bar of soap, it was still not accepted. I asked the reason. I was told that my being a "white" was the problem. I didn't know what it meant to be white. I remained perplexed about the whole situation. I felt unwanted, and toward the end, I moved to live inside the park with other staff.

By the third year, college became more interesting. My English had improved, and I could follow the lectures more easily. Besides, the whole college experience was halfway done. In the winter, I applied to study at the Merrill-Palmer Institute for Social Work in Detroit. For some reason, I had the need to travel as often as possible. Life in Detroit was the best learning experience of my life. I was extremely oblivious about the American social fabric. It was during those years that I began reading about the different groups residing inside the United States. Living in Detroit and walking around the inner city was a shocking experience. I was absolutely stunned to find out there were actually poor people in the U.S. How could that be possible? It was like a puzzle to me that a rich country like America had poor people. At first, I thought perhaps they were African nationals living in the U.S. In comparison to my experience with the indigenous Americans in Mesa Verde, the "Africans" of Detroit were friendlier toward me. I made a lot of friends just hanging out on porches and gossiping.

The third summer, I applied to go to Maine. I had heard wonderful things about Maine. I wanted to live somewhere close to the ocean. Once again through the Chamber of Commerce, I found a job at the Bar Harbor Restaurant. We were six waitresses working in two shifts and sharing two rooms in the back of the restaurant. My two main challenges working in this fancy restaurant were learning about drinks and demonstrating to tourists how to break a lobster properly. Both were new to me. The biggest tips came from tables with drinks. However, waitresses were to bring the drink order, and then they were expected to put the appropriate garnish on the appropriate drink. For example, I had to learn to which drinks lemon, onion, or a cherry should be added. At times, I didn't have a clue about the type of drinks being ordered by customers. I was simply mimicking the name of the drink. Often, I put the wrong garnish on the wrong drink. The bartender was often furious with me. But after two months, I got better at it. The second dilemma was showing customers how to eat lobster. The other waitresses were from Maine, and they were expert in cutting the lobster with the right squeeze. Often I mashed the lobster and so ended up losing a lot of tips. But eventually I learned how to do it. Coming from a landlocked country, eating lobster was a treat. I loved it. Besides eating lobster, on our nights off, we used to cruise around Bar Harbor Street, which was packed with tourists.

One evening we entered a dance saloon, with three young men playing guitar on stage. During the break, one of the players came over and asked me to dance with him. I accepted the offer. The song was "Sitting on the Dock of the Bay." He then came and sat at our table. He was studying political science at the University of Oklahoma and his father was the head of Acadia National Park. He was pleasant and kind. His name was Richard, and he invited me to visit his family. His mother was an Italian, and his father was of Swedish decsent. The other two players were his brothers, and knowing his family was a pleasure. The rest of that summer I used to visit the family on a daily basis, and then it was time to leave for the last year of college.

I couldn't wait to complete the college experience and leave for home. Every holiday of my senior year was spent with Richard's family. They were the most gracious and kind people I knew in those days. My mother, my siblings and their families, and a cousin who was madly in love with me, all were present for my graduation. Right after the ceremony, my mother told me calmly that as much as she was proud of me for completing my four years of college, it was not good enough. I had to earn my master's degree before returning to Kabul. This was hurtful. However, she promised that I could visit Kabul the following summer. After the graduation, we all left for New York, and from New York, my mother, my sister, and I left for Bar Harbor to visit Richard's family. During that visit, Richard proposed, but my mother declined the offer. Mother wanted me to return home.

In the summer of 1971, I visited Kabul after five years. Kabul wasn't the same. My acne scars and my shaggy hippie look were not appealing to my family or friends. My outlook on life had changed after college. My idea of fun was no longer attending fancy parties and hanging around with the elites of Kabul. My appearance became an embarrassment to my mother. Relatives kept asking why I kept a shaggy look. The general expectation for those returning from the West was to have them resemble the beautiful Americans of the movies and magazines. People were shocked to see me more resemble the "locals." Everything about Kabul, about Afghan culture and lifestyle, was considered to be lower-class when compared to things European and American. No one really asked much about my learning experiences. It was all about my looks and my clothes. They were curious about the American lifestyle and the latest fashion. The environment felt as strange as the American climate had once seemed to me. I returned to the States after a month of living in Kabul in order to complete my double master's degrees.

After graduate school, my mother was waiting desperately for my return to Kabul. She was disappointed and depressed after her sons' refusal to return to Afghanistan. Both of my brothers had married Western women, and even though my younger brother returned to Afghanistan for a short one-year period, he joined his wife and son a year later in Germany. My mother and I were left to make the best of things by ourselves. I was the only family member who was looking forward to the return to Afghanistan.

However, returning as a young unmarried girl was difficult. Reconnecting to my past and to my school friends was a challenge. I tried to avoid leading a privileged life by avoiding driving a private car to work and eating at local restaurants. I also stopped attending events in luxurious places, such as the Intercontinental Hotel, or celebrating the Christian New Year among a circle of elite families. In those days, celebrating any Afghan holiday was considered not "cool." For example, participating in the traditional Afghan New Year's events, such as going to the Red Tulip Ceremony in Mazar-i-sharif or going to Ziarat-i-Sakhi Sahib, was considered mundane and low. Ostracizing myself and wanting to be like the majority of regular Afghans left me in a peculiar position.

Perhaps one of the advantages of having left Afghanistan was learning to see my country and its social structure from a different angle. To have lived in the United States in the 1960s as a "foreign student" or "other" gave me a deeper understanding of what it meant to be a marginalized person. These experiences led me to relate differently to the realities of my life upon my return to Afghanistan. I became more conscious of my social position and that of others surrounding me. Had I not left Afghanistan, I would have accepted the social injustices and social inequalities of my country as the "norm." The displaced years of my life in the U.S. brought a broader perspective on many issues upon my return to Afghanistan.

My mother was disappointed about this change. My "hippie" outfits, my inclination to wear local cultural outfits, and my critique of elites trying to act anything but Afghan led to much tension among relatives. To be elite was to be "Western." For example, at local Kabul cinemas, ordinary Afghans were not allowed to attend the theater wearing local outfits. They were forced to wear European attire. So outside the theaters were piles of secondhand American outfits for Afghans to rent in order to watch a film.

My mother was disappointed in me. After she had spent so much money on me, I returned acting low-brow. She wanted me to become educated in order to bridge with the elites of Kabul. She saw me as an opportunity to gain access to power. I did not want to open such doors. She always said I would have been much better off had I not left the country.

AMAN MOJADIDI

In this vividly written essay, Aman Mojadidi shares his return to Afghanistan during the Soviet Afghan war (1979–89). He offers an important testimonial on what the Soviet war in Afghanistan did to the people there: farms and water poisoned by toxic aerial sprays that killed entire villages, the beginning of wars that are yet to end. This is one of the few testimonies we have regarding the Soviet Afghan war and its impact inside Afghanistan.

Home

We leave the house in Peshawar early, right after morning prayers, before the sun becomes an amber disc filtered through layers of thick brown haze. I climb into the back seat of a Toyota Custom pickup and am immediately flanked by two AK-47-wielding mujahideen, rebels from the Afghan National Liberation Front (ANLF). Aql Khan and Baznoor stand their Kalashnikovs between their legs and smile at me, while another mujahid in the front seat whose name I don't know coordinates with the other vehicles through a high-band walkie-talkie. A minute later, six vehicles carrying twenty mujahideen and me pull out in a cloud of dust onto the main road heading toward Torkham, a lawless zone nestled between this stretch of the Northwest Frontier Province and Afghanistan's border. It's barely seven a.m., but the streets are already filled with people as they spill out of overcrowded buses and climb into three-wheeled rickshaws. Within the hour we pass through Torkham, my eyes falling upon stall after stall with names like "Ahmed's Arms Store," selling large bags of chars-e-Mazari and a range of popular weaponry from landmines to rocket-propelled grenades. The perfect one-stop jihad shop, where you can get sweet, sticky Afghan-made hashish and cheap Russian-made AK-47s before crossing through the Khyber Pass.

The driver picks up speed, and we all sit in silence for much of the way. I look out the window as the dry, barren landscape passes by in a dusty blur. One of the vehicles behind us radios that they're stopping at a fruit stall to buy a bag of *kinos,* so we pull off to the side of the road to wait. I get out of the truck, and not far from the roadside my eyes fall upon what must be hundreds of tents. But not the kind of tents I'm used to, waterproof, with windows, screens, and zippers. These are a patchwork of different-colored materials and old clothes sewn together into make-shift shelters with a certain tragic beauty in their design. I ask Baznoor who they are, and he says they're Afghans who have fled their villages due to the war and set up camp here where it's calm. I walk a ways toward the tents, and by this time our presence along the road has attracted the attention of several of the camp's children, who have begun excitedly running toward us.

"Hello, Mister" is the first thing that comes out of their mouths, not thinking that I am Afghan. I reply in Dari, "Your English is very good. Tell me more." One of the older children, his clothes dirty and much too small for him, says, "How are you?" and "What is your name?" Behind the caked-on dust and smeared grease, his face is aglow at the opportunity to use his language skills. "My name is Amanullah. What is your name?" "My name is Kanishka," and at this point he stops, those four phrases having exhausted his knowledge of English.

I think of his name and how easily it flows when spoken. Ka-nish-ka, tolerant king of the Kushan dynasty, largely responsible for the spread of Buddhism throughout Central Asia, including what is now Afghanistan. I stare at the gathered children for a moment and am overcome with an uneasiness I can't quite define. I wonder if I'm the only one who's uncomfortable.

Aql Khan calls out that we're leaving. The children walk with me to the truck, and looking back as we're pulling away, I see the mujahideen who had purchased the fruit toss a bag out the window. The kids are wrestling over who'll carry it back to camp as dust clouds envelop them, and the tents in the background slowly disappear.

We're a good hour and a half inside Afghanistan now. We've been driving straight and fast for the last thirty minutes, heading in the direction of Jalalabad. The road is slightly bumpy but still well-paved, although every fifteen minutes or so we have to swerve around a crater left in the road by any of a variety of mortars and rockets fired in this war. The bumps and swerves make me drowsy, slowly lulling me to sleep despite my attempts to stay alert. My head banging into the ceiling of the truck abruptly wakes me to find that in veering away from one rocket crater, the driver has inadvertently driven into another shallow hole in the road.

In between laughs, my copassengers ask if I'm okay, and rubbing my head, I can't keep from laughing myself at the thoughts that went through my head when I was so rudely awakened: *Were we fired on? Are we hit?*

A few minutes later, we're pulling into our first stop on this journey, an ANLF mujahideen training camp in the middle of a field of tall, yellow grass by a swiftly moving river. We're greeted by maybe eighty to one hundred rebels of all ages. Some come forward to hug and shake hands, while others hang back with looks of curiosity mixed with suspicion on their war-weathered faces. I shake hands with a boy who couldn't be older than twelve, equipped with an AK-47 slung over his shoulder. I'm told by a mujahid standing next to me that the boy's family became *shaheed,* martyred, when the Soviets bombed their village. The young boy's eyes are hard, his face aged, and he refuses to smile. Maybe he's unable to.

I'm taken on a tour of the training camp, a relatively bare fitness course with homemade pull-up bars, balance beams, and old tires to skip through. Besides this there are several types of weaponry, such as surface-to-air missile (SAM) launchers, which appear to be huge machine guns mounted on stands, and a sizable arsenal of other assorted small arms. After prolonged encouragement I agree to take pictures with me holding an AK or perhaps posing with a three-legged machine gun. It's a strange feeling posing with weapons, and I feel uncomfortable in a way that's hard to explain. I consider myself a pacifist and wonder if this breaks some sort of nonviolent code.

It's after noon by now, and I'm told we have to get back on the road if we're going to make it by sundown to the base camp where we'll be spending the night. I give back the Kalashnikov rifle that still hung over my shoulder, only now realizing that I have been carrying it around with me for at least the last half hour.

It's not until we're driving again for about ten minutes or so that I realize why we had to leave in order to get to base camp by dark. All of the sudden, the asphalt road simply ends, slowly deteriorating and fading into what becomes a path comprised of jagged stones and river rocks. Although the distance is actually only another seventy-five miles or so, it takes us several hours to navigate over the terrain and arrive at our destination. At first I'm not sure what's happening when we turn off the main road and onto a dirt path lined with what look like eucalyptus trees that seemingly leads nowhere. Then we pass through gates under an archway of sorts, an entrance guarded by two rebels, and I notice the skeletal remains of a bombed-out village lying just ahead. We meander through the village and on to what appears to have once been a *masjid,* but is now part of a base camp for ANLF rebels. We're here.

It's getting dark, and preparations are being made for dinner. The cook picks a karakul sheep from the herd and leads it behind the building, where he will *halal* the animal and prepare it for cooking. I'm curious and would like to follow him, but Baznoor tells me we should sit with the commander of this camp, as he's been waiting for our arrival. For the next hour, we sit and listen to the commander tell us about recent skirmishes that his men have been involved in with the Communist forces around Jalalabad. By this time, 1990, the Soviet troops have withdrawn from Afghanistan, and the war is now primarily between the Afghan resistance and the pro-Communist Afghan Army, which is still receiving significant aid from Moscow.

I become less interested in his stories, and more in tune with the chorus of hunger pangs taking place in my stomach. As I'm listening to what could be something from Bach in D-minor emanating from behind my navel, we're summoned to dinner, a plentiful display of stewed meat and bread. Some vegetables and fruit are brought out in honor of the guests, but out of a natural desire not to get a running belly in the middle of rural Afghanistan, I stick with my meat and bread. Bananas, however, I'm told are okay to eat because the fruit is fully encased inside the skin, safe from the microbes that could wreak havoc on an untrained digestive system like mine. So for dessert I pick a couple from the pile and cautiously eat them both. In the end, the bananas are somewhat small but perfectly sweet.

After dinner, as I'm leaning on a pillow drinking green tea, I begin to wonder where I'll be sleeping for the night. There doesn't seem to be much shelter around, and there are by now probably up to a hundred mujahideen who have trickled into camp throughout the evening. Without electricity, and with a need to rise early and get moving again, bedtime arrives not long after darkness settles in. I follow the others to an outdoor area where several *charpaey* are set up with blankets, but no pillows. Our beds are ready.

As I'm lying in the open air of this bombed-out village, looking up at the sky, the stars seem closer and more reachable than I've ever imagined they could be. I reach out toward this celestial field and pluck one like a spring flower right out of its black velvety bed, secretly saving it for a future wish. Then I notice the wind as it approaches the village through the front entrance, proceeding down the tree-lined lane that leads to where we're camped. It begins quiet and distant, detectable in the leaves of treetops long before it can be felt on your skin. Growing louder as it comes closer, closer, a warm rush passing over you, through you, and on to the next bombed-out village. I wonder whether there will be anyone there to listen. The blanket of stars and the soft lullaby of whispering leaves soothe me to sleep before too long, while the quiet voices of others in the camp slowly fade into the dark.

It's just before dawn, and the camp is already stirring. I try to go back to sleep but fail miserably, so I sit up in the *charpaey* and put on my new black Chuck Taylor Converse low-tops. The mujahideen have already begun loading the vehicles for our trip forward to Jalalabad and are preparing breakfast. Breakfast, it turns out, is several cups of sweet milk-tea in cheap "Made in China" porcelain, bone-colored with little pink roses around the rim of each teacup, and some stale sweetbreads and cakes that someone brought back with them from their last trip to visit their family in a Peshawar refugee camp. And then there are the flies. The sweetbread and cake are covered under a blanket of flies, while the rim of my teacup is invisible beneath their bristling fur as they fight frantically for the sweet, milky residue left behind from each new sip. I refuse to just turn my breakfast over to the insect kingdom and so simply follow the others, fanning away the flies before each sip or bite, allowing them to settle in again, and repeating this ritual until I'm done.

After breakfast I team up with Farid, a young mujahid with shoulder-length hair and dark *kohl* around his eyes, and help load up the last of the supplies that are being taken to the front-line base camp we'll be visiting. Farid tells me he's twenty-one years old and that after his parents were killed in a Soviet bombing raid when they first invaded in 1979, he dropped out of school and joined the mujahideen. At the age of ten, he began as a kind of servant boy, wiping down weapons, serving tea and water, carrying ammunition. Now, eleven years later, Farid can drive a tank, can break down and reassemble a Kalashnikov AK-47 "in less than three minutes," and is particularly skilled at firing SAMs. But he can't read, and the only words he can confidently spell are his name and "Allah."

Farid's staying behind at this camp, and before leaving I notice he's wearing a pair of old, worn, brown sandals. It looks as though our feet are about the same size, so I take off my right sneaker and tell Farid to try it on. I ask him if he likes the sneakers, and although he's older than I am by two years, he quietly replies, "Yes, sir." The sneaker fits, so I tell him that I've been looking for some sandals just like his and ask him if he'll trade with me. All of the sudden, at least ten other mujahideen who have been observing what's going on immediately come toward me, waving one of their sandals in the air and telling me how much better their sandals are and what a better trade it would be. Laughing, I tell them all the deal's done with Farid, as he quickly puts on his new black Chuck Taylor Converse low-tops.

We're not on the road long before we pull into a large, relatively green area where the gray remains of several buildings sit quietly amid shady groves of trees. I'm told that before the jihad, this used to be a lavish resort getaway frequented largely by foreigners, including Russians. In fact, I'm told that the place itself was part of a development project carried out with the cooperation of the Soviet Union. The project included a plentiful farm where orchards of pomegranate, olive, and almond trees, among other varieties, covered large parts of the property. Two of the larger buildings, including the one we're standing in, were a hotel and a movie theater. As I stand amid the roofless rubble that was once a state-of-the-art, modern movie house, I try and imagine the place filled with finely dressed people as the latest Western film plays on a big screen. The image fades before it fully takes shape, the current reality of the place difficult to ignore.

"Who bombed this place?" I ask. I learn that after the jihad started, the mujahideen began to make use of the farm. They got food from the orchards and fields, water from the wells, and shelter from the buildings. When the Soviets realized this, they bombed the buildings to deny them shelter, poisoned the orchards and burned the fields to deny them food, and contaminated the water supply to deny them water. They even blew up and leveled the bigger trees so mujahideen couldn't hide in them with rocket launchers and shoot down helicopters. This was a skill, I had been told, that the mujahideen had gained quickly. I look over toward the mujahid who answered me, and he adds, with a look of angry disgust in his eyes, "They burned our whole country." I think of the irony in destroying something you helped build and am reminded of yet another development project: The Soviet Union built a well-paved road cutting down into Afghanistan from Tajikistan in the north to facilitate trade, commerce, and travel. On Christmas Eve 1979, the Soviets used the same road to roll their tanks directly into Afghanistan as part of a full-scale invasion.

I walk out of the theater and into what was once an almond orchard. The trees are bare, and the decomposing shells of long-ago-fallen almonds litter the ground. I bend down and pick up a black, shriveled pod. Even after the poisoning, children came to the farm to gather nuts and fruits to eat, unaware of what the strange spraying over the fields meant. Dozens of people in the surrounding villages died before the cause was understood. After that, hungry children watched as what looked like perfectly good foodstuffs fell from the trees, shriveled up, and rotted.

We're back on the road, still heading toward a front-line base camp in Samarkheil, outside Jalalabad. Thinking back on the farm we just left, I realize how green it actually was there in comparison to the barren, dusty terrain surrounding me once again. A deceptive green, as everything from the treetops to the soil to the deepest roots is now dangerous. What once grew there and what could be grown, both rendered equally inedible for years to come. Even the ponds where fish could once be caught, surrounded by beautiful, tall, green grass, are littered with metal, cylindrical canisters that leaked poison into the water, killing all the fish. I wonder if life will ever return to the farm.

Since we entered Afghanistan, all of the areas we have passed through, and continue to pass through, are controlled by the mujahideen. The city we're heading toward, Jalalabad, has been volleyed back and forth between the pro-Soviet government troops and the rebels for the last several months. Three days ago it fell to the government troops again, and the mujahideen retreated to their base camp in Samarkheil, on the outskirts of the city. The road grows even worse as we approach Samarkheil, with huge bombed-out sections that have us veering in large, wide circles for the last half hour. The road we're traveling on is now an arrow-straight stretch that leads directly into Jalalabad.

But before the city is even in plain view, I see several dozen mujahideen standing around, on, and alongside the road, with several Toyota pickups parked under the shade of a couple nearby trees. Once we reach them, we pull off the side of the road. I can now see that there is a very wide, dried-out wash that intersects the road at a perpendicular angle. The now empty, dirt-bottom wash once flowed beneath the road through two side-by-side tunnels approximately forty to fifty feet apart.

Having stayed the previous night in a relatively nice camp, with a wall surrounding the village, I don't expect what I see in Samarkheil. I get out of the truck and am led toward the tunnels. The one closest to the city has clearly been hit, and the road has collapsed into the wash, leaving a pile of rubble, atop which rests another Toyota pickup. Camp is a makeshift shelter set up beneath the road, inside the wash's other tunnel.

Large stones are stacked into the walls about chest high, creating an enclosure with a narrow space left as an entrance and exit. Inside, dusty but beautiful dark red rugs with traditional geometric designs cover the ground. A few pillows are strewn about the edges, and a small arsenal of AK-47s, SAMs, and their launchers leans against all four walls.

I am struck for a moment by the sheer number of weapons I have been around in the last two days alone and feel as though I am being given a glimpse of how it must be when weapons are a mere part of your day-to-day reality. They already don't seem as threatening to me as they did before, and I find myself perfectly comfortable being around, and carrying, a Kalashnikov.

"Agha saib, Agha saib!" I step outside to where someone is calling me and find several mujahids gathered around what appears to be a sort of rocket launcher, with twelve hollow cylinders, slightly rusting around their circular edges, attached together to form a square, resting on a sturdy base at about a 45-degree angle. "Do you want to fire on them?" I'm asked. I respond, "On who?" and am immediately handed a pair of binoculars, while someone points in the direction of Jalalabad. I look through the scopes and bring the blurry beige image into focus, only to see several tanks lined up in a horizontal row facing the camp. I look without the binoculars and see nothing, then look back through the lenses at the potential targets.

In the meantime, a couple mujahids have brought out three rockets and placed them next to the readied launcher in case I'm game. "Sure, let's fire on them," I say. I tell them I don't know how the weapon works, and without warning, one of the mujahids takes the first rocket and places it into a cylinder. The rocket is ejected out of the launcher with a roar, and flames come shooting out the back of the cylinder in a rush, kicking dust and dirt up and around us all. The mujahid responsible is doubled over laughing, as are several others, a prank that is apparently often played and yet never gets old. Much more nervously, I pick up a rocket, slip it into the cylinder, and run hunched over from the launcher with my fingers in my ears as the rocket is catapulted by fire toward the army tanks. A third person fires the last one, and rather unceremoniously, we return to the camp beneath the road for a little green tea.

"I just did jihad," I think to myself in half disbelief, as the tea burns its way through my throat and into a slightly upset stomach. "You're a mujahid now," Baznoor is saying, his words filling me with a deep sense of simultaneous belonging and betrayal. I think about the war and the hell it unleashed upon my family. Assassinations, disappearances, and beheadings were common occurrences. Whether monarchy or mujahideen, Afghans were seen by the Soviets as the enemy, and they suffered as a result. For that, the one rocket fired upon a distant tank hardly even seems enough to satisfy my desire for retribution. And an armed resistance seems like the only way to truly pay my respect to relatives lost at the hands of the invading Soviets. But engaging in an armed struggle goes against every belief I have in the power of nonviolence to bring about change in the world. It becomes hard to swallow, and my head begins to hurt. I close my eyes for a moment and gently pull myself out of the ethical maelstrom that's been triggered inside of me. Opening my eyes, I take another sip of tea and distractedly engage with the group that's sitting with me beneath the road.

After several minutes of small talk about what's been happening with the front line, the predictions for regaining control of Jalalabad, and the need for replenishing the ammunitions stockpile, whose current level has become a point of concern, I hear a distant boom and feel the ground beneath me rumble softly. We stand up and look out the "window" of the camp into the seemingly endless barren field beside us. Someone points, and in the distance I can barely make out a cloud of dust slowly dissipating into thin air. The tanks surrounding Jalalabad, the ones I fired on maybe a half hour before, are returning fire. Return fire, a concept that just happened to escape my mind when I had the bright idea of firing on them. "Of course they'd want to shoot back," I think to myself now, as another explosion of dust, this time closer, billows into the air. "Don't worry," a mujahid says to me. "They always miss."

I think of the other tunnel next door filled with road rubble, serving as a parking space, and ask him about it. "Oh, they got lucky once," he says, smiling. I watch as the tank shells steadily make their way closer to the camp, the last blast shaking it enough to topple over a few of the rifles leaning against the wall. Then, suddenly, there's a strange noise directly above our heads, like a heavy weight grinding deeply into the road, followed by a more distant blast that seems to come from behind us. "Where did I pack that star from last night?" I think to myself. "Time to make a wish."

Next thing I see outside the camp is a pickup truck overloaded with young mujahideen racing out into the open field, drawing wide figure-eights and other erratic moves, kicking up a storm of dust and hollers. They're drawing the tank fire away from camp, making themselves a moving target out in the open, like a game of cat and mouse, except the cat is a tank and the mouse a truck full of teenagers. Playing by the rules, the tanks fire a couple of unsuccessful rounds toward the truck and then seem to tire of this game. It's silent once again, and the truck returns to camp.

Stepping out from under the road to see what happened above where we had been sitting, I see a short, narrow, deep gouge in the asphalt staring back at me from the road, like a giant finger had come down to taste the gray, gravelly frosting that protected us. Some mujahideen had gone down the road to investigate the blast we heard earlier and noticed remnants of a tank mortar resting in the bottom of a fresh crater. That mortar was what landed above us, except that it didn't hit nose first. Rather, it belly-flopped its way over us and on down the road, where it left its proper mark. Had it done so on first impact, it would have surely collapsed the road in on those of us standing beneath it. They almost got lucky again.

With what resembles cynicism, a mujahid asks, "How does it feel to be home?" The question sounds as if it has come from miles away, traveling on the breeze and slowly blowing across my ear. I look around me at the group of armed rebels, their faces dusty and war-scarred. The wind is whipping sand into earthy spirals that disappear into a sky that, though calm and blue, feels heavy above me. Dizzy, I sit on a rock to steady myself as an uneasy awareness of my own privilege washes over me. And slightly nauseous, I lay my AK-47 on the ground and think, "I *am* home, and yet I can't wait to get there."

YASMINE DELAWARI
JOHNSON

*Yasmine Delawari Johnson's empathy for the girl from the National
Geographic cover, later identified as Sharbatgul, leads her to tell the
story of Afghans who survived. Delawari Johnson compares her life to
Sharbatgul's life: they are the same age; one escaped, and one
remained behind. This sisterhood she feels unfolds layers of guilt, love,
and a sense of responsibility for Afghanistan. Sharbatgul's face, to
Delawari Johnson, embodies the history of Afghanistan.*

The Girl with the Green Eyes

When I was twelve years old, my parents' friend Debra Danker published
an article on Afghanistan in *National Geographic*. When the article came
out, a beautiful girl stared back from the cover, "The Girl with the Green
Eyes." Debra told me we were the same age, but she didn't seem to be
my age. She seemed older.

At the time, I was performing in a play called *Nanawatai,* by William
Mastrosimone. I played a young Afghan girl who is killed by the Russians.
I stood on the stage of the Los Angeles Theater Center and wondered
why I was here, in America, and she was there, in Afghanistan. What if
Mom and Dad had decided to stay in Afghanistan? Would I be the girl on
the cover of a magazine, and would she be the girl pretending to be me
in a play?

She followed me for many years. When I was in eleventh grade, I was
assigned an art project. I drew her. She stared back at me day after day in
Mrs. Mealiffe's art class. I carefully drew the shape of her face. We were
sixteen then. My drawing of her picture seemed to have aged with us.
Her face was a little longer and her eyes a little older.

She went on to become the most famous photograph in the history
of *National Geographic*. Her face continued to follow me. I would see her
staring back at me from the shelves of Barnes and Noble. She was on the

cover of the *National Geographic's* book of photography. She'd fall out of people's magazines onto the ground. She'd appear in little postcards asking me to subscribe to *National Geographics.* There were posters of her, notecards with her face, and one man even had a tattoo of her.

Then I saw her on another book, a book of Steve McCurry's portraits. On the back of the book, I saw the only other picture I had ever seen of her. She was pulling her red scarf over her mouth. Finally, she seemed twelve.

I went to hear Steve McCurry speak about the new book. I listened as person after person asked questions about her. He talked about the letters and phone calls he continued to receive. People wanted to adopt her. People wanted to send her money. People wanted to marry her. I remember the phone calls and letters my dad got about her, back when we were twelve. Someone even asked whether she might want to model. I nervously asked Steve McCurry a question,:"Whatever happened to her?"

Now we were both twenty–eight, or at least, I was. "Is she still alive?"

He answered. That photograph was taken in a refugee camp in Pakistan, along the border. He said that after the Soviets left, many refugees went back to Afghanistan. He had gone back but had not yet found her.

My mind reeled. What happened to her? Does she have any idea that the world knows her face? Is it better if she doesn't know? We live in a world where a beautiful face on a magazine cover means something. But here was one of the most incredible faces ever to appear on a magazine, and she was lost. Not only was she lost, but everything she symbolized was lost, so easily forgotten. I imagined going to Afghanistan in search of the girl with the green eyes. I wondered if she was a mother, a wife. And all the while, I continued to enjoy my freedom.

She was twelve when that picture was taken. It was 1986. She had already lived through six years of war. She looked older than I did. It was in her eyes. From the ages of six to twelve, she had seen war, death, her home destroyed and her family slaughtered. She was scared and living in a tent in Pakistan. She had walked for days to get there. Alone. I had lived in a house on a Southern California cul-de-sac. I had my mommy and my daddy. I was in carpools. I watched *Little House on the Prairie.* I had slumber parties.

Why her and not me?

Two decades later, the answer came. He found her. Steve McCurry went back with a camera crew and found her. I should have been happy. She was alive! For so many years, I had thought she was dead. I looked her up on the Internet. I was shocked to see her beautiful face. Her skin was like leather. We were the same age. She had two children and a husband. She was very religious. So why did I feel disappointment? I think I liked keeping her just as she was at twelve. I don't think I was alone.

I got a lot of phone calls from friends: everyone knew that I wanted to go find her. They all said the same thing: "She looks so old." Of course she looked old; that's what war does. Doesn't anyone get that? Tragedy ages people. Look at any person on the news who is going through some hellish loss—they age in days. She had a solid twenty years of death, war, weather, and hunger.

People could empathize more with the beauty with the green eyes. We don't like harsh-looking people in this country. We like pretty people. We like flawless skin and piercing green eyes. We liked her better when she reminded us of Helena Christensen. No one said it out loud, but it was true.

The guilt flooded me. It was not new guilt. It had been there since we first met at twelve. I spoke to her in my head, in my prayers . . . I'm sorry I never saved you or even tried to save you. I wonder how much money everyone made off of you. How many careers were launched? Steve Mc Curry's, yes. How many book sales for *National Geographic?* And the only person who did not profit is you.

This parallel life we had lived, my sister of sorts, my connection to a world and a war so far away. I tried to relate to her. We shared the same blood, Afghan blood, but our lives could not be more different. And with each year that passed, I tried to live my life. My American life, my ballet lessons, my yearbooks, my college years, Manhattan in my twenties, but she was always there. A reminder of what could have been just a random twist of fate. And the question that had been there so many years before remained unanswered.

Why her and not me?

ASADULLA ABUBAKR

Asadulla Abubakr is the author of the successful book Islam vs. West: Fact or Fiction? (2009), which offers a history of Islam that debunks stereotypes. In this essay, he remembers the Soviet Invasion of Afghanistan in 1979 and shares his journey to here and how his life changed after September 11, 2001.

The Irony of Life and the Survival of the American Dream

December 24, 1979, was another ordinary day for an eight-year-old child, except the day itself wasn't ordinary. Overhead, close to Kabul International Airport, Wazir Akbar Khan, where the world seemed to be, there were an unusual number of frequent flights by large airplanes, both arriving and departing. The vibrating sounds of their engines were extremely intriguing and exciting. I loved to hear them transverse the sky, and as they did, the air transmitted their intense energy to the windows and walls, which vibrated in an exciting melody. Ironically, I was anxiously waiting for the next invading flight to cross above our house. For three days the flights continued. On the evening of February 27, I was abruptly awoken by sounds, echoes, and reechoes of the intense gun battles that had begun in the presidential residence, Tape-Taj beg. The Soviet invasion of Afghanistan had begun. Throughout the night, traces and sparkles of bullets and rocket fire seemed like a huge celebration, but it wasn't a celebration; it was an invasion! We were in the middle of a battle zone; Sherpur, a military barracks, was only two blocks from our house, and the presidential palace was less than a mile. The intense military activity was confusing, not only for me but also for my parents. Years later, I became aware that even Hafizullah Amin, the ruling Communist leader, was baffled. The following day, the sounds of ammunition were silent, and a new Communist puppet president, Babrak Karmal, was installed.

In the subsequent days and nights, the mood in our house was tense. My parents knew that their hope for a return to the freedom we had enjoyed prior to the Communist coup of April 1978 was futile. The Soviets were a superpower, and to expel them and their puppets would require an intense rebellion, along with unwavering support from the international community. My parents were aware of the iron-fisted subjugation of Soviet republics behind the curtain the Soviets had created in Europe. To say the least, the overall mood was depressing. The Soviets and their Communist allies created an environment of paranoia. Intermittently, I could overhear adults whisper about who had gone missing, and how they might be in line for imprisonment or death. One day, my mother, who was an elementary school teacher, came home sooner than usual, and I could hear her tremulously whisper to my grandmother: "Today, a Jeep full of police came to the school asking for me." She seemed terrified, and I could hear it in her voice, but luckily, she said, it was a case of mistaken identity. At the end of the conversation, they decided to quickly visit every local primary school in her district and look for the individual with the same name. They wanted to warn her that she was in danger. Years later, when I approached my mother about the events of that day, she said they went to three elementary schools and weren't able to find her.

Meanwhile, my father was approached in his office by intelligence officers of the Communist regime who accused him of disseminating anti-Communist leaflets. He was transported to the local police station, interrogated, and luckily released. After being released, he came back to his office—he was an entrepreneur—only to find that his car, a Mercedes-Benz, was missing. He called the local police station to report his missing vehicle, and the reply from the interrogating officer was, "Forget about it if you know what's good for you." After hearing those words and experiencing the interrogation, he understood that the country we knew was no longer, and it was time to leave. His resolve became further solidified as news of my uncles' harassment by the Communists trickled into our house.

As those dark days befell us, they had a huge psychological impact on us children. Our parents weren't the same. The mood in the house was one of fear and uncertainty, as I am sure it was throughout Afghanistan. My mother and father instructed us not to say anything negative about the new regime. They pretended to be happy, but we knew they were not. If anyone inquired about our family's attitude toward the new regime, we were instructed to be full of praise. It was an open secret that the Communists were utilizing children to acquire information about household anti-Communist activities. My older brother and I were instructed not to let anyone know about my parents listening to the BBC or any foreign radio stations. The general population was afraid that their contacts might be agents of the government. It seemed that the walls had ears. We were physically free but mentally imprisoned. Every word uttered in public or private was calculated and purposeful. It was a constant contest to prove your loyalty to the Soviets and Communists and your disdain for democracy and capitalism.

As the weeks passed, I heard stories of people missing, an insurgency developing, and life becoming more and more constraining—unless you became a Communist. Surprisingly, even children were being indoctrinated in Communist ideals. Our schools were drumming the beats of the greatness of Communism and the genius of Marxism, and the "destructive" and "inhumane" imperialism of the West. In the midst of all these events, life felt uncertain, and psychologically you were afraid that your parents could be the next victims of the Communists.

It was time to leave Afghanistan for the United States of America, the ideal of freedom, democracy, and tolerance. Our last night in Kabul, February 22, was energetically charged. Kabul spontaneously became alive with shouts of "Allah-o-Akbar!"—God is great. In defiance of Communism's atheism, the entire city of approximately five hundred thousand citizens was out, some on their roofs, some in their backyards, and others in the streets, echoing in unison, "Allah-o-Akbar!" That night provided an opportunity for me and my older brother to get out our anger and frustration toward the Communists, who had made our childhood so miserable. I remember shouting loudly in cycles, uncontrollably, until I couldn't speak.

The following morning, my father drove us to a compound on the outskirts of Kabul where we boarded a secret compartment of an eighteen-wheeler truck and set off for Pakistan. During the journey, my mother was instructed to give my younger siblings Valium for sedation. Unfortunately, after several hours, the sedation began to wear off. At one of the last military checkpoints, my five-month-old sister woke up to the external sounds of the border guards. As she was about to cry, my mother placed her hand over her mouth and begged her to stay quiet, meanwhile giving her more Valium. We were all frightened; it was a horrible experience. We were close to being caught, and the consequences were uncertain. Miraculously, after an hour or two, we were able to cross the disputed border at Khyber Pass and continue to Peshawar. After a journey of close to twelve hours, we were finally in Peshawar, where our guide was waiting. As I got out of the truck, I realized I hadn't urinated for close to twelve hours. My bladder was achingly full, and the only thing I could think of was how to relieve myself of the severe lower abdominal pain.

After two months in Peshawar, my father arrived from Afghanistan, and we drove toward the U.S. embassy in Islamabad to obtain a visa. After obtaining a visa, on May 5, 1980, we arrived at New York's JFK Airport. At last, we were in the land of the free and the home of the brave. Fortunately, Wazir Akbar Khan was more like Woodside, New York, rather than Peshawar or Islamabad, Pakistan. Because we arrived in May, we were not enrolled in elementary school until September. The five idle months were boring and grueling. Back in Afghanistan, we were used to living in a house with our own rooms, a spacious backyard, and many friends. In New York City, we had three bedrooms for seven people, no backyard privileges, and no friends. I felt like a caged animal, but what could we do? We had nothing to do, and since we didn't speak English, we were constantly in search of other Afghans. Unfortunately, we found only two families, and neither had kids our age! Our painfully boring days felt like eternity. The highlight of the day was watching, on a twelve-inch black-and-white TV, *The Price Is Right* in the morning and *Spiderman* and *Josey and the Pussy Cats* in the afternoons.

After our first few days in NYC, my dad set out to find work. He literally walked the streets of Queens Boulevard soliciting work, finally finding it at a car parts dealership. I remember him walking inside the house with a wide smile, telling my mother he had found a job. He used to be an employer, and now he was an employee, but it didn't seem to dent his ego. His motto in Pashto, passed down from his father, was and is, "Wogata feel wokhra!": Acquire and eat an elephant. And that was exactly what he was going to do.

Our lives slowly started to settle. New York became our city, and America became our country. As time passed, more and more Afghans started to arrive, and finally we moved from Woodside to Flushing, where a small community of Afghans was forming. By this time, 1986, we were well adjusted, yet our minds were still disturbed by the chaos that was going on in Afghanistan. We never really intended to stay permanently in the United States. My parents' hope was that one day we would go back to the "good life." Unfortunately, with every year that passed, that hope became less and less realistic.

Over the years, we became less comfortable with Dari and could only recall a few words of Pashto; we were more comfortable with English. Afghanistan became a foreign country in a fading memory. At times I had to make sure that my recollection wasn't a dream and that I wasn't fooled by my fading memories. Nevertheless, gradually, we became proud Americans. America became the center of the universe, and I spontaneously and consciously defended it when the opportunity arose. I especially noticed this with my visiting Afghan-European relatives. It became obvious at some point that even minor criticism of the U.S. was insulting. Love for most American values and opportunities, and American sympathy toward and commitment to Afghans and their plight, made me feel so indebted that by age fourteen I wanted to join the U.S. Army and defend the country from Communism. Nevertheless, at the end, I chose medicine, the profession of my childhood dreams, instead of the profession I sought because of emotionalism.

By the time I was ready to finish high school, I was a typical American teenager with a deep attachment to Afghanistan. Not a single day passed without my checking the magazines, journals, or newspapers to which I had access for news articles, essays, or commentaries about Afghanistan. In the evenings, I was glued to the TV for news from Afghanistan. I remember flipping channels between Peter Jennings of ABC, Tom Brokaw of NBC, and Dan Rather of CBS. When there was a news story, I was overwhelmed with joy.

Once I became a college student at University of California, Davis (UC Davis), reading about Afghanistan became an obsessive passion. I remember walking through the aisles of the library looking for any book that had information about Afghanistan and/or Afghans. I am certain that by the time I completed my biochemistry bachelor's, I had read either completely or partially every book whose title included the words "Afghan" or "Afghanistan." By my early twenties, it was becoming obvious that I was a patriotic American with a significant attachment to a nation where I had lived as a child, which was now starting to feel more like a dream than reality.

After completing my degree at UC Davis, I became a student in the chemistry master's of science program at California State University, Hayward, now known as California State University, East Bay (CSU, East Bay). At this point, my life was more focused on formulating a career than on engaging in historical, political, or social interests. I knew that these years were going to be defining for my future profession. I had the limited intention of becoming a chemist, but I had every intention of becoming a physician who understood chemistry. I completed my master's program with great satisfaction and entered St. George's University School of

Medicine. After four years of medical school and three years of residency, the first year at New York Hospital, Queens, and the last two years at Kern Medical Center in Bakersfield, California, I joined Kaiser Permanente as an internist in 2000. At this point, my life was stable, and everything was going as expected.

On September 11, 2001, I was awoken by my sister's call from Virginia. She was crying, "We are under attack." After seeing the devastation and carnage in New York and Washington D.C., on TV, my first instinct was that we were probably being attacked by Timothy McVeigh–type terrorists. As events unfolded, it became clear that nineteen men of Arab descent had brought devastation to America. I was extremely angry, since, as a Muslim, I knew I was going to be associated with these terrorists, even though I am not an Arab. And sure enough, I had colleagues come to my office asking me, "Why did they do it?" As if I knew! September 11, 2001, changed my life as much as it had changed on February 24, 1980.

After twenty-one years, life was again becoming psychologically stressful. The mood of Muslims was tense and disoriented. Psychologically, you were suspected of being one of "them," as was evident from George W. Bush's declaration, "Either you are with us, or you are against us." Once again, as with the rule of the Communists and the occupying forces of the former Soviet Union, Afghans were challenged to demonstrate our loyalty. The media was constantly coupling the words "Muslim" and "terrorist," just as the former Communists used to couple "capitalist" and "imperialism." Thus, in my childhood, if you were considered a capitalist, you were automatically accused of being an imperialist; now, as soon as people realized you were Muslim, you were coupled with terrorism and terrorists. Regrettably, every Muslim was considered guilty until proven otherwise. Thus, all Muslims became a target of subtle and not so subtle accusations and suspicion. The average Muslim became afraid to identify with Islam, just as the average Afghan became fearful, under the former Soviet Union's occupation, to be associated with capitalism and democracy. Disgusted with the degree of false information, and the rampant false stereotypes about Muslims, I decided to write *Islam vs. West: Fact or Fiction?* The purpose of the book was to demonstrate that we Muslims are not innately against the West. On the contrary, we thank the West for helping us. Specifically as an Afghan American Muslim, I want to thank the United States for helping save us from the clutches of Communism and despotism.

Nevertheless, after 9/11, America wasn't the America I knew growing up. In my mind, it had transformed into a police state almost parallel to the former Soviet Union—not to the same degree, but it was inching that way. Once again uncertainty permeated the community, and interrogation and arbitrary incarceration, in the name of fighting terrorism, became a possibility. The fears were further solidified in 2006, when Amnesty International accused the United States of violating basic human rights. In its report, it expressed concern at a wide range of practices, such as secret and incommunicado detentions, the use of interrogation techniques that violate the prohibition on torture and cruel punishment, and the policies of "rendition."

As under the former Soviet Union, even borrowing books from the library, or obtaining information online, became intimidating. Some people even curtailed going to the mosque, or donating to one, to avoid being profiled. The aura of intimidation and fear curtailed people from observing their constitutionally guaranteed right to freely practice their religion. Unfortunately, these are the same concerns that the world expressed toward the former Soviet Union. Of course, the root cause of this paranoia is the terrorists who set rolling the wheel of suspicion, not necessarily the system. Nevertheless, in my mind, George W. Bush was becoming the U.S. Brezhnev, and I was hoping for a U.S. Mikhail Gorbachev to shatter the mountain of suspicion and uncertainty that we lived beneath.

My prayers, like, I am sure, the prayers of countless of other Americans and non-Americans, were answered when Barack Obama became the president of the United States of America. The hope is once again that America will wear the mantle of liberty, prosperity, and happiness, free of uncertainty. After seven years, once again I feel like I can walk the streets without looking over my shoulder. Once again I am experiencing the psychological freedom we yearned for between 1978 and 1980.

As a child, I lived through the psychological stress of Communism, and as an adult, I experienced 9/11 and the subsequent suspicions and bigotry. The similarities are striking, but in both cases there was a light at the end of the tunnel. In the former, the light at the end of the tunnel was arriving in America; in the latter the light was the end of the rule of George W. Bush and his cronies. Now once again I find myself living in an America that provides a home for the hungry, poor, and suppressed peoples of the world. I can admit that since January 20, 2009, I can breathe again. And importantly, I am proud to admit that I owe everything I have or have achieved to the opportunities that were provided by America and my fellow Americans.

KHALIDA SETHI

*Khalida Sethi uses questions to guide her narrative about her mother
and growing up in Queens. There is shame in this telling of the story of
her mother's hard work trying to live the American dream and raising
her children. But as she grows and begins to see her mother in herself,
the author ends with a great sense of pride in having such a mother.*

My Mother

*Why do your hands always smell like onions and Brucci lipstick, and why does
olive skin always remind me of poverty?*

Every wrinkle in my mother's hands used to embarrass me. Parent-
teacher night was a nightmare of Persian accents and bad, slow English. I
would die if my teachers found out where I came from. I hated my
mother's hand-me-down clothes (that acid-washed denim skirt set my
aunt was too good for). I hated the smell of Brucci lipstick because I
hated the smell of ninety-nine cents. My mother was a barrage of ninety-
nine-cent scents like knock-off perfume sprays and Wet n' Wild blush.
She tried so hard! And I tried so hard to make it all go away. I marvel at
the luxury of the Jordache Gitanno jeans and L.A. Gear sneakers that my
sister and I wore while my mother wore hand-me-downs.

*Why do you have to look at the price tag and carry on about it when you
know you won't buy it anyway if it isn't on sale!?!*

Her complaining about prices made my brother, my sister, and me
avoid going shopping with her at all costs. We didn't have much of a
choice. We were all under the age of twelve, and it was New York City.
There was no way our immigrant mother was going to trust the city to
bring us back to her as fully Afghan as when we left. She was right about
that. I hated the way my mother was treated when we did accompany her
as she shopped. I never equated the dirty looks my mother got at shops
and restaurants with racism and xenophobia. I simply internalized them
as a flaw I was determined not to inherit.

*Don't hit your sister today! It's Eid, for God's sake! Khak da sarit! Don't
make me get my chablak!*

Eid-ul-qurban is a holiday when sacrifices are made and charitable giving is a religious duty. My face burned as my relatives fulfilled their charitable-giving obligation by bringing my family groceries or bags of sacrificial lambs, literally. I hated the way my mother thanked them instead of being insulted. At school I would brag about phantom shopping trips to Macy's and refuse to hang out with people who were decidedly poor. I remember that phase of my life as the first in which I actively tried to be an American. Internalized classism is a prerequisite of Americanization.

Here is a picture of your uncle's bride-to-be in Pakistan. Look how light her skin is! She has hazel eyes too. What a lucky thing to have found her!

I grew into high school and realized that I wore Brucci lipstick—brown shades made my skin look lighter—because it was affordable. My hands started smelling like onions, which are the basis of all Afghani cooking, because my mother just didn't have the time to cook with the two jobs she was forced to work. This was her American dream. I hated every minute of her sacrifice and the pressure it put on me to excel at school. We were constant burdens to her family, who would have to come over and look after us three kids and my ailing father. My mother managed to get her associate's degree, her bachelor's degree, and her master's degree while I pined away for brand-name clothing and Americanized parents. While I cried over not going to the prom because "Muslim girls just don't do that," my mother was making sure she could make enough of a salary to put me through college. My face burns with that shame now. Afghan women are good at feeling shame. It's one of our high selling points.

I remember the moment when my teenage American embarrassment left me. I was sixteen, going through puberty, and staring at myself in the mirror of my family's Queens apartment. I realized that I had inherited the olive skin I hated so much. I looked exactly like my mother, a smaller version of my mother. And the thought made me happy, much to my surprise. I see my grandmother when I look at my mother, and I see both women when I look at myself. This knowledge has carried me far. I had inherited and rejected the poverty of self-hate that comes with olive skin in my family. This didn't bring about instant self-love and the end of internal conflict though. As much as my family loved me and supported me, they still drilled into us Western ideals of beauty. My sister suffered far more than I did because of her weight. Only my brother was exempt from strict beauty standards. He was required only to be tall and have a good work ethic. I remember wishing at the age of ten that I had been born a boy. It seemed as if there were miles and miles between me and the standard of beauty that would make my mother less embarrassing to me, my father well again, and the strains of being fresh off the boat in America less hard to bear. As if blond hair, fair skin, and blue eyes would make the world a better place. In a way, this has come to be true as I've gotten older. Women with names like Khalida don't exactly get a lot of employment call-backs or much of a chance. Being a woman of color has definitely made me work ten times as hard. It's a shame that a child of ten had to discover and internalize that.

If he is your third cousin I'm meeting for the first time, why is he still considered my uncle? Why can't I answer honestly if he asks me how I'm doing in school?

When I look at pictures of myself growing up in the 1980s in New York City, learning English for the first time and adjusting to a whole different culture, I'm astonished at how hard my mother tried. Her infinite fatigue shows in these pictures. She tried so hard! Her constant weight battle, her attempts to home perm her hair and tailor old clothes so that they looked new again, amaze me. I am humbled by the way ninety-nine-cent makeup looks like Sephora on her. She was my age in those pictures. I am twenty years old today. I can't imagine living the life my mother lived then. I don't have any responsibilities to anyone except myself. But of course this is not really true. All Afghan women have strict responsibilities to their immediate, extended, and long-deceased relatives—"What would your grandmother say!" You know what I mean. I haven't turned twenty-six in a strange country, faced strange new forms of racism, hate, xenophobia, classism, newly formed rebellion in children unable to understand, and had to support the entire family on a secretary's salary. I haven't been that tired yet. And so this is the American dream. This is why my mother endured, survived, and is revolutionary beyond any activist I've ever met. How my children will be forced to thank her one day! But because my mother will probably end up reading this, and because it is apparently shameful for an unmarried Afghan woman to talk about children, I'll just say that I have grown to silently thank every wrinkle and sign of sacrifice on her hard-working hands.

RAMEEN JAVID MOSHREF

Rameen Javid Moshref is the founding director of the Afghan Communicator, an Afghan/Afghan American organization. He worked as an activist and writer for a decade before returning to work in Afghanistan. His work has been devoted to cultural dialogue between the United States and Afghanistan. In this essay written in 2000, Moshref traces his steps to America and how he struggled to fit into his new home. A historian by training, Moshref sketches out the complex history and culture of Afghanistan and Afghan settlement in America.

The Odyssey of Coming to America

The Afghan community is a relatively new community in the U.S. Afghan Americans still do not have elected officials. People still call us Afghani, which is actually the Afghan currency. Others say Afghanistani, but the correct term is Afghan. With about two hundred thousand Afghans living all over the U.S., we have traveled a long way to be here.

Following the Soviet war and its systematic bombardment of the countryside in the 1980s, an Afghan exodus began to the Afghan cities, neighboring countries, and beyond. Following the Soviet departure in 1989, the civil war further destroyed the landscape and social fabric of Afghan society. From the refugee camps of Pakistan to the growing communities of Northern California, Afghans are one of the largest refugee groups in the world.

Remembering my own experiences in the mid-1980s, the pro-Communist Afghan military stood with their trucks in crowded places and stopped young men who they thought were fit to serve in the military and forced them into their trucks. After a few weeks of training these boy soldiers were given a gun and rushed to their deaths on the front lines. I was becoming military age and was about to be conscripted into the Afghan Communist army—not because I was eighteen years old, but because my legs had enough hair for me to be considered a man and given a rifle to shoot fellow Afghans fighting on the other side, as the

Mujahidin. My parents thought it was time for us to leave, as they did not want me to end up on the front lines, to be used as a guard of the pro-Communist revolution, fighting other Afghans in a war that no one understood.

In 1983, I finished the eighth grade and was heading to a junior high school for ninth grade before going to high school. The lack of textbooks in schools forced some students to copy textbooks, word by word, in their own notebooks for daily assignments. I remember borrowing a friend's Persian literature textbook and rewriting the lessons in my new hardcover two-hundred-page notebook, which was becoming really popular among students. When I was halfway through the academic year, my family told me to stop going to school because we were going to escape to Pakistan across the border, and then to the U.S. I was disappointed at not being able to show off my new notebook. On my last day of school I gave my black, hardcover, red-fabric-bound, two-hundred-page notebook to one of my classmate friends, who could not believe his eyes. When he asked the reason, I told him I was leaving for Pakistan. It was common for many Kabulis to secretly leave for the border. I told him not to tell anyone, as we were afraid that if the government found out, they would jail my family, since it was not permitted to leave Afghanistan without an exit visa—acquired through much bribery and through knowing the right people in the right places. I saw sadness in my friend's eyes as he accepted my notebook. I too was sad, not only about losing my notebook but about losing all my friends. I also left behind memories of my childhood, which the continuous war permanently destroyed, slowly fading away from my memory with the passage of time.

My family secured the help of a guide who could smuggle us out of Afghanistan through Kandahar or Jalalabad, two Afghan provinces that border Pakistan. Seven members of my family and four family friends boarded the bus to Jalalabad. The bus station was a dusty field from which buses left in different directions. Before I boarded the bus, my father pulled me aside and told me, "Son, since I am staying behind, it means that you are the oldest and therefore the man of the family now. Take care of your mom and brother and sister. I tried to teach you toughness and responsibility as you were growing up. You are becoming a man now. Take good care and watch out for the family." I said okay then, not knowing the heavy burden he laid on my shoulders, but that promise changed my life and the decisions I would make. I left Kabul and my childhood in the summer of 1984. I did not see my father again for another eight years.

Our experiences on the way to Pakistan, and living there, are themselves book-worthy. In the interest of time and good humor, I will forgo describing those events.

By September 1985, I entered a Queens high school, starting in tenth grade. The whole system was different. Afghanistan had a nine-month-long academic year, and the passing grade was forty out of one hundred; students stayed in one classroom, while different teachers came in at different times to teach different subjects. When a teacher entered a classroom, all the students would stand up as a sign of respect. The teacher then would permit the students to sit down. When I first went to high school here, I stood up immediately when a teacher entered the classroom, while all the other students would sit down when they saw a teacher. One of the teachers warned me that she would not have students stand around once she was in the classroom. Confused and disappointed, I stopped standing for my teachers. In Afghanistan, after grade school, boys and girls went to different schools until they reached college. Schools were off during the winter because they were not equipped with heating systems. I did not know how to behave around girls in the same school. In Afghanistan girls used to sit in the front row, and it was not considered polite to talk to them very much. No boy would admit he liked girls; it was very improper. In the U.S., boys and girls flirted and went out and held hands. I remember one of my classmates asked me if I liked girls. I was very embarrassed to hear such a question, and I immediately said no. Needless to say, I did not have many friends until I was in college.

The Afghan community has been struggling with its identity. To describe oneself as not Afghan anymore would evoke the concept that there is a standard against which one's Afghanness can be measured. Growing up in Afghanistan for fifteen years of my life, there was not much discussion about who or what is an Afghan. Most identified with their ethnic groups, tribes, regions, neighborhoods, or even streets. Television came to Afghanistan in the late 1970s, on a limited basis. Radio was more common, but still not widely listened to. Therefore there was not a large medium of communication through which people could reflect on their identity. The fact that more than half of Afghanistan was illiterate did not help the growth of a national ideology and national consciousness either.

Afghanistan is made up of five major ethnic groups and about fifteen minor ethnic groups. The largest minority, and the one always dominating Afghanistan's government since its creation in 1747, is the Pashtuns. Pashtuns are a tribal people living predominantly in southern Afghanistan.

Tajiks or Persians make up the second-largest minority. Most Tajiks are city dwellers, and they do not belong to any tribe or clan. Hazaras, who are descendents of the Mongol armies of Changiz Khan, which swept through the Muslim world from East Asia in the thirteenth century A.D., make up the third-largest minority. Hazaras live predominantly in central Afghanistan. The Uzbeks and Turkmens live in north and northwestern Afghanistan. There are also small minorities of Arabs, Jews, Kargizis, Hindus, and Sikhs living in Afghanistan. Intermarriage between Afghan minorities is not uncommon, but people largely marry within their families to preserve family wealth and to resolve domestic disputes among themselves.

By the late 1970s more and more Afghans were slowly venturing out of their villages to travel to the cities, and city dwellers were going abroad to neighboring countries and to the West for travel, education, and business. It was in this environment that the Communist regime took power in April 1978; the following year the Soviet Union invaded. Forcing its communist and socialist ideology on peasants and landowners, the pro-Communist government of Afghanistan threatened the patron-client relationships between farmers and landlords, which had existed for hundreds of years. As the government escalated its efforts to violently stomp out the landowners and the feudal elements by bombing, killing, and incarceration, it alienated many ordinary people and scared more people into taking up arms. The Soviets, in turn, with their invasion and systematic bombardment of the countryside, bolstered the ranks of the Mujahidin. Meanwhile, the U.S. saw Afghanistan as a battlefield where it might pin down the Soviet Union during the Cold War, calling the Afghan resistance groups, the Mujahidin, holy warriors, fighting for Islam against the evil Soviet Empire. In the early 1980s, the U.S. supplied Soviet-style weapons and provided training for the Afghan Mujahidin to fight a guerilla war against the Soviets. In 1986, the U.S. supplied the Mujahidin with land-to-air Stinger missiles to end Soviet air superiority.

The situation in Afghanistan worsened as the pro-Communist regime was divided into two main factions, the Khalq (People) and the Parcham (Banner), which started to root each other out through killing and incarceration. The few educated Afghans who still remained neutral and still lived in the country were either killed or fled Afghanistan.

The first stop for most Afghans on their way to the West was either Pakistan or India. Iran was isolated by the West, and no aid agencies were based there to assist a flood of Afghan refugees coming across the border.

Further, in India and Pakistan, there were agents and loyal fans of the various Mujahidin groups. They further manipulated, cajoled, and harassed Afghan refugees for their personal gain in the name of Islam and nationalism. Most Afghans have painful and bitter memories of their refugee years at the hands of both Afghans and non-Afghans.

As they came to the West, Afghans were only too relieved to be away from the preying eyes and hands of various groups. Most isolated themselves from the Afghan community or any other group, having many unpleasant memories from the past. Thus, there never developed a sense of community, and there were no successful organizations to orient incoming Afghan immigrants within Western societies. Most had to rely on the experience and whims of the relatives who had come before them. Afghans coming to New York were encouraged by other Afghans already here to get involved predominantly in opening fast-food restaurants, driving taxicabs, or working behind pushcarts. Today, a great number of independent fast-food restaurants and coffee trucks are Afghan-owned and -operated.

Forced to support their families, the young men went to work, since their parents could not find jobs in their fields and could not learn English fast enough for many other jobs. As most young Afghan men worked instead of pursuing an education, their sisters attended school. While young men were mainly employed as manual laborers, and their mentalities did not change very much, young women entered more fully into American society and developed more common U.S. values and norms similar to those held by mainstream culture. This resulted in a male-female gap among young, single Afghan American that still exists to a certain degree.

Furthermore, a lack of effort or resources necessary to introduce the older generation to American culture left many older Afghan Americans dependent on their children and grandchildren. Even a simple doctor's visit, or the translation of letters from English, left many parents feeling dependent and therefore alienated from and resentful toward Western culture. Seeing how their children turned out in the U.S., as opposed to the environments they grew up in, most parents have enforced strict curfews and rules on their children, which keep many young people from doing what their peers are doing. Such restrictions further widen the gap between the new generation and Afghan culture.

Much of the generation gap is due to miscommunication between the generations. They do not speak each other's language, not only because of the language barrier but because they are in two completely different states of mind. The older generation grew up obeying their parents and elders in Afghanistan. It was common for parents to decide whom their children married and what they studied in college. Now, not only do parents no longer have control over their children, but they are becoming more dependent on them. Afghanistan, to most teenage Afghan Americans, evokes a set of old-world values and memories remembered only by their parents. The mainstream media's images of Afghanistan and its negative portrayal of Islam have alienated many younger Afghans, who cannot relate to recent events. Consequently, some young Afghans have become more active, while others wish to melt away in the crowd. Regardless, the most serous challenge facing young Afghans is a continuous and fruitless dialogue about their own future. It is hoped that recent events can change that for the better.

In 2004, Rameen Javid Moshref returned to Kabul, where he currently lives. This essay was written in January 2010, capturing the anxious relations between Afghans and Afghan American returnees.

Who the Hell is the Foreigner?!

A while back I was riding in a taxi, sitting shotgun, in Kabul when a policeman stopped the car near Zanbaq Square, leading to the Ministry of Foreign Affairs. We were in the first car that he stopped, and behind us the traffic came to a standstill. Apparently some nobody, who by the miracle of today's connections had become somebody, was passing through and imagined that someone else would want to waste a good bullet on him. It seems that it has become a symbol of power and prestige to stop traffic, and the longer you hold people in traffic the more important you are. God forbid anyone think that serving people or accomplishing the tasks noted on one's job description would be a measure of success or importance.

Directly behind us was a NATO armored military vehicle. The armored vehicle's driver signaled us to move aside so he could pass. The poor taxi driver dutifully obliged and advanced. He had not moved a meter up before the policeman slapped the hood of the car, ordering him to stop immediately! Then the policeman angrily came over to the driver to scold him. The driver apologetically said that the foreigner has asked him to move up. The policeman, all steamed up, exclaimed, "Who the hell is the foreigner?!"

I was both scandalized and amused, at the same time, by this statement. It was one of those rare moments when so many thoughts and feelings rush through you that you can't react or reply properly. Not that anything that I had formulated would have mattered to this policeman in a traffic rush. Ever since hearing this statement, I find new places in me that twitch. Retelling the story to friends sometimes gets mixed reactions. I especially loved the reply of one person to whom I told the story later on: "Tell him the foreigner is your daddy," or more literally, "your mommy's husband." In Dari that would be *shoi-e nanait*.

What bothers me the most about the policeman's statement is its blatant hypocrisy, which seems to have gripped almost everybody in Afghanistan these days. There is a sense of people distancing themselves from what goes on around them and a hypocritical sense of self-assurance that they are doing good but the system is corrupt. No one actually thinks that getting a large salary and being responsible for a key position means you have to do anything useful in return. The foreigners blame the Afghans for being corrupt, dismissive, or incapable, while Afghans think foreigners are overpaid, overappreciated, and inept, not to mention morally loose. Each side blames the other for what is happening without looking at themselves.

In reality, the policeman works for a government that was brought to power by foreigners, and the whole government system was modeled after a foreign one. The constitution and the parliament were designed by foreigners. The cabinet was arranged by foreigners. Even the policeman and his military colleagues were trained by foreigners, and the policeman is paid by foreigners. If the foreigners did not like something, they would quite literally tell the policeman's president to shape up or else. Worse yet, this president claims Afghanistan as sovereign and capable one day, but the next day asks the foreign army to stay in Afghanistan for the next fifteen to twenty years because the Afghan army is not ready to defend this sovereignty.

In the past, I have criticized the blunders of foreigners quite often and rightfully so; it is they who laid or helped lay the foundation of post-

Taliban Afghinistan and who support those in power, who are corrupt through and through. However, I am not blind to the fact that Afghans have been disorganized, unmoved, and complacent partners in this process. Afghans do not provide an alternative, as most are too busy collecting scraps from the *khaariji* tables and missing their chance at something greater.

Lacking a national identity and constantly being disappointed by the so-called representatives of the people, Afghans do not have much left to be proud of. Not ever having been conquered or colonized would be a huge accomplishment if it went hand in hand with national independence or at least a strong sense of national identity. Ask thirty million Afghans to define being Afghan, and you will hear thirty million different definitions. If not even two Afghans think alike, how can Afghans rule themselves, and how will they be ready take over from NATO?

There is no way Afghanistan will be a sovereign or self-governing state if this situation persists. Perhaps the foreigner is all too familiar with this and wants it this way. A strong Afghanistan is really not in the best interests of the region, which has a lot more strategic importance at the moment than Afghanistan does, and the foreigner is all too willing to trade Afghanistan for favors.

Most of this reality is lost on the young generation, whose members are either complacent, wishing someone would do something but expecting high posts after this dream revolution takes place, or directly benefiting from this chaos, thus preferring to maintain the status quo. Alas, financial gains are defining and effective incentives, overwhelming consciousness and a sense of justice. One might have assumed that free will and intellectualism would have yielded independence-loving and sovereignty-inclined ideologists, not self-interested individuals with compromising principles who are eager to pass the buck.

The statement "Who the hell is the foreigner?" and the pride at never having been colonized would be more worthy from people who actually control their destiny. In the title of another article, "Make Sure What You Are Laughing At Is Not Your Own Beard," I tried to underline this very concept, which I am repeating once again, but from another perspective. Before I encouraged more transparency and justice from the foreigner; this time I am asking for Afghans to look more realistically at ourselves.

The claim of national pride, if not earned, does not actually translate into real national pride. Freedom is a sacred privilege that is earned with sacrifice, and maintaining freedom is a constant struggle. People are defined by their everyday actions and choices. The greatest gift to pass on to our children is freedom and the pride of sovereignty. That road starts with one small action before the other. In the immortal words of Martin Luther King Jr., "I have a dream" that one day Afghans will realize their own value, each others' value, and the value of their country.

SAHAR MURADI

Sahar Muradi's loving story of her grandparents is an account of how one displacement creates many smaller displacements. The exile from their homeland has not ended in a solid new home for Muradi's grandparents. Instead there are many little displacements as her grandparents shuffle from home to home around the United States, staying with a different relative every few months in order to maintain family relationships. For Muradi's grandparents, constant movement means that they have no settled roots, even if their children and grandchildren do. They are living in the limbo of hope, a hope that one day they will return home.

The Things They Wait For

My grandparents start early every morning. At *sahar*, the first light of morning, he in his undershirt, she in her white *chador*, entering each day with a groan as if disappointed by the reality of morning after the long possibility of night. They wait for dawn, for the first prayer.

After *sobh* and the arrival of the sun, after they have stood in the tub and washed their arms up to the elbows, their scalps down the center, and their feet between their toes, after they have laid down two tassled rugs and knelt, lowered their heads and prayed, "Allah o' Akbar," he boils water for *chai-sia*, and she takes out the white cubes of *qand*.

For one hour they sit at the table beside the window, dipping their *qand* in their *chai* and resting the white dice on their tongues where the sweetness quickly sinks. They sit in the quiet and wait for the rest of the house to wake up.

Sahara comes down the stairs and heads straight for the TV. "Salaam," she manages, and they are thrilled for miles. "Eggo?" he asks excitedly. My grandfather is the only person Sahara allows to prepare her waffles. "Awh!" she answers, unaware it is informal and therefore impolite. He toasts two perfectly, low-medium heat, and cuts them into small chewable squares. He pours the syrup and puts the plate into the microwave, fifteen seconds, just as she demands. My grandmother watches him, shifting her teeth inside her mouth, then looks at Sahara, who sits five inches away from the screen, eyes fixed, unblinking. "Sahrawh jaan, iqah nasdeek nashee, chishmai't gharab meysha!" Sahara looks up, smiles inadvertently. She understands every word, even moves back two feet, but her mouth is incapable. Suddenly the timer rings. "Ay-nah!" announces my grandfather and brings Sahara the plate, handing it over without wanting to leave. "Tashakar," she manages and smiles back. And that is it; they are done for the day, their mouths like two dead fish facing one another.

Between the first and second prayers, between the second and third prayers, their hours pass slowly. She watches soap operas on Telemundo—Spanish or English, she cannot tell the difference—watches quietly until the undoing of zippers, the hints of skin, or even the subtle slide of the tongue forces out a trail of reprimands in Dari: *Have you no shame? Have you no morality? For God's sake, keep your tongues inside your own mouths!* She puts her hand to her cheek, the white *chador* between her fingers, and watches on.

All day they wait to be taken out. In New York, they wait to visit others, like them, who wait to be taken out. In Florida, where there aren't many other Afghans like them, they wait for us children to come home and for my parents to get off work. When he is down in the summertime, my grandfather will ask me to drive him to my parents' café in Fort Lauderdale. The restaurant faces a pond whose edges are lined with mangroves, in the center of which stands a sole twisted tree, spotted white with cranes. In the water are turtles and bright, freckled fish. Three wooden benches line a platform over the pond. We make the half-hour drive, and after greeting my parents, my grandfather immediately goes to the middle bench that faces the tree in the center. He sits there, staring out for hours, more content than I see him anywhere else. *For me,* he says, *this is life.* He compares the view to a royal palace, to Zahir Shah's castle in Kabul. In fact, when he wants to go there, he asks to be taken to Castle Sultanati.

At dusk, they take out their rugs again and kneel for the fourth time. Afterward, in those small hours before everyone disappears again to their separate rooms, we come together to eat. My grandmother shuffles alongside my mother, stirring the lamb curry and shaking cumin into the pot of rice. My grandfather sits at the table with his son, my father, discussing the workday or the stock market or the news. The rest of us help set the table. No sooner do we start eating than they begin telling stories. My grandfather tells a joke about the beggar who thinks he hears God talking to him, but it turns out to be a swindler up in a tree. We ask my parents to repeat it in English, and we laugh and ask him to tell another one. We listen on over second and third helpings, over *chai* and *tarbuz*. This is what they miss. In Kabul, even after they had moved out, my parents had dinner at my grandparents' house almost every night.

Here, most of my grandparents' conversations take place with each other, before the television set, or at the window, in the quiet pools where memories and losses collect.

She has lost the color in her hair. Long white threads spool out of her head, knotted and twisted under her veil. She can feel the difference from when she was just a *dughtar* in Kabul and her hair swept full and brown across her back. Now my grandmother buys henna and rubs the brown mud into her scalp until it shines like bright copper pennies melted down. She does this every three months.

He has lost his eyesight reading the news. He follows the situation very closely, eager to find out when they can return. Every Monday he checks the mailbox for the *Omaid Weekly,* an Afghan paper printed in Virginia. In Dari, *omaid* means hope. My grandfather has been reading the papers for twenty-two years.

NADIA MAIWANDI

Born on the West Coast, Nadia Maiwandi writes about her experience facing racism post-9/11. She introduces her experiences as an Afghan American after sharing hate mail that she received when people found out she is Afghan. In this essay, the "girl with the Valley Girl accent" shares her experiences as an Afghan American post-9/11.

The Enemy

Let the bodies hit the floor in Afghanistan.
Let the bodies hit the floor in Iraq.
Let the bodies hit the floor in Pakistan.
Let the bodies hit the floor in Iran.
Let the bodies hit the floor in Yemen.
Let the bodies hit the floor in all of the UAE.
We should wipe this scum off the face of the earth!! I personnally don't care about their babies, mothers, brothers, dogs, cats, or whatever. They should all die a horrible and torturous death and then writh in the pits of hell for all eternity . . . I can't wait to see you die for your country asshole. I'm living right now for that very moment. The hatred your people brought to this country was BROUGHT here by you. You are the only one to blame for the consiquence of this action. I recommend you consult your Koran for some solace before you die, bastard.

UNITED STATES OFFICIALS NEED TO DEPORT EVERY ARAB BACK TO THEIR DIRTY SANDY ASS COUNTRIES SO THEY CAN BURN WITH THE REST OF THEIR PEOPLE. DIE RAG HEADS!

The above sentiments have been overwhelming my email accounts since September 11. I am a member of several Afghan or Muslim e-groups discussing the continuing tragedies in our homeland or the true peaceful teaching of the Quran. People outside these communities for a long time

128 ◆

largely overlooked such groups. They were of little concern until September 11, when the forums became an easy target for bloody calls of revenge. Suddenly, our membership numbers are doubling and tripling, as cowardly hatemongers, nameless and faceless, crowd to wish for our deaths. In the first couple of weeks, it was constant: every five or ten minutes another message came through, each more profane and bloodthirsty than the other. And messages are still coming.

I wish I could shut off my computer and escape it, but unfortunately, it's on my TV screen, in the market, at the restaurant, walking down the street . . . There is no safe place. Being a Central Asian Muslim after September 11 is dangerous. The first few days were especially volatile; stillness followed any Central Asian or Middle Eastern person who dared to be in public. I remember going to a popular Indian restaurant in mid-September to find it eerily empty at lunch hour. I remember fearing for the Arab brother who pumped my gas as he looked at his feet, trying to go unnoticed, and the Muslim sisters who passed me on the street, defiantly wearing hijab.

I am the child of Afghan immigrants who came to America in 1966. Even though I was born here and my first and only language is English, I am constantly asked, "Where are you from?" and "How long have you been here?" My six-year-old nephew, Alec, now third-generation American, is quick with the answer to this question he has been asked his whole life. I look at him, so young and far removed from Afghanistan, and wonder if he even knows where it is—where this mysterious "home" of his is that he will never visit.

It is clear to me that we are not "from" here; that we will never be so, no matter how many generations later. But never is it made more clear to me than at a time like this: when someone in the Middle East or Central Asia strikes out or defies the U.S.

Suddenly, I am not a cute little novelty anymore, but THE ENEMY. Me? The girl with all the rock albums and the annoying Valley Girl vernacular?

But it is a change I know all too well, from the Iran hostages back in 1979, when I was a child in grade school, and all the hatred for Iranian people that followed, to the bombings of Libya in 1985, to the Persian Gulf War in 1991, to today. The shift is always sudden and deliberate. America needs to come together and unite against THE ENEMY, and I am that.

The anti–Middle Eastern sentiment of the past pales in comparison to that today. Growing up, a couple other Central South Asian kids and I were taunted for our ethnicity ("Iranian" was the worse you could be called in the late '70s/early '80s), and I knew some kids deliberately avoided me for being THE ENEMY. But a collection of hostages, or a defiant world leader from the past, does not equate with thousands dead on American soil, as on September 11. So has the retaliation changed; the avoiding and insulting have today sharpened into hate crimes against Middle Eastern/Central Asian Americans.

Reports of hate crimes came through faster than the Arab-American League could get them down. People were beaten to death or shot, and there are still reports of harassment and threats. Mosques are being graffitied with death threats or burned down. Muslims feel trapped in their homes, afraid to venture out for fear of America's reaction.

"Where did all this racism suddenly come from?" a concerned American friend asked me. I smiled. "It's always been there," I told her. "It's just more acceptable to speak it now."

America has some serious race issues with Middle Eastern people, and this is clear. I remember the LA disk jockey Rikki Rachman describing this some years ago as "the last acceptable prejudice." It wasn't politically correct anymore, he argued, to make fun of people of any other ethnicity or people with disabilities—but no one would check you on racism against people from the Middle East.

I think there's some truth to that. We are the newest community to the States and are still somewhat unseen, unknown. Crimes against Middle Eastern people are met with little resistance from the community. We are not marching in the street, angry and demanding respect. Instead, we are inundated, dealing with cultural and language barriers, making ends met, acclimating to the new environment, yet still keeping what we like about our culture. We are barely creating our own neighborhoods and have been here for too short a time to have a voice in the country. In fact, many Middle Eastern/Central Asian folks are trying not to call too much attention to themselves; my own Afghan American community often tells me to keep a low profile, not to make too much noise.

America has yet to see us as American citizens, as diverse individuals. The Middle Eastern/Central Asian area is the largest chunk of Asia, spreading from Turkey to Pakistan, from Georgia to Egypt. There are billions of people who fill these regions, all with different customs, languages, races, ethnicities, value systems, and the like. Many religions make up the region, not just Islam, although there are one billion Muslims all over the world (one-sixth the Earth's population). So, I wonder, how can we be all the same?

I heard no Central Asian or Middle Eastern person cheer when the bombings occurred. What I did hear was a lot of shock, grief, and anger, and shortly thereafter, fear for their safety. The people in America are here because they want to be. They want a better future for themselves; they've run from persecution by their governments or escaped miserable conditions. They are not people trying to destroy America, but to make America better for future generations.

When I read sentiments like those quoted above, it strikes me as wholly ironic that it is we who are characterized as "barbarians," "terrorists," "evil," and "uncivilized." All these are catchphrases for residents and descendants of the Middle East and Central Asia, so much so that any of these words automatically brings to mind images of Arabic-looking people. I don't ever remember the word "barbarian" or "terrorist" used as a substitute for Oklahoma bomber Timothy McVeigh's name. Instead, he was simply referred to by his name, or known as the "bomber."

But with this new war on the Middle East/Central Asia and its people, there is a ray of hope. The Afghan crisis has been spotlighted more than ever—even more than when the Taliban annihilated the Buddhist statues of Afghanistan last March, an event that sparked a condemnation greater than that precipitated by the regime's annihilation of the Afghan people. Through responsible media coverage and trustworthy education, concerned members of the international community will no longer think of disregard for human life as leading to atrocities that take place "over there," and are subsequently irrelevant, but will instead begin to realize that true evil cannot be contained within borders.

And many more Americans do "get it" than ten years ago. Although I don't remember reports of hate crimes during the Persian Gulf War, the American public's attitude at the time supported whatever violent and counterproductive actions the president called for. I got into heated arguments in cafes and on campus because I refused to lower my voice and support the deaths of innocent Iraqis. This time, on the contrary, I have been offered the love and support of my close American circle; even people I have not seen for years have sought me out to make sure I am okay. They seek discussion with me and want to hear about the plight of the Afghan people. I am further encouraged to see antiwar protests, media segments addressing the true teachings of Islam, and the movement of some to educate themselves on a region of the world they know little about.

Perhaps we have grown, and our past mistakes have taught us something. But this is only the first step. We cannot forget that there is racism in this country that allows the death of anyone who appears to be Middle Eastern or Central Asian. We cannot forget all the thousands of people who are scared to leave their homes, who feel they must conceal their ethnicity or dress differently. We cannot forget the kind of hatred that swallows our world when a handful of people disregard human life. We cannot forget that our ignorance allows us to harm people, whether directly through hate mail, harassment, or violence, or indirectly through the silence we keep when we are witness to these crimes of ignorance.

ZOHRA SAED

In this journal entry documenting the weeks after 9/11, Zohra Saed explores the desire of Afghans to claim America as home during the most anxious moments after the catastrophe, which Saed witnessed firsthand. There is an echo of helplessness in her words as she wonders whether poetry is enough to bring together these two divided parts of her identity at a time of possible violence toward Afghans and Muslims in New York City.

A Week Later

TUESDAY, SEPTEMBER 20, 2001

One week after the destruction of the World Trade Center, I take the 6 train to the downtown Manhattan area with my Afghan American friend Shekaiba. Since the Wall Street station has been shut down, we pass by in seeming slow motion; we emerge from the Bowling Green stop. Shekaiba and I don't know what to expect after seeing so many images of this area on television—a place reserved for grieving families, eager journalists, and heroic firefighters. I take out two surgical masks from my bag. I grabbed them from my dad's dental supplies drawer as I was going out the door, a precaution against the potentially toxic air and something I had seen people wearing on the news. Shekaiba and I come out into a section of the city that has more police officers than pedestrians. One six-foot-tall officer gives directions to a woman two feet away from him through a bullhorn. Yet she doesn't allow the force of his triply amplified voice to distance her from him. She hangs by so close that her face is crinkled from discomfort.

Shekaiba and I are lost in this new labyrinth of yellow tape and police blockades.

As we walk toward Wall Street, what strikes me as especially sad is not the dusty streets—I expected this, so I am wearing my boots today; it is the dust on the store awnings. It looks as if a dam broke loose and an ocean's worth of dust crashed its way through a narrow urban canyon. The acrid smell in the air makes my eyes burn and the sides of my nose, even beneath the mask, sting. It is unlike anything I have ever smelled before in my life—is it melted steel? My head aches and throbs. Yet people are there, going to work and standing outside smoking cigarettes—a mute collection of faces still raw from an immense shock.

They look at Shekaiba and me as if we are the rookies on the block. Apparently, everyone else has already given up wearing their masks, except for a few. We may be passé, in refusing to remove ours: the air is too thick. Everything seems normal—that is, if I don't catch my reflection, and if I avoid noticing the military presence at every other intersection. Here is a scene I never imagined: two Afghan women walking around with surgical masks just around the corner from the mall on South Street Seaport and asking directions from American soldiers. No one has checked for our ID—although I have three forms of picture ID ready, just in case.

TUESDAY, SEPTEMBER 11

While crossing the Manhattan Bridge on the Q train, along with other straphangers, I had seen the Twin Towers burning. However, following New York train etiquette, I took a few looks from under a woman's arms then returned to my book, just as everyone else returned to their newspapers. No one guessed the magnitude of what was to follow. The Fire Department would handle it. As New Yorkers, we carry an air of invincibility. It was terrible, but nothing the FDNY couldn't handle. So I turned my head down to my book and prepared my lesson plan for later on in the afternoon. The class I was teaching? Arab American literature.

At my office at the City University of New York Graduate Center, where I work as an academic advisor to undergraduates in the baccalaureate program, I enter to find the secretary frantic. I can hear her screaming, and she frightens me enough to weaken my knees. I still have no idea what is going on. Has there been some awful fire? I turn the radio on in my office, and all I hear is about the Pentagon. I say, "Just tell me what is going on in New York!" And then I hear the words again: a plane crashed into the Twin Towers. The last time I heard it, I thought it was a joke, a conductor's monotone voice having broadcast this brief bit of info as we crossed the bridge and entered the Canal Street station: "We are experiencing train delays because a plane crashed into the World Trade Center." But my ears didn't fully absorb the message. Now I am standing in my office and listening to the news about the plane crashing into the Pentagon. Now I'm so frightened my stomach is about to cave in. All I want to do is go back home, but all the routes have been shut down. And I can't get a call out of the city to Brooklyn. I open my email to find a message from a friend from college, Yuichi, in Japan. He asks me to write him back to tell him that I am okay. He says that he is worried about me and worried about New York. I haven't seen him in years, but receiving his email here at this frightening moment means more than any present in the world. I write back that I am stuck in Manhattan and can't find a way back home.

For three hours, I am unable to get any phone connection to Brooklyn. In the meantime, I have made friends with a postdoctorate fellow, Sunita. I am calmed by her reassuring voice, the only voice that hasn't become thin and shrill with fear. She advises that we go downstairs and that we carry a radio with us. So we end up downstairs, walking for an hour aimlessly in and out of the building, wondering if it is safer inside or outside, and taking turns holding a portable radio with the plug dragging around on the floor. We can't find any outlets, and we do not have batteries. Yet we cling to the radio as if it is some form of security blanket. We spend a few hours together, walking north, eating pizza, and discussing Bollywood films to distract ourselves from events. But even this discussion touches upon Bollywood's fascination with suicide bombers, from *Fiza* to *Mission Kashmir.* It is Fashion Week at Bryant Park. A photographer comes to sit with us. We only know this because he announces himself as a photographer and then sits down to tell us that it is probably Palestinians. Sunita and I get angry and tell him to get lost. Sunita argues with him some more when he doesn't back off. I sit in my seat, exhausted with wondering how I will get home to Brooklyn.

Sunita and I end up walking back to the Graduate Center to listen to the news in the auditorium. I run into a Turkish friend of mine in the chaos of people out on the street. She tells me that a suicide bomber has attacked a police station in Istanbul. I tell her that on Sunday, suicide bombers disguised as journalists assassinated the anti-Taliban opposition leader Commander Ahmad Shah Massoud. Both of our lips turn even paler from fear. A faraway threat has come to our town.

Sometime in the afternoon, I have lost track of Sunita, so I walk by myself from 34th Street across the Manhattan Bridge into Brooklyn with a mass of other displaced workers. Rather than following everyone in their migration to the north of Manhattan, I go south, away from the shadow of the Empire State Building, to Dekalb Avenue in Brooklyn. For some reason, everyone thinks the Bronx will be safer than Brooklyn at this time. Alone and frightened, I am convinced that New York City is going to crack beneath me like an egg. As a little Afghan girl in Brooklyn, I grew up with the dual visuals of American fear films revolving around nuclear war (*The Day After* being the most frightening) and the real bloody war in Afghanistan broadcast on the nightly news. As a seven-year-old, safe in the red brick of Sheepshead Bay, I was an insomniac, fearing a Soviet invasion or the end of the world. In my childhood nightmares, my fear was not of death but of separation from my family. After seeing the Twin Towers burning from the Q train, which passes over the Manhattan Bridge, these old sensations return.

Several times on my walk across a bridge littered with empty film canisters and Red Cross water cups—I suppose a moment of crisis in NYC calls for water and snapshots—I look over my shoulder, incredulous that something like this could strike New York. It is something out of a science fiction novel. Hollywood and fantasy fiction are our only reference points for such an act. I pray with the others crossing the bridge that no one will attack us. Then, at the very end of the bridge, humanity resurfaces and offers water, kind words, restrooms, and warm support for us—a mass of disheveled and frightened workers finding our way home. It is these acts of kindness that give me faith that the world is not over.

After the longest, most frightening walk of my life, I come home to death threats from people who grew up with us. I come home to cold stares on the streets—these from acquaintances, since, like many Afghans, I have ambiguous racial features. I am not attacked on the basis of my face, only for the sake of my name and where I was born, Afghanistan. These are only verbal threats and harassment, but they cut deep since I grew up with these people's children and thought of them as surrogate aunts and uncles. I ran errands for them and got in trouble alongside their children for staying out too late or stealing Icees from the nearby Teamo shop. Another friend, who is Turkish, refuses to speak to me and tells me not to call her again because she is in the process of getting her Green Card and thinks speaking to an Afghan at this time will prevent her from being approved.

The director of the Asian American Studies Program at Hunter, Robert, calls me to ask how I am and to say that perhaps I should let some time pass before I go back to teaching. He is worried about any potential anger that students may have against Arabs and against me. I am nervous, too, and not sure what answers I am expected to give my students. Would poetry have answers to quell racism?

Already, reports of physical violence and vandalism of property against visibly Muslim, or South Asian, or Middle Eastern Americans drip through the phone lines. "Be careful." I hear these words more and more as the day progresses. A warning for my safety not only as a New Yorker but as a Muslim Afghan New Yorker, a combustible combination in these days when fear has dug so deeply into our hearts that it threatens to congeal our blood.

SATURDAY, SEPTEMBER 15

After four days of remaining indoors, I venture out with my family. We go to Flushing, Queens—the heart of the Afghan American community in New York—with the pretence of going to stock up on ethnic groceries. In actuality, we go to check up on our community, but we are afraid to admit that it needs to be checked up on. To admit this would be to verify the rumors we hear through the insulated walls of our home in the midst of Sheepshead Bay—a mix of newly immigrated Russian, Albanian, and Turkish families, set upon an older layer of Italian American and Jewish American families—all of whom we grew up with, playing on the streets. As in many places, in Sheepshead Bay, we are one of the few Afghan families anyone has met (ever).

I don't know what we expect to find in Queens, after hearing so many stories about Arab, Afghan, and Pakistani stores being attacked, but the Afghan shops still seem intact, and people are smiling and overcharging us lovingly. We check the Kouchi (Nomad) Market on Kissena Boulevard, the Bakhtar Market on Main Street and the Ariana Halal Meat Store on Main Street, near the Queens Botanical Garden. All are fine. All refuse to talk about any incidents. Everything is fine, so say the large flags in their windows and their neatly compressed smiles. It is difficult to pry through Afghan etiquette when one is a young female equipped with fragmented Dari trying to break through to the heart of the matter. The nearby Hindi video and music shop displays not only an American flag but an Indian flag as well—to avoid being misrecognized, assuming that an angry mob is an educated mob that knows the difference among a Muslim, a Hindu, and a Sikh.

Main Street, which is usually filled with Muslims in hijab, is now empty of ladies perfuming the air with a spill of ornate languages. I see three women in total: women who have come out in a group of three, with large men accompanying them. Everyone has flags up, but it seems part of Muslim Americans' survival to carry one prominently. One Afghan woman in an Indian shop is dressed modestly in Western clothes. When her two almost-blond-haired boys speak to her in Dari, she shushes them up and speaks to them in English. The English language winds around them throughout the store—a young mother protecting her two boys, who can potentially pass as white Americans.

All of these women I see are out only to shop. The nearby Queens Botanical Garden, once filled with families taking their children out for strolls among the flowers, seems reserved for wedding parties. The park behind the gardens is empty, except for the ice cream truck with its rather grossly out-of-place music. The day is tinged with autumn. Sitting like this, so close to my family, so far away from the pain of the past few days, makes me feel so fortunate to be alive and so fortunate to be able to love. This comfort is something that soothes the painful ruptures of the last week.

One of my last memorable images of Queens is of a South Asian man, strolling by himself down a quiet street with card-paper American flags stapled together to make a hat. He makes me laugh and point. But a little further down, there is a group of white American men waving flags with signs that say, "GOD BLESS AMERICA!!!" God should bless America, but in these days of simplifications and Us vs. Them, do I have the right to claim America as my own in order to bless? And what about Afghanistan? Do I have the right to bless Afghanistan without being pointed out as a traitor? Can I put both these flags on my car and not worry about vandalism? The men on the street are average lower- to middle-class white Queens residents. Their beer bellies look ready to bust at the seams from so much patriotism. A frenzy of beeping cars and shouting men creates more traffic. They smile broadly at our car and shake their fists in the air, a sign of unity. I wonder if they would be so happy to see us if our car weren't fluttering with little flags, or if I had veil on. But it is not fair of me to make assumptions about what their head and hearts are like. I think of the South Asian man in the American flag hat, walking with his hands crossed behind his back into a narrow street in Flushing. He was simply wearing a talisman to protect himself from zeal and the frightening noise of scenes like this. On the Belt Parkway, I see the smoke fill the red horizon, reminding us of the deep wound in Manhattan.

TUESDAY, SEPTEMBER 18

The streets of downtown Manhattan are cluttered with generators. The sound outside is not the usual New York noise pollution. There are no snippets of conversations, or car horns, or streaming voices from radios. The loud noise of the area comes from a crescendo of generators outside of each building that has survived. Here even the buildings sag from the weight of witnessing such a tremendous loss. Monstrous machine sounds and smells rule the streets. This keeps Shekaiba and me quiet. As we struggle to find the radio station on Wall Street, we realize that we have lost our sense of direction, until we see Trinity Church and, behind it, a gauze-like memory of smoke emanating from the destroyed buildings.

Finally, we find our way into the building, stepping over layers of extension wires. Upstairs, we find that everything is out of synch—the phone connections are bad because of the explosion, and the guests haven't been interviewed. Shekaiba and I come into a studio that is frantic with attempts to replace the interviewed guests. Shekaiba reads poetry by Afghan Americans, which recounts their childhood memories in Afghanistan. I read poems about growing up in Brooklyn. Of course, such childhoods seem so distant from what we had recently experienced, but then the poetry makes more sense as the program goes on. It adds a different dimension to the words "Afghan" and "American." Certainly, they aren't as flammable together as the world has believed over the past week. But how much of a difference does this poetry reading really make?

FAHIM ANWAR

This young Afghan American comedian's first YouTube production, "Afghan Wedding," a humorous look at, as the title says, Afghan weddings, became an instant hit among Afghans, Afghan Americans, and Americans. Fahim Anwar then produced a few more short videos for YouTube that were also successful: "Afghan Wedding II," "Afghan Christmas," and others. The first Afghan American comedian, Fahim Anwar has made quite a successful career. Here he shares his experience as a young Afghan American and his love of stand-up comedy. In the realm of comedy, there is no hyphenated identity; there is only a comedian.

Stand-Up Comedy

Webster's defines "Afghan American" as . . . just kidding. I heard it's good form to start every single paper with "*Webster's* defines." I am an Afghan American. My dad came to this country from Kabul when he was eighteen for studies and later sent for my mom. I was born in Everett, Washington (Seattle to anyone I meet outside the state). My upbringing was typical of any American family, with a little Afghan culture sprinkled in. We mostly spoke English in the household, which is probably the one regret my parents and I have. My Farsi is pretty atrocious. I can say pleasantries well enough and get by, but a sustained conversation with a distant aunt or family friend terrifies me. "Just smile and nod," I always tell myself. It is an interesting predicament being Afghan and not being able to speak the language well. The dynamic is completely different than if a white person were attempting to speak Farsi with an Afghan. Much leeway would be given to them, as it's endearing in itself that they would even be attempting to speak Farsi. When you're Afghan, speaking broken-down Farsi with another Afghan, there is little to no leeway. You can almost hear the other person's inner monologue: "Oh my God, his parents must have fed him nothing but paint chips as a child." My mom would always tell me to practice by speaking around the house or with people at get-togethers. The problem was whenever I would say something in Farsi or I'd answer one of her Farsi quiz questions correctly, she would start clapping and make a big ordeal out of it. This was all very sweet of her but made me feel like I had suffered severe brain damage in some sort of motorcycle accident and was slowly regaining my motor skills, since any milestone was met with thunderous applause. The reason for this language deficiency was my brother's late speech development. He wasn't talking for the longest time, and when my parents took him to the doctor, he said my brother was probably getting confused by the Farsi and English being spoken at home. My parents decided to stick with English, and that kind of set the tone for me once I came into the world. As we grew older, my mom would urge us to learn Farsi, but at that point it was kind of a lost cause. She promised to buy us a Sega Genesis if we learned it, but even that wasn't enough. My brother and I missed out on many other consoles because of this. Super Nintendo, N64, Sega Saturn, and Dreamcast all passed us by. Eventually, we got old enough to where we just bought our own Playstation when that came out.

I think because I grew up tucked away in Washington, I turned out a little different from Afghans born in Afghan epicenters like the Bay, SoCal, or D.C. I've been told that I sound "white" by other Afghans, which I always found to be a ridiculous insult. What's the alternative? Sound like Eminem? Or would they rather I sound like Borat? Everyone is a product of their environment. The Afghan community is rather small in Washington. About one weekend every month, my family would pile in to the Dodge Caravan and drive to someone's house for an Afghan party where a number of families would mingle as their children, including myself, ran wild. This was really my first introduction to the music, the dancing, the generous portions of food, and of course the two-hour goodbye. I always looked forward to those parties because I would get to play with my friends until two a.m. The only thing I didn't look forward to was the three-mile Rooy Mochy line I had to go through before getting to run upstairs. Rooy Mochy (how it sounds in English) is the double cheek-kissing that has become oh-so-fashionable in the entertainment industry these days. I always feel like a piece of our culture has been ripped off every time I watch a late-night talk show and the young starlet kisses the host before sitting down. "THAT'S OUR THING!" These parties growing up prevented my family from being completely culturally insulated.

I enjoy telling people I'm Afghan when they ask. There aren't too many of us, comparatively, so people are always intrigued. They often want to get my take on the current situation overseas and know more about the country. After 9/11, though, I was a tad more hesitant to reveal this information. Luckily, that reservation was short-lived after I realized that the people in my town were educated and could make the distinction between a handful of people and an entire race. I've heard some terrible post-9/11 stories, but I was fortunate enough to not encounter any hints of racism. My dad was expecting the worst. I actually woke up to 9/11 when my mom shook me and held out the phone, telling me my dad was on the line. I had no idea what was going on. "Don't go to school!" he told me. He thought I would get beat up and ostracized, which is funny now, looking back, knowing how little trouble I had.

I've always been a pretty creative person and have gravitated toward the arts since I can remember. I'd do all the talent shows. I was involved in pep assemblies, video productions, orchestra, and drama. My parents were always supportive of these endeavors until I gave indications that I might want to make a career out of one of them. I was at that point in my life when you have to decide what you want to do for the rest of it. I had three contenders: directing, acting, and writing. You might be better off telling an Afghan dad you're gay than telling him you want to study one of these majors at university. He was not going to have any of this. My parents were going to pay for my college, but they were not going to pay for any of these majors. In a perfect world I would have been a doctor, dentist, or lawyer, but sometimes children come out with brains of their own that steer them in different directions. I understand where they were coming from though. They had come from Afghanistan to make a better life for their children, and I could seemingly be throwing it all away as a failed director/writer/actor. In hindsight, I'm glad they didn't let me go through with any of my initial choices. After thinking it over, I realized I could do any or all of these three things on my own time, without having to go to school for them. My parents wanted me to have a degree with teeth in case things didn't work out, and I figured these passions could be pursued on the side. My best friend, who lived across the street from me, was studying to be a mechanical engineer, so I figured I'd do the same. It would get my parents off my back, and I'd get to spend a lot of time at school with my friend.

Around my senior year of high school, I started doing stand-up comedy. I think at first my parents thought it was just a phase and I'd soon outgrow it, but weeks turned into months, then years. My dad has never been a fan of me doing comedy; he's learned to accept it, but a career in entertainment is often viewed as low-class in Afghan culture. My mom is a little more accepting. I remember coming home late from shows and my mom having stayed up, coming to me to say, "Your father is worried about you. What is this comedy? Is it worth throwing your life away?" Comedy was viewed like heroin addiction. I never saw the problem. I was studying engineering and had this hobby on the side that made me money on occasion. With time, it just became known that stand-up is something I do, and I could not be swayed. All arguments had proved futile.

I graduated from the University of Washington in spring '06 and landed a job in Los Angeles, which had been my plan all along. One can do only so much in Seattle to further one's comedic career. Finding it harder to get stage time in LA, I decided to start doing Internet shorts as well. I had an idea for an Afghan wedding tutorial, teaching people the ins and outs. I filmed it all in my apartment, edited it, and secretly posted it to my Myspace account to see whether there would be any sort of response. I hadn't posted any video of my comedy prior to this, because you leave yourself open to severe criticism when you post anything of artistic value on the Internet. People can be incredibly vicious when hiding behind a screen name, and I didn't know if I wanted to leave myself so vulnerable. Within a few short days, the Afghan community had embraced it and posted it everywhere. This gave me the confidence to release some of my stand-up material and become more willing to produce the short ideas that came to mind. My comedy as a whole isn't very Afghan. It's more reflective of how American my upbringing was and how much like my audience I am, rather than how different. I may have a joke about being Middle Eastern here or there, but as whole it's very universal. My goal is to have people coming out of my shows thinking, "That was a funny comedian," not solely a funny Afghan comedian. It's kind of ironic how the most successful video I've ever done is "Afghan Wedding," because it doesn't exactly fall into this philosophy. It was an idea that people seemed to latch onto more than others, because it spoke to a group that had never been represented before in this comedic medium. I feel pressure from the Afghan community to make many more Afghan-themed shorts, but it's not me. I don't like being pigeonholed, and it's not my voice. These people are hungry for something I can't deliver. Still, there are many Afghan Americans like me out there who send emails and comments expressing their appreciation for my style of comedy, relieved that I'm not pandering. I'm just happy that I can serve as an example for younger Afghan Americans: it is possible to follow your passions outside of the Afghan realm.

TAREQ MIRZA

Tareq Mirza's account of his trip back home at the height of "mass returns" to Afghanistan during the reconstruction era captures the exhilaration of this time. He reveals all the complexity of returning and reclaiming a homeland one has never seen before. Mirza's honest and humorous narrative is about finding a place where you fit that may not be one place at all, but a conglomeration of many places. This was originally published in Snapshots: This Afghan American Life, *edited by Mir Tamim Ansary and Yalda Asmatey (2008).*

Journey to Afghanistan, September 2002

I sat quietly in the room, waiting. The plastic chair rocked back and forth on its bad leg as I shifted around. Other than the chair and the table a few feet in front of me, the room was barren—an out-of-the-way room in an out-of-the-way place. After several minutes the door opened, and two cleancut men wearing khakis and dress shirts walked in. The first man set a handgun down on the table and dropped a pair of handcuffs next to it. An obvious ploy to intimidate me, it was working. The other man had my backpack and was looking through its contents. The first man turned to me and said, "We're FBI agents, and we want to ask you some questions."

"Okay."

"So, your name is Tareq Mirza?"

"Yes."

"Why are you going on a trip to Afghanistan?"

"Because I was born there and haven't been back since I was three."

The second agent paused his search through my bag and looked at me. "You don't look Afghan."

Before I could answer, the first agent chimed in: "You know they're going to kill you over there."

Then the second agent pulled earplugs out of my bag. "What do you need these for?"

"It was one of the suggestions on the list my tour gave me."

I became more nervous. I had done nothing wrong, yet here I was being interrogated by FBI agents. It felt like I was in a scene from a movie. What made the situation even more disturbing was that I was in Newark Airport almost a year after 9/11, headed on an art and culture tour of Afghanistan. A week earlier in San Francisco, when I had decided to undertake this dangerous trip, I had not realized the danger would begin before I left the country. I began my trip at the San Francisco airport with two other Afghan friends, Farhad and Shafi. I had met both of them at the Society of Afghan Professionals, an organization of young Afghans trying to help their community in the Bay area. We had departed on September 5 and would be arriving the next day in Newark, New Jersey, where we would be meeting the other members of the tour, comprised of Afghans and Americans from various backgrounds who were interested in assessing the state of art and culture in wartorn Afghanistan.

"What do you need a money belt for?"

"It was on the list from the tour company also, for safety."

"You're not going to be safe over there unless you have a flak jacket and an M-16," said the first agent.

"Not a lot of money for a money belt. You only have seven hundred dollars in here?" said the second agent.

"It's a lot of money to me."

"Why weren't you sitting in your seat on the airplane?"

"I was told the old man sitting next to me needed the aisle because he used the bathroom often."

I thought back to when I was sitting on the tarmac for three hours on Air Malaysia 747. No one knew what the holdup was or what was going on. Then police officers started boarding the plane, taking people off one at a time. I saw two officers board and take my friends Farhad and Shafi off the plane, and an unsettling feeling came over me. I had a feeling I would be next. Another two officers boarded and made their way to my row. They stopped and looked at the old man sitting in the aisle seat.

"Sir, would you please grab your belongings and come with us?"

The old man looked up at them, confused. It didn't seem like his English was good enough to understand them.

"Sir, please get your things and come with us."

I finally got up the nerve to interject. "That was my seat. We switched because he needed the aisle. I think you are looking for me."

"Are you Mirza, Tareq?"

"Yes, that's me."

As I got up and grabbed my bag from the overhead compartment, I could feel all the passengers' eyes on me. As far as everyone was concerned, I was probably a terrorist, caught before I could do any harm. I was taken off the plane and searched at the gate. The entire contents of my bag were meticulously removed and scrutinized. All of this took place in front of a full terminal of onlookers. One by one all the members of the tour, both Afghan and American, were taken off the plane and searched. Then our entire party was led to a secure part of the airport, where they sat us all in a room with armed guards. Then one by one they took people out for questioning.

The questioning over, they took me back into the room with everyone else. We were detained for a total of nine hours. Then the head of customs at Newark Airport told us we had been cleared and were free to go. They arranged transportation for us to JFK, where we could make another flight bound for Afghanistan. As the plane took off, and my fear and anxiety over the day's events subsided, I realized that I was finally on my way to Afghanistan. But the unsettling feeling never left me. Up until that day, I had always considered myself an American. I had moved to the United States when I was six years old. At the age of eighteen I had become a U.S. citizen. But leaving New Jersey on that plane, I came to terms with what my passport said on its first page: I was a U.S. citizen, but a U.S. citizen who had been born in Kabul, Afghanistan. And I would always be treated as such.

The pressure building in my ears woke me up. The Ariana Airlines 737 was making its descent into Kabul Airport. I was tired and had not slept much in the last forty-eight hours. Our departure from JFK in New York had taken us on a seven-hour flight to London, followed by another seven-hour flight to Dubai. Our layover in Dubai, scheduled to be an entire day, had been cut down to four hours. We had all decided this was enough time to get to the hotel, shower, change, and make it back to the airport to catch our plane to Kabul. At that time, Ariana Airlines only had one departure from Dubai to Afghanistan, once a week, early Sunday morning. The three-hour flight took us across water and vast mountain ranges. I stared out the window, my Nikon SLR in hand, ready to take any interesting pictures. As we made it through the cloud cover, and the city of Kabul slowly took shape, a strange calm came over me. I was coming home for the first time to where I was born. The calm did not last, as my viewfinder was soon filled with wrecked aircraft, tanks, and other debris, scattered on either side of the runway. It was a clear reminder that this was still a country at war, having been so for over twenty years.

I took my first breath when I stepped out of the plane; the Kabul air was clean and dry. I took a moment and surveyed the landscape, mountains in every direction, sparse vegetation and sand blowing in the slight breeze. It reminded me a bit of California. We were all guided to the terminal by soldiers carrying AK-47s, another reminder that we were in a hostile land, yet I felt at ease. Inside the terminal was a madhouse, chaos in motion. Soldiers were directing people, airport personnel were stamping passports, guides were finding their tourists, and a sea of cabbies were offering their services. We all stood around confused, not knowing what to do or where to go. Our tour guide, Nilofar, made her way through the dense airport traffic and found us. It was reassuring to see a familiar face. Nilofar was a friend from the Society of Afghan Professionals who had relocated to Kabul and was working for our tour company. She was accompanied by Ahmed, one of her tour drivers. Ahmed was twenty-one years old, but looked and acted like someone who was at least thirty. Most of the people I encountered on the tour had this same premature aging, a tragic result of living through many years of war.

We arrived at the guesthouse in Wazer-Akbar-Khan without incident. This house, like all in Kabul, was a compound, with seven- to eight-foot brick walls around the house and grounds. It was a large guesthouse with all the amenities that we enjoy in the West. It had a full kitchen, a living room with TV and video player, seven guest rooms, and two bathrooms with showers, although the hot water only ran during the night because the house did not have electricity by day. We were all shown to our rooms, where beds had been made for us. I dropped my bags, took off my coat and shoes, and dropped face-first on the bed. It had been over two days since I had gotten any rest. I passed out within minutes.

"As khodam ko tashodi?" What mountain did you climb down from? I said to Shafi in Dari as we sat in the backseat of the tour van.

"Forget about the mountain; one of those camels will be your wife." He replied in Dari, pointing at a group of camels. We both laughed hysterically. It was strange how being in Kabul just two days had made me want to talk Dari as much as I could. I rarely spoke it back in the U.S., but in Kabul it just felt natural. We had just set out on our drive around the city. Since our party was big, we traveled in a convoy of three vans everywhere we went. Our joking subsided when our van stopped at an intersection and was surrounded by beggars reaching their hands into the windows. We had been warned not to give money while in the vans, because more beggars would come. It was sad to see the women in burkas with their children on the streets begging.

After a quick tour of the city, we were taken to the hillside. Here we stopped and began our climb up the hill to take a look down at Kabul. As I made my way up the rocks with my camera slung over my shoulder, I encountered a little boy.

"Do you need help? Follow me," he said in Dari. Then he turned and led the way up the hill. I followed him up, making sure not to miss any steps. When I got to the top, where he was standing, I took out a few afghanis and offered him the money. He shook his head and refused.

"Neh tashakur." No thank you, he said.

I insisted, and he finally accepted the bills. Then he walked down a little, put his hands on his hips, and stood overlooking Kabul. He was but seven years old, but even at that age he had strength, pride, confidence, and the hospitable nature that is a trademark of Afghan people. I pulled my camera out and took a picture of him, with his arms at his sides, silhouetted against the city below him.

A place we frequented every afternoon after our tour was done for the day was *kotche morghau,* or Chicken Street. It was considered the tourist street where you could buy various Afghan clothing, rugs, trinkets, *pakools* (Afghan hats), or anything else you were looking for. Here we saw foreigners from various NGOs, tourists, ISAF soldiers and U.S. soldiers walking the street.

"How much for these?" I said, gesturing to two soccer balls in a bag.

"Twelve dollars each."

"I'll give you ten dollars for both."

"No, both for twenty."

"Twelve dollars for both, no more."

"Sorry brother, but I cannot do that."

"Goodbye then," I said as I made for the door.

"Okay brother, come sit and have some tea. I will give them to you for eighteen."

"No, thank you," I said as I left the store. Bargaining was normal practice in Kabul. In fact, if you did not bargain the merchants had no respect for you. All the merchants on Chicken Street sold their goods to foreigners in dollars. Since the afghani was not a stable currency, everyone in Kabul preferred U.S. currency. I was beginning to realize that while I was Afghan and spoke almost fluent Dari, it was easy for native Afghans to single me out as a foreigner. Perhaps it was the goatee or the glasses I wore, or the way I carried myself and the accent I spoke with that I did not realize. It became clear that I would not blend in no matter what I did.

The next day we went to the remains of Darul Aman Palace, translated as "the abode of peace." Darul Aman had been built in the 1920s by King Amanullah Khan in order to modernize Afghanistan. It had been a beautiful and majestic structure, built in a neoclassical style on a hilltop in the western part of Kabul. Throughout the many years of war it had been reduced to a shell filled with rubble. Our vans drove up to the main entrance, where we saw an Afghan soldier sleeping on a small cot. He was startled awake by the sound of the vans and jumped to his feet, removing the AK-47 from beneath the pillow he had been sleeping on. He didn't look more than eighteen years old, standing there with machine gun in hand. We all exited the vans and made our way through the building. We walked through the halls, carefully maneuvering through concrete and rebar. I took many pictures of the palace, trying to capture the beauty it once had. On some of the walls there were illustrations of tanks, guns, and soldiers fighting. It almost seemed like an account of what had happened. As we boarded the vans and drove away, I took a picture of the entire palace and thought to myself how strange that a palace named the "abode of peace" had been riddled with fires and destruction for its entire history. It was a testament to its construction that it was still standing after all those years.

"Indian movie again!" I yelled out.

"Yes, another Indian DVD," said Nilofar.

"It's not a DVD. It's a video CD. That's why there are two discs."

"It says 'DVD' on the label."

"Yeah, but that's a video CD player, not a DVD player. And just because it says it's a DVD doesn't mean it is one."

"Can you both shut up so we can watch the movie?" Farhad said.

After the long days traveling around Kabul, it was nice to relax at the guesthouse at night, although we really couldn't go out if we wanted to since the curfew was set for ten p.m. No one could be out later than ten p.m. without proper authorization. We would all eat a meal together prepared by the cook. Traditional Afghan dishes, eggplant, spinach, rice, and bread. We did not eat meat much at night since it was considered a luxury, and it was difficult to get good meat unless you ran a restaurant. After dinner, we would have either watermelon or cantaloupe. This was because both were closed fruits that had not been washed with Afghan water. We had been told when we arrived not to drink the tap water, as it was rich with bacteria that we had never been exposed to and would most likely make us sick. But we did use the tap water for making tea; most of the bacteria would get killed when the water was boiled. It was strange that the Afghans in the tour group would stay up very late into the night, socialize, and watch movies, while everyone else in the group went to sleep early. This divide between the two groups intensified throughout the trip.

I sat there perplexed, staring at the two older Afghan professors sitting in front of me. I was trying to help them with the computer in their office.

"The problem is . . . this is . . . over here you can't . . ."

I quickly realized that my vocabulary in Dari was horrible and that I couldn't even convey simple concepts without throwing English words into a sentence. This was never a problem in the U.S., because everyone to whom I spoke Dari most likely knew English as well. We had come to Kabul University to talk with the dean. He had given us an overview of the difficulties the university was having. The biggest problem was a lack of the funds necessary to rebuild and modernize the school. The other major problem was that all the students wanted to learn English, but most of the books in the library were in Russian. No matter how much I tried to search for the right words to convey that the computer needed a boot disk, I came up with nothing.

"I'm sorry. I don't know the words in Dari."

"It's okay, my son. It's okay," they both said, smiling at me.

I shook their hands, said my goodbyes, and headed for the library on campus. We had been sent a list of supplies that the library needed in order to fix basic electrical problems so the students could study at night. Knowing the situation in Kabul, it was a bad idea to give cash to anyone, because it most likely would not end up being used for the intended purpose and would just find its way into someone's pockets. We decided the best thing to do was to buy the supplies ourselves and deliver them.

As I made by way across the campus toward the library, I felt the eyes of students staring at me. I had accepted that I was a tourist and would be treated as such, but the looks were different now. I got the impression that I was not welcome there. Upon reflection, this made sense. My family and I were part of the fortunate few who had been able to get out of the country when the war started. And now, after twenty-four years, I was back to visit. To the Afghans who had endured the constant fighting and terror, I no more belonged there than did the foreigners from the various NGOs. Twenty-four years of constant war was a barrier beyond race, ethnicity, and color. It was a psychological barrier that would always keep us apart. Only the younger generation could change that, a generation not ravaged by war.

"Thank you all very much for your generous donation," said the man at the library. The custodian of the library was away on a trip, and this gentleman was filling in for him until his return. I arrived just in time to help carry in the supplies we had purchased.

"You're welcome. We are sorry we could not have done more, but hopefully this will help the students," said our tour guide.

It was a good day; we had made a small contribution to help others. Many months later we would learn from Nilofar that the library had never been repaired and that the man had taken all the supplies, sold them, and kept the money. This is a small example of the rampant corruption that plagues Afghanistan and is a hindrance to its progress.

A few days later we went to the orphanage in Kabul. We were greeted by hundreds of children running to the vans as we drove up to the playground. They crowded around us as we stepped out of the vehicles. They smiled, laughed, and welcomed us, while the more reserved ones looked on from swings, slides, and monkey bars.

"Salaam. Salaam," their voices rang out.

The head of the orphanage walked up and greeted us. "Salaam, thank you for coming. We don't get visitors often here, but I am glad to show you around and answer any questions you may have."

"How many children do you have here?" asked Farhad.

"We have over nine hundred children here. Some are here only by day while their parents work. But most are without families and live here year-round."

We were taken into the main house and shown the facilities and children's rooms.   "There are not enough beds for all the children to have one of their own. Sometimes we run out of food and try to ration what we have. As you can see, the conditions are barely livable. But this is all we have, and we do not have any more money. But this is not the worst of it. Winter is coming in a few months, and there are not enough blankets and warm clothes for all the children."

Our entire group contributed as much money as we could to the orphanage. The gesture probably helped us feel better more than it did the orphanage much good, but any money helped.

The last day was difficult. I was leaving Kabul, the place where I had been born twenty-eight years earlier. There was a part of me that was tied to Afghanistan and did not want to leave. But I also knew that I would never be accepted there. To them I was a foreigner and would perhaps always be viewed as such. As I boarded the plane at Kabul Airport I realized I was caught between two countries. I had left the United States feeling as if I were no longer an American. Now I was leaving Kabul feeling as if I was not an Afghan either. I represented a generation of refuges that would always be caught between two worlds, never completely belonging to either . . .

ARIANA DELAWARI

Ariana Delawari interweaves her own voyage to Kabul with her grandfather's voyage to Boston from Afghanistan. Delawari's parents returned to live in Afghanistan and be part of the reconstruction. Delawari has followed her father's footsteps by remaining committed to educating people about Afghanistan and followed her mother's revolutionary spirit. A colorful family history begins with a bit of copper, Abraham Lincoln's beard, and faith in God.

A Penny

It was late when we arrived in Delhi. The line to get through customs was long and slow moving. There was an express line for wheelchairs. Pretty soon about a dozen different families had obtained wheelchairs and were putting their eldest relatives in them. It was my first encounter with the haphazard, chaotic airports of the east that I would later grow to love and appreciate. At the time I found it very annoying. It was a few months after my college graduation. My mother and I were on our way to Afghanistan. We stopped in Delhi to visit the Taj Mahal. The streets smelled of smoky earth, spices, and sulfur. Definitely a scent I had never smelled before in any other land and have not smelled since my visit to Delhi. It was at least one o'clock in the morning when we got to the hotel. I was so relieved to have arrived after the long journey. We were the only ones in the brightly lit dining room. My mother ordered us parathas, dahl, and warm shir chai to drink. I was so excited. Everything about the trip was so familiar yet so new. It was like all of the glimpses and tastes of my heritage I had grown up with were adding up in their original form. How traditions change or get lost in translation over miles of land. "My father used to make paratha—he used to pour the butter onto the dough," my mother said. "On cold days, when it was snowing out, he would rub butter on our skin. He wanted us to feel safe." Her eyes drift off when she talks about my grandfather. Though I never got to meet him, I can feel his presence. There is something so beautiful about the way a person describes someone they love.

Mirzah Mohammed Beg was born to an Iranian mother and a Pashtun father. His mother died when he was a child. His father was a merchant. In 1925, when Mirzah was sixteen years old, his father came home with a trunk full of goods. A coin rolled out of the trunk, and Mirzah picked it up. He was deeply taken by the face on the coin. He said to his father, "This man looks like a holy man." His father explained that the coin was a penny from the United States of America and that the man was Abraham Lincoln. He translated the words "In God we trust." Mirzah replied, "What an amazing land to have God on their currency. I must go there someday." Two years later he snuck onto a ship in the ports of Karachi with his best friend. All they had with them was a bunch of bananas and a loaf of bread. Mirzah traveled like this for thirty-three days. His friend was caught and sent back home. When Mirzah arrived at the ports in Boston he stuck a newspaper underneath his arm in order to look like the British travelers on the boat. As he stepped off the gang plank he waved wildly to an imaginary friend and called out the two words of English he knew: "HELLO JOE!"

Whenever I drink shir chai (which translates to "milk tea"), I drink it slowly. It's my favorite drink. Afghans and Indians boil the loose tea with the spices and sugar and slowly add the milk. When you boil the milk in the tea all of the flavors combine and make it much creamier and tastier than the Western way of drinking tea. We grew up with it both ways. My mother and father lived in London for a while. So some of the time it was English breakfast tea, and other times it was Asian black tea. Always with milk, cardamoms, and sugar. And always out of bone china tea cups. When I was a kid my mother taught me to read the bottoms of the cups at estate sales. She collected Royal Albert china and all kinds of antiques. On special occasions, my father would make real shir chai. He would go to Chinatown and buy this special green tea, which would actually turn red when he boiled it. Then he would add cardamoms, milk, and sugar. He would make a huge pot of it and have a party. I remember those Saturdays in our old house in La Canada. I loved those Saturdays. He would start cooking early. The kitchen was big and tiled in French blue and bright yellow. My mother loves Monet. She loves art. She loves anything historical. She loves revolutionaries and visionaries.

We sat in the dining room on that particular night in Delhi, which would be the first day of the most significant journey of my life, and I felt so excited and so full of wonder. It was days away from my twenty-second birthday. I asked her to tell me about my grandfather. I knew that my mother had visited the Taj Mahal with her father, but I didn't realize that she had taken the trip when she was twenty-two years old. Our ancestors were Moghuls. They were among the men who built the Taj Mahal. She told me a story of a man walking past her and trying to brush up against her body. She said she turned around, and her father was holding him up in the air by his neck, cursing him in Hindi. She laughed in her street-savvy, Jersey kind of way. My mother has a peaceful heart and a fighting spirit.

When Mirzah got off the boat in Boston, he took a train to Bayonne, New Jersey. He had an Italian friend there. When he got off the train he walked across the street to an Italian bakery. The Restivos, a Sicilian couple, owned the bakery. They hired Mirzah to help out and gave him a little room to stay in. They had a daughter named Pauline. Mirzah told his friend that he would marry Pauline someday. He said she looked like a woman from "the old country." She had long auburn hair and green eyes. His friend told him he was crazy. A Sicilian Catholic would never marry a Muslim man. Pauline's mother really liked Mirzah, but no one else wanted her to marry him. So when they did get married, everyone was pretty shocked to say the least. They had twelve children together. Eight sons, four daughters, and two miscarriages. They barely had enough to feed their children. Mirzah was working as a longshoreman. He was a proud and generous man. My mother says he would buy all of the children on the block ice cream. She says he used to cut up newspaper into the shape of money. He would fold the fake notes into a bundle and put one real bank note around it. They were the only Muslim family in Jersey. The priest used to visit their home every week trying to convert them to Catholicism. Mirzah would curse him and push him out the door. My mother's teachers used to send notes home with her saying that she was malnourished. She says that every day the children in her class would get graham crackers and milk for a snack, but she never got to have any. Her mother Pauline would say, "We can't afford it." My mother would grow to dislike the word "afford." Her father would have to leave on the ships. When she was four years old she would sit on the steps in front of her home and look across the Kill Von Kull Bay dreaming of going to the other side of the world. When she was sixteen years old, she ditched school one day and snuck into the American embassy to see Ernesto Che Guevara and Fidel Castro speak. She dressed like a beatnik and posed as a journalist. She didn't speak Spanish at the time, so she asked them questions in Italian. They were very amused by this. My mother met Malcolm X while she was studying international relations at UCLA. She challenged him at a rally and said, "Why is it that you can come to my mosque, but I can't come to your mosque? What you are preaching is racism, not Islam." At the time, he brushed off her comment. A few years later she ran into Malcolm on the steps of a mosque in London. He pointed at her and said, "UCLA." She was amazed that he remembered her. He apologized for not listening to her at UCLA. He had just returned from the Hajj to Mecca and had completely changed from his journey. He told her that he knew he would be killed by his own people. When my mother asked him if he was afraid, he answered, "Never fear your destiny." He was killed a few months later.

We took a car to Agra from Delhi and a rickshaw from our hotel in Agra to the Taj Mahal. The whole thing seemed so mysterious. I felt so vulnerable in the rickshaw, riding along a dirt road in the black of night with an occasional small fire or kerosene light shining from a street vendor's tent. As dark as it was, I could feel and hear the presence of many people around me. The Taj Mahal is constantly bathed in a soft glow. In moonlight and sunlight it is surrounded by the same dreamy soft light. It is a combination of the tiny flecks of light in the marble and the love that inspired its creation. My mother explained that it was built by the Mughal emperor in memory of his wife. It really does feel like a dream or a memory, untouched by anything surrounding it throughout time. I felt that way in that moment with my mother. I had just graduated from college. My father had moved to Afghanistan a few months earlier to be part of the reconstruction of the country. I was moving my mother there and visiting the land I was named after for the first time in my life. "Ariana" was the ancient name of the land. It means "land of the Aryans." I was born in Los Angeles ten months after the Soviet invasion of Afghanistan. Our relatives fled their homeland and came to live with us twenty days before I was born. I stood beside my mother in Agra, looking at this great white wonder, feeling deeply rooted in the past and completely uncertain about the future. My own personal future and the future of our world. I had always lived in the same city as my parents. Now they would be fourteen thousand miles away, living in a war zone. But there was hope in the glow of the Taj Mahal. Built with love, it has remained protected by seen and unseen forces and has withstood the test of time. I thought of the Towers and wondered if they would still stand had they been created for love rather than being constructed for commerce. It is this difference of spirit and intention that I felt in the east.

When my mother was twenty-two years old she moved from California to Afghanistan to work for USAID. She had been living there for about six months when she met my father. She wanted to visit the Kuchies (nomadic people), but she only spoke Dari and they speak Pashto. An American painter she was friends with said, "I know just the person to come along and translate, Noor Delawari." When my mother opened the door to greet my father, she found a young scrawny Afghan man wearing singlasses, blue jeans, and an ascot scarf. Her first words to him were, "I just want you to know that I HATE Western Afghans." When they got to the Kuchie tents, the tribe leader offered my father three camels for my mother. My parents were best friends during the two years that my mother lived in Kabul. When she left he was devastated. He went on to study at the London School of Economics. Several months later he received a telegram that my mother would be in Paris traveling. He met her there, and they knew immediately that they were in love. They got married shortly after in London and stayed there while my father finished school. They moved to Glendale, California, in 1970. My father became very successful as the vice president of an international bank. My mother opened a toy store. They had my two older sisters and moved to the beautiful, conservative suburb of La Canada, California. In December 1979 the Soviets invaded Afghanistan. On October 1, 1980, all of my father's relatives fled Kabul and moved into our home in La Canada. Twenty days later I was born. I was born the year that my father's obsession with saving his country began. My mother calls Afghanistan "the mistress" in her marriage. In the early years my father organized peace organizations and demonstrations at the federal building in Westwood. He was referred to as a sort of "godfather" for Afghans who came to California to start their new lives. We had parties every weekend with love music, and all of the Afghans in Los Angeles would come over. It is still easier for me to fall asleep when there is noise and people around. My mother called me "Baghali" as I was constantly held by someone. Later I recall my father making trips to meet with congressmen in D.C. or King Zahir Shah in Rome. There were constant meetings, appearances on Afghan radio stations, dinner conversations. And there were many prices to pay, namely high-profile banking jobs lost due to the constant distraction of philanthropic efforts, in turn leading to constant arguments with my mother. To my mother Afghanistan was the mistress in her marriage. To me Afghanistan was my orphan sister. Adopted by our family. Shaping everything forever.

On September 11, 2001, I received a phone call at seven a.m. from my father. Two planes had flown into the World Trade Center in New York. My mother and sister were there at the time. My mother later said that she and my sister turned to each other and said "Osama Bin Laden" simultaneously. Just two weeks earlier than the attacks, my father asked me to proofread a letter he had written to Diane Feinstein titled, "Bin

Laden's War in Afghanistan." I remembered how I had complained about proofreading it. I was rushing out the door to meet with friends. "Please, Ariana," he said. "This is important. You're an English major." I took it from him reluctantly. Later a few CIA operatives showed up at my dad's work questioning him about the letter, how he knew so much about the situation. My father held out boxes of newspaper clippings and said to the men, "How DIDN'T you know about it?" My father moved to Afghanistan a few months later, in February 2002. My mother sold everything they owned: their cars, their house, and all of their furniture. She posted a sign at the top of our driveway in La Canada that said: "Moving to Afghanistan: Everything must go." My father immediately began working with the minister of finance to implement a new afghani banknote. Prior to this change, the exchange rate was sixty thousand afghanis to one American dollar. This vast difference made money cumbersome to carry and was not conducive to economic growth. My father implemented a change of currency so that the new afghani rate would be six hundred to one dollar. The money was minted in Europe and flown in on private planes. The old notes were simultaneously destroyed—some shredded, mostly by women whom he had hired, and the rest burned in large clay ovens he had built. He had to travel to the different provinces and tell them about this change. People were digging up their gold and finding their hidden notes from up in the rafters of their homes. There were cartoons drawn as diagrams for the large population of illiterate adults, victims of twenty-two years of war and lack of education.

I had planned it so that we would arrive in Afghanistan on my twenty-second birthday. It was the first time since the year of my birth that Afghanistan was free. It was my first opportunity to see the land. My father and I share the same birthday. When we got to the airport in Delhi they greeted us with an immediate denial of our boarding passes. "We have no reservation for you, madame," the man said in a monotone. This was a major problem, since Ariana Airlines only flew out of Delhi every four days or so. My mother argued with the man, and I stormed off, fighting tears of frustration. I remember walking up to a coffee cart where they had a brightly colored instant coffee and hot chocolate machine. I bought a hot chocolate for a few rupees and walked back to the line. By the time I got back my mother had caused such a commotion that the airline had found an Afghan man from the Afghan embassy to come and talk to her. He was a kind, mild-mannered man who ended up knowing my father. We boarded the plane shortly after. I was sure to cover my head with a chadori. I remember being so shocked that the men and women had to sit separately on the plane. The plane was worn. The upholstery was faded and ripped in places. Ariana Airlines had earned the name "Inshallah airlines" due to the condition of the planes and various times when a pilot would run out of fuel and have to stop unexpectedly in different cities to refuel (this happened to me on a later trip, when all of a sudden we were stopping in Islamabad). They served us delicious home-cooked sabzee, palau, and naan wrapped in a makeshift paper-plate and silver-foil package. I was so excited. I couldn't believe that I was finally getting to see Afghanistan. My whole life came into focus flying over the Hindu Kush. I could see my life like a map—all that had led me to that flight and all that lay ahead. The responsibility. The possibility. When we landed and walked down the steps my father was already running toward me with red eyes and open arms. I felt the size of his mission in the weight of his heart.

I have traveled there four times since that trip, documenting my journeys in photographs, writing, and music. My mother has been working with the United Nations on various projects to re construct the country. My father became the governor of the Central Bank of Afghanistan in 2005. During his time as the governor, his signature was printed on the afghani. For my mother, a penny had brought her father from Afghanistan to the United States, and an afghani had brought her husband back to Afghanistan. And for me, that sister I had never met but always loved had shown herself, never to be forgotten again.

HOMIRA NASSERY

Homira Nassery, a long-time Afghan American activist, celebrates the first Afghan election in Kabul post-Taliban. This elated document of that moment is testimony to the hope and potential Afghanistan had at this point in history. In light of the recent election fraud allegations in Afghanistan, this testimony to Afghans' belief in the vote in 2004 seems even more heightened in importance.

Voting in Afghanistan

I wake in a foul and grumpy mood because I had to leave my radio and mobile on in case of alarming evacuation news and both had spilled forth the most inane messages. People sent me messages like "Vote 2day for a better 2morrow." Well, I was planning on doing that anyway, thank you very much. Or "Plse do not go out before 11:00 a.m." Right, like I need more direction in my life. I hate my life: what the hell am I doing by myself in this dreary place, so devoid of beauty? Every turn, every breath a struggle, from my evil uncles trying to kill me, to getting my staff paid on time, to simply trying not to breathe funky odors. I mean, really, princesses don't do war zones very well. I keep thinking of my lovely house in D.C., the precious *NYT* delivered to my door on Sundays, sinking into its folds for hours, devouring the life of the intellegentsia, marking which books I would read, watering my lovely orchids, spraying the bromeliads, taking my beloved Jazz out for her walk to the dog park where all her denizens would be waiting for her, then hiking the billy goat trail at Great Falls with my friends, catching a movie and drinks, just chillin'. Maybe a massage or facial if I felt ambitious. My bossa nova on the stereo, automatically gliding into the blues, then J. Lo revving me up, just the pure loveliness and indolence of time on my hands, with so many options to craft it. Sunday nights with HBO . . . Oh electricity, how I took you for granted!

Instead, I have chronic diarrhea, opt to hear jets roaring overhead, shaking the windows, helicopters chopping about our hills in Wazir Akbar

Khan, and the night before, just a tiny rocket that went over our house before it exploded in a thunderous crash as it landed next to the German embassy. These are not normal things for a princess. I woke that night, heard the crash, listened to the loudspeakers, got confused. Maybe it was Azan and time for the morning prayer? But it was only 1:15 a.m? I registered that I was alive, but nothing came across the VHF radio to inform me. Should I call Hawa and Nadeem and ask them what it was? What would I do if it had hit my house? Wanted to call my mom, but what could she do? Lost in an Ambien Klonopin cocktail haze—very necessary to get anywhere near sleep here—I checked on my cat and went back to bed.

Hey, I'm not complaining. I chose to be here. I'm just reflecting. So the day of the vote, and the days before, we are told it's "white city"—can't go outside, period. Not to work, not to market, not to exercise, not to just feel part of the community. Naturally, I have to violate this little rule since I am Afghan and I am registered to vote. Careful not to make too much of a fashion statement, I opt for my baggy Chicos pants with the inspirational leadership quotes on them in English, a drab black smock, and an even more drab mud-colored giant scarf to cover the offensive fact that I am female. I try, but I simply cannot leave the house without lipstick. Every cell in my body objects to effacing myself that much. I try to make it muted, but Mulberry L'Autumne beckons me. I immediately feel 30 percent better.

Okay, just go out and get it over with. You might get hurt, killed, whatever; it's a job, just do it. What are the options? Hide in the house until it's over? Watch it on TV? I had just read that one of my best friends in Kandahar had publicly announced that she would not vote because of the threat of violence. This hurt me to the core because I know how committed she is. I know the reality of the provinces, but if she can't vote, then I have to. Ziajan comes out to walk me to the WAK masjid, where the polls are set up. Oh, how I hate the staring. I hardly ever walk anywhere precisely because of this, the feeling that I am a freak show, all covered up, sure, but they can still tell I'm a freak: it's in the way I walk, the way I don't avoid their eyes, the way I challenge them to even try to provoke me, my ready retorts to the smallest offense, and poor Ziajan, he has to put up with all my neuroses. My levels of irritation reach a crescendo. God will reward him especially richly in heaven, Inshallah.

We get to the masjid; there's a truck full of women wearing chadaris. If only I had my camera, which I still don't know how to operate. In the dark, dusty atmosphere of WAK, they look like flowers, brilliant blue nasturtiums. I smile at them, starting to feel better. Go get in line with the women. There's an older Hazara gentleman who has brought twenty of his womenfolk to vote. I ask him, "Did you instruct them in who to vote for?" He looks at me and says, "Madam, I cannot even instruct them to simply broom the carpet. How can you expect me to have that kind of influence on them?" I smile, start talking to the women in line, all chadari-covered. They ask me why I came back after thirty-six years in the U.S. I stumble, and try to go back to my usual line about wanting to rediscover my home, help out, etc., but I see how stupid they must think me. To have a chance in the great lottery game of life to get out of pure hell: what on earth compelled me to come back? I start wondering myself and play with my shoe in the dirt, feeling rather stupid.

Then I see the woman who did a crappy interview of Karzai the night before—my housemates and I were apoplectic at the bias and negativity of her questions. I can't believe I have a chance in real life to confront her and tell her exactly what I feel. I introduce myself, deliver the message; she makes comments about journalistic fairness, how she asked the other candidates the same questions, etc. I say, Well, the other candidates' responses to your questions weren't aired on international BBC. She says she's known Karzai for years, and it didn't mean anything. I'm so unimpressed. Who cares how long you've known whom? There's professionalism, and there's ugly baiting. I give her my name; she asks for my opinion of the elections. I say pure success, optimism, a turning point in our history, not perfect by any means, but if you could have told me five years ago I would be voting in Kabul, I would have told you to increase your medication. I persist, tell her I'm disappointed in her. Want to tell her she needs botox and an eye-lift really badly too, but restrain myself.

Then waiting in line, some of the older ladies start to take their chadaris off and talk to me. One lovely old (maybe thirty-four?) woman, with to-die-for cheekbones but no teeth, tells me that she's illiterate, and she feels bad because she might not be able to tell the candidates apart. I assure her there will be pictures for her to go by. Then the uncommonly handsome young army officer observing us tells her, "You might be illiterate, but your children won't be." This kindness pierces my frozen heart. He is from a different ethnic group—there was no need for him to extend himself to her like that, and I didn't even think to say that, but that effort, that small attempt to reach out and assuage someone else's feelings of inferiority, reminds me of what my people are like. I know why I'm here, and I know why I love this place so much. Wild, wild horses couldn't drag me away . . .

Waiting in the queue outside, I congratulate every woman who comes out with a big smile and a Mubarak basha! They smile back at me and thank me. I go in and vote. My body's trembling. I can't believe how lucky I am to be part of this historic moment. I know the facts, I know we aren't really ready for the elections at this point, it's part of fortifying U.S. foreign policy, etc., but now that we're here, doing it, let's do it right and quit with the kvetching. Everything's done properly, my finger is still marked from the correct ink they used, my card is punched. It never felt like this in the States when I was voting for poor Dukakis, bless his heart. I look at the list of candidates, so professionaly prepared, that ballot, and I put a big X in my selection box, then add a happy face, then circle the picture too, just in case someone doesn't get it. Thank God for the pictures—I'm illiterate in Farsi too! I fold the paper, say a little prayer, and then kiss the folded piece big and bold with my Mulberry lipstick. Only then do I drop it in the box. To no one in particular, I say, "Here's one for peace and justice." I want to go outside, celebrate, let out a war cry, and give high-fives to everyone. Yeeeee-haaaaa! How fabulously cool is this moment?

HALIMA KAZEM

Halima Kazem returned to Afghanistan to work as a journalist and part of the Afghan government. She has since written numerous articles on Afghanistan and coproduced a documentary, Frontrunner, on Massouda Jalal, the first Afghan woman to run for president in Afghanistan. Kazem, as she recounts here, overngiht became a yoga instructor for her coworkers in Kabul.

Afghan Awakening

Just before dawn the cry of the muezzin, calling Kabul's faithful to the first of the five daily prayers, awakened me. I arose—a painful process given that I'd spent the night with only a two-inch mattress shielding me from the hard wooden plank that served as my bed—and put on my yoga clothes. No Lycra sports bras or hipster yoga duds, though; in Afghanistan, I practiced in a loose knee-length tunic and wide-leg pajama pants, always prepared for an interruption from the gardener or doorman of the guest house where I stayed. Heavy damask curtains kept nosy neighbors from peering into my second-floor room. Sitting on the prickly handmade carpet, I dropped down to Child's Pose and greeted the day.

I moved slowly into Janu Sirsasana (Head-to-Knee Pose), then Paschimottanasana (Seated Forward Bend), grateful that my New York gym had offered yoga and that I'd taken enough classes to feel at home in the poses. In a country where security is a real concern, a casual jog in the park or a visit to the male-dominated gyms is unheard of for a woman. A jump rope, a few rusty dumbbells, and yoga were my only hope for exercise. Besides, time was at a premium, as I had two jobs—freelancing for the *Christian Science Monitor* and training Afghan journalists to dig deep and fearlessly report the truth.

In the United States, my yoga practice had been for stress relief and fitness, plain and simple. But when I lived in Afghanistan from 2002 to 2005, my time on the mat offered a chance to connect with myself, after what was often a tense awakening—to the sound of rockets exploding nearby or to yet another day without electricity. As I folded into Prasarita Padottanasana (Wide-Legged Standing Forward Bend), humility set in: I thought of Khala, our cleaning lady, who had walked an hour and a half to arrive by 7:30 to serve us green tea, and who made but three dollars for a twelve-hour day. She was one of the many examples I found each day to remind me of how privileged I was.

Often, it was during those moments of relative peace in the morning that I would connect with this sense of gratitude: for the guesthouse, for one thing, a sanctuary where I was able to talk with my husband, who as a non-Afghan was under scrutiny every minute he spent in public. And for the new connection I felt with my mother and father, who had left Afghanistan twenty-five years ago and barely recognized the country I described in phone calls home: I finally had a reference for all the stories they had shared about the *watan* (homeland). Somehow, the parts of me that were Afghan and the parts that were American were beginning to meld. And in the quiet of my practice, I could feel the union solidifying.

AN AMERICAN IN KABUL

After a long Balasana, Child's Pose, I donned a headscarf that wrapped around both my head and my torso and left for the office. Often I would walk the ten minutes from my guesthouse to Kabul's busy Shar-e-Naw (New City) district, home to hundreds of traditional handicraft stores, Kabul's only mall—and Pajhwok Afghan News, the agency where I worked. Making my way through the pothole-ridden streets, I passed heckling shopkeepers, skipping schoolchildren, and groups of beggars. I was covered from head to toe, but still my presence attracted attention, mostly from men curious about "international women." Although I had been born in Afghanistan, the twenty-five years I'd spent in the United States had created differences that most Afghans could recognize from a block away.

"Look how she meets our gaze when she walks by," said an antique-gun dealer, as he set up his window display. Though I'd become accustomed to the leering, name-calling, and even occasional groping, I wondered whether the boldness I exhibited—unafraid to meet a man's eye—might eventually help Afghan men view women as strong, confident human beings.

By the time I arrived at the office, my body had forgotten the asana, and I was already tense. As a newsroom trainer, I worked with more than fifty Afghan men and women—a multigenerational melange of journalists from the country's various ethnic groups—to build the first independent Afghan news agency. To teach them modern journalism concepts while doing my own job as a reporter required near-limitless energy and patience.

"Good morning, Ms. Halima, how was your evening? How has your morning been? I hope you have a blessed day," said Najibullah Bayan, the forty-two-year-old news director, in his ritual stream of greetings. Long employed by the government news service, Najibullah had remained in Kabul during some of the heaviest fighting. His worried eyes and soft voice signaled the complexity of his life and the resiliency of the Afghan people. Seeing him, I found myself wondering, as I so often did, how I would have withstood so much turmoil, violence, and suffering. Would I have shrunk in the face of war? The resilience of the Afghans humbled me.

Sitting at my desk, surrounded by the chatter of the younger female reporters greeting each other, I fell into deep thought. What must life have been like for people like Najibullah, who had watched bombs obliterate neighborhoods and seen people die on the street?

"Ms. Halima, Ms. Halima, it's time for the morning editorial meeting. Are you coming?" My daze was interrupted by a perky nineteen-year-old business reporter from my training group. And so the endless meetings began.

PILLS OR POSES

Already my chronic back pain was getting the better of me. Between meetings, I sneaked a Bharadvaja's Twist on my chair.

"Here is a tablet of Panasol," said my colleague Zarpana, her green eyes filled with worry. She didn't understand why I was contorting my body in strange ways.

"No, no, I don't take pain medication until I absolutely have to," I told her in Dari, the lingua franca of Afghanistan. "I'd rather do these yoga positions." Zarpana dropped the pills back into her purse and shrugged. She started to walk away but then quickly turned around and asked me, "What is this 'yooogaaa' you keep talking about? Is this some sort of medicine that we don't know about?"

"Yoga is a way to relax through stretching and meditation. It's exercise for the body and mind," I said hesitantly. I wanted to explain yoga as simply as possible but wasn't sure how to help her understand. I avoided giving much background—if the handful of women gathered around my desk knew that yoga's roots were linked to Hinduism, they would be offended.

"Most Afghans think that exercise is just for men. They don't see a need for women to exercise," said Forozan Danish, a young reporter who covered sports for the news agency. "Exercise is not just for fun but for good health too. If we tell the men that we can have healthier children if we exercise, maybe then they will agree to let us exercise," she said, half giggling and half confident that she had the answer.

Historically, the conservative Afghan culture has never encouraged women to participate in leisure activities like sports and exercise. In the 1960s and '70s, girls' schools introduced physical education, and girls began playing sports as part of their school activities. But this came to a halt in the early 1980s as the Soviet-Afghan war heated up and the Afghan government was destabilized. During the late 1990s, the ultraconservative Taliban regime outlawed most public outings for women, including going to school or even leaving the home without the company of a close male relative.

Zarpana and Nooria, another reporter, complained of back pain and stiffness. They reached for their purses and the painkillers that they were always offering me. I decided to offer them an alternative: "Instead of the pills, why don't we try to do a few stretches together?" I asked.

I then showed them a Standing Forward Bend. When Nooria, thirty-two, an education reporter and the mother of five, tried to imitate me, her headscarf nearly slipped off. She crouched by her desk and wrapped the pink chiffon scarf around her head and tied it tightly under her chin. In my eagerness to teach the women about yoga, I'd forgotten the difficulty of doing poses with a headscarf on.

I could tell the women were interested but were nervous about an impromptu lesson in the newsroom. "Why don't we go to the conference room for a few minutes so I can show you some of these yoga positions? Please come only if you feel comfortable," I said.

THE ACCIDENTAL YOGA TEACHER

Continuing past a group of curious men, seven women followed me up the cracked marble steps and into the room we normally used for training workshops. Once inside, I removed my headscarf and rolled up my sleeves. Forozan, the young sports reporter, and a few others followed my lead, but Nooria and Zarpana just stood there. "I can't take my jacket off—I have a sleeveless tank on underneath. I'm a married woman. What if someone walks in and sees me?" said Nooria.

Determined to help them experience a bit of yoga, I closed all the curtains and locked both entrances. "Now you have nothing to worry about," I said. The women immediately took off their headscarves and jackets, revealing brightly colored tanks and T-shirts.

"Find a comfortable spot on the floor, but make sure you can see me," I said nervously. Since 2000, I had studied yoga sporadically while in graduate school in New York City, mostly as a way to manage neck pain associated with the stresses of my studies. However, I was usually in the back of the class, struggling to hold the basic poses. Never did I imagine I'd be leading a yoga class, much less one filled with Afghan women.

"Let's start with Hero Pose," I said. The women looked at my position and maneuvered gracefully into Virasana. "Now close your eyes and take some deep breaths through your nose and let them out through your mouth."

The women quietly did what I suggested, and we continued for a few minutes. I could sense that they were relaxing, as their breathing grew longer and deeper with each passing minute. I loved these women like sisters—we had gone through tough months together organizing the news agency. And my interest was always in expanding their horizons, encouraging them to be less dependent on others and more capable of helping themselves. I had always hoped that I could help them professionally and intellectually. Like most returning Afghans, I had arrived with the express intention of transferring knowledge and giving back to a country that has been repeatedly robbed of its potential. But I never believed a transfer of knowledge like yoga was possible; certainly it hadn't been my intention.

"Now kneel, spread your knees just a bit, and bend down until your forehead touches the floor," I said encouragingly. "This is called Child's Pose."

Zainab and Forozan looked at each other and giggled. "Are we praying, or are we exercising?" asked Zainab, whose father was an imam (Islamic religious leader) at a local mosque.

Confused for a minute, I then realized that Hero Pose and Child's Pose are similar to the physical movements performed during Islamic prayer.

"Maybe God thought about our back pain when he designed the prayers," Zainab said.

I hadn't thought of the poses in that way before and wasn't sure what an imam or even a yogi would think of the idea, but I was happy that she had created a connection that seemed to please the other women. We continued through a few more poses and then returned to the newsroom before our coworkers became concerned about our absence.

During my six months at the news agency, we managed to meet a few more times and practice a few different yoga postures. I encouraged the women to practice at home as often as they could, knowing that it was practically impossible for those who were married and had kids.

Two years later, when I return to the news agency to teach an advanced course in business reporting, Zainab and Forozan tell me that they occasionally practice a few of the yoga poses I taught them. "What we remember more was that we had fun learning and that you cared about our well-being enough to teach us yooogaaa," Zainab says.

The funny thing is that it was the women at the agency—all the Afghans I met, really—who taught me to care enough about my own well-being to truly embrace yoga. I had always devoted myself to my studies, my professional life, the world of the mind and intellect. I put my physical and spiritual health on the back burner. But living in Afghanistan, I came to see that in order to share my intellectual interests and professional knowledge, and even just to survive the stresses of the place, I had to incorporate yoga more regularly into my life. Practicing on my own has naturally led to a greater appreciation for the quiet moments in my life, even when I'm in the States.

That this revelation would have occurred in Afghanistan still surprises me, but perhaps it shouldn't: going back to your roots opens you up to aspects of yourself that you might not ever have known were there.

WAHEEDA SAMADY

Waheeda Samady's literary dedication to her father's hard work in this new country seems to be a motif in these narratives about the first generation, the parents who came to build a life for their children. In this essay, she tells the story of how her loving cab-driver father raised a daughter who became a doctor and who chooses to wear hijab, or the veil. This tender essay breaks stereotypes of the supposed "oppressive" Afghan male. Samady replaces this stock image with a gentle father who has sacrificed his life and his body for the sake of his children. This was originally published in Snapshots: This Afghan American Life, edited by Mir Tamim Ansary and Yalda Asmatey (2008).

The Cab Driver's Daughter

He has one of the most sincere smiles I have ever seen. Suddenly, you realize how all the wrinkles got there. We go about our lives normally. My father goes to work. I head off to class. The morning mingling consists of "good luck on your test" and "hope business is good," with one response to everything: *Insh'Allah*. God willing. I get into my mini–SUV and head off to medical school. I groan about the lack of sleep, the lack of time. However, I drive off to what has always been my dream, a wealth of knowledge, ample opportunity, and limitless potential.

My father gets into his blue taxi, picks up his radio speaker, and tells the dispatcher he's ready. Then he waits. He waits for someone to go somewhere. He waits to pay the next bill. He waits to go home to my mother, the woman he calls "the boss." Maybe today will be a good day. He will call her up and tell her he is taking her out tonight. He can do that now that we're all grown up, now that he doesn't have to save every dime for the "what ifs" and the "just in cases."

There is very little complaining in his car. His day starts off with a silent prayer, then a pledge: *Hudaya ba omaide hudit*. God, as you wish. Then he hums; then he sings. Some songs are about love and some about loss. They are all about life. He sings. He smiles the whole time.

My father is the type of person who is always content to listen, but I love when he speaks. There is wisdom there, although he does not intend there to be.

"What's new?" he'll ask over a Saturday-morning breakfast.

"Not much," I reply. "My life revolves around these books, Dad. There is little to say unless you want to hear about the urinary tract."

"You know, when Ghandhi's minister of foreign affairs died, his only true possessions were books. It is the sign of a life worth living," he replies and begins to butter his toast.

Sometimes, the years of education and learning shine through the injuries and lost dreams. I get a glance of the man who existed and the one who never will. Who would he have been, I wonder, if the bombs hadn't come down in 1978? What if I could take away the time he spent in a coma, the years of treatment and surgery, the broken bones and disabilities? What if there were no refugee ghettos, no poverty, no fear or depression written in his life history? Who could he have been? The thought saddens me, but it intrigues me as well. Is it possible that he is who he is because the life he has lived has been filled with such tragedy? Perhaps these stories were the making of my hero.

Sometimes he'll tell me about his college days, about an Afghanistan I have never known and very few people would believe ever existed. "In the College of Engineering, there was this lecture hall, with seats for roughly one thousand students," he says as eyes begin to get bigger. "At the end of lecture, the seats would move. The whole auditorium would shift as you spun along the diameter. The engineering of the building itself was very interesting . . ." He continues to describe the construction details, then sighs, "I wonder if it's still around."

There is a pause. For twenty-five years I have tried to say something in that silence, but I have never quite figured out what to say. I guess silence goes best there. He is the next one to speak. "You see, even your old-aged father was once part of something important."

When he says things like that, I want to scream. I don't want to believe that the years can beat away at you like that. I don't want to know that if enough time passes, you begin to question what is real or who you are. I am unconcerned with what the world thinks of him, but it is devastating to know that he at times thinks less of himself.

We are the same, but we are separated. People don't see him in me. I wish they would. I walk in with a doctor's white coat and smile, a suit, my Berkeley sweatshirt and jeans. High heels or sneakers, it doesn't matter, people always seem impressed with me. "Medical student, eh?" they say. "Well, good for you."

I wonder what people see when they look at him. They don't see what I see in his smile ... how could they? Perhaps they see a brown man with a thick accent; perhaps they think, *Another immigrant cab driver.* Or perhaps it is much worse: maybe he is a profile-matched terrorist, aligned with some axis of evil. "Another Abd-ool f———-g foreigner," I heard someone say.

Sometimes the worst things are not what people say to your face or what they say at all; it is the things that are assumed. I am in line at the grocery store, studying at a café, on a plane flying somewhere.

"Her English is excellent; she must have grown up here," I hear a lady whisper. "But why on earth does she wear that thing on her head?"

"Oh, that's not her fault," someone replies. "Her father probably forces her to wear that."

I am still searching for a profound thirty-second sound bite to use when I hear comments like that. The trouble is that things like that never take thirty seconds to say. So I say nothing, but silence does not belong there. I want to grasp their hands and usher them home with me. Come, meet my father. Don't look at the wrinkles, don't look at the scars, don't mind the hearing aid or the thick accent. Don't look at the world's effect on him; look at his effect on the world. Come to my childhood and hear the lullabies, the warm hand on your shoulder on the worst of days, the silly jokes on the mundane afternoons. Come meet the woman he has loved and respected his whole life; witness the confidence he has nurtured in his three daughters. Stay the night; hear his footsteps come in at midnight after a long day's work. That thumping is his head bowing in prayer although he is exhausted. Granted, the wealth is gone and the legacy unknown, but look at what the bombs did not destroy. Now tell me, am I really oppressed? The question alone makes me laugh. Now tell me, is he really the oppressor? The question alone makes me cry.

At times, I want to throw it all away: the education, the opportunities, the potential. I want to slip into the passenger seat of his cab and say: This is who I am. If he is going to be labeled, then give me those labels too. If you are going to look down on him, then you might as well peer down on me as well. Close this gap. Erase this line. There is no differentiation here. Of all the things I am, of all the things I could be, I will never be prouder than to say I am of him.

I am this cab driver's daughter.

BISMILLAH IQBAL

In this raw and honest testimonial of assimilation, Bismillah Iqbal shares the story of the first ten years of his life in Philadelphia, Pennsylvania. Philadelphia's inner city brought pressures and circumstances that were entirely foreign to this Afghan family. Iqbal tells his painful story with nonchalance and a touch of lightness that leaves the reader feeling hopeful, despite the challenges of adjusting to life in the United States. This was originally published in Snapshots: This Afghan American Life, edited by Mir Tamim Ansary and Yalda Asmatey (2008).

Hope Street

The journey from Kabul to New York took us two years. I won't go into all our difficulties, except to say that the time did not pass pleasantly. I was a carefree seven-year-old when we left Afghanistan, an anxious nine-year-old when we arrived. No one met us at JFK Airport. We sat down to wait. What were we waiting for? I didn't know. When I asked Dad about it, he just muttered something about "some nice people." I could see that he was nervous, and that made me nervous too. The hours passed, and my butt went numb, sitting on those hard plastic airport chairs. At one point, I overheard my mother asking what we were going to do about money. Dad assured her everything would be okay but didn't say how.

Finally, two men in a van picked us up. Who they were or where they where taking us, I didn't know, but that was my normal state. We drove for three hours, because our destination was not in New York but in West Philadelphia. The men dropped us off in the pitch-black dead of night and drove away. We walked up two flights of stairs and entered our new home. Even in the dark, I could see that the apartment was completely empty. Dad hit the light switch—nothing happened. He moved the switch up and down: still nothing.

"Is this America?" I asked Dad.

"Can we go back?" said my sister.

Dad didn't say a word to either of us. He just took our only suitcase inside, and our new life began. The next day, a local church supplied us with a bunch of mattresses, and just in time because on our third night in America, Mom started having contractions: she was pregnant with her fifth child. We didn't have a phone, so Dad went out to look for help, leaving my sister Parveen in charge. By the time he came back, fourteen-year-old Parveen had delivered our family's first American citizen: Azam.

I remember how the sheer abundance dazzled me the first time I went to the supermarket with Dad. Look at all the milk! Look at all the everything! I couldn't believe my eyes. Shelf after shelf of . . . *stuff!* My mother had often described heaven to me as a place with rivers of milk. Standing in that supermarket, I could believe we were in heaven. "Is this America?" I thought.

We had started home with our groceries when all of a sudden an African American guy came up behind us and asked my father for a light. My father was wearing a suit jacket, as many Afghan men do. When he took out his lighter, his food stamps showed. In a flash, this guy grabbed the stamps out of my father's pocket and took off. My father just stared after him, not even bothering to chase after him. I felt dazed, but then, dazed was how I mostly felt during our early days in America.

West Philadelphia was just a pause for us. After only two years, my father decided to move us to North Philadelphia, where the rents were cheaper, even though the neighborhoods were much worse. We ended up in an old, broken-down, two-story place on Hope Street, and there we spent the next eight years. The house had three bedrooms and one bathroom. A large crack ran down the front of it from top to bottom, and the whole building looked like it was about to tip over. A sewer pipe ran right across the basement, and when that pipe broke (as it often did) the basement flooded with sewage. Dad had to fix it himself, and I always served as his assistant. How I came to dread that basement!

Dad had a room to himself. My brother Ibrahim and I shared another room, because we were the oldest boys. The rest of the pack, all six of them, jammed into the third room with Mom. That's right, six! Mom had given birth to two more children after Azam was born, Fatima and Ahmad Shah (and would have one more later on). I don't have to tell you life was tight in that third room!

North Philly was a little more diverse than our old neighborhood. We had black people, white people, and Puerto Ricans living around us, but we still didn't fit in, because we were none of the above. Most people thought we came from India—if they were told that we were from "Afghanistan," they just scratched their heads. They didn't know where that was.

The summer after ninth grade, my father decided to get me a job working in a hot dog stand owned by a Pakistani friend of his. The "stand" was a metal booth in front of a busy hospital. In the summer, it heated up to about 120 degrees in there. I worked twelve hours days and made two hundred dollars a week—and I worked hard! I had to wonder: was this really how hard people had to work to make a measly two hundred dollars? After two weeks the owner let me go (he said I was too slow). I had never been so glad! I hated that job, hated the heat! It reminded me of Pakistan.

Losing the job, however, left me at loose ends. Then one day, my friend George said, "Hey, you want to help me in my business?" I needed the money, so I said okay.

George's "business" was selling crack cocaine. In the beginning, I was just a lookout. I stood on the corner while the older boys sold drugs, and every time I saw a cop, I yelled "Agua!" which was code for "here-comes-a-cop." For this "work" I got paid two hundred dollars—a day, not a week.

This job opened doors. George trusted me because I didn't cheat, didn't try to rip him off, and didn't do drugs. Soon enough, I was moved from scouting to bagging, a mark of trust. I would be given a whole kilo of cocaine, and I would divide it up into little "dime bags."

After six or seven months, George and the people he worked for promoted me to dealing. I became one of the guys standing around in the street waiting for white junkies from the suburbs to come by. We worked on commission, getting dime bags for seven dollars and selling them for ten. Believe me, they sold like hotcakes. On a busy day, I could make anywhere from four hundred to one thousand dollars.

At one point I had a ring on every finger, gold medallions, lots of bling. Even though I was only fourteen, I drove one of my friend George's many cars. It was just crazy how easy it was to be doing that—and how hard it was to not be doing it. In that neighborhood, if you weren't on the corner selling crack, you were in an aluminum hot dog stand, working twenty-hour days, in 120-degree heat, for less than minimum wage.

Even with all the bling, I couldn't get a date. I just didn't have much confidence in myself. I came across as a tough guy because I knew certain people, but I wasn't tough at all. The actual tough guys accepted me and liked me, though, and the more they trusted me, the more I wanted to be trusted, so I did my best not to let them down. Looking back, I find that whole era very strange, yet I understand why I fell into it. The temptations were just so strong. In junior high, all my clothes came from thrift stores. We never went to barbers because we couldn't afford it. The first pair of sneakers my father ever bought me brand-new was in eighth grade. Besides, by the time I was in high school, I had expenses. My father insisted on my paying rent.

There's one day I'll never forget. I was at George's place, working at my daily chore of bagging cocaine. I had about two kilos of white powder sitting there and maybe twenty thousand dollars in cash, plus some guns. Suddenly, I heard the dut-dut-dut-dut of somebody knocking. I went downstairs, opened the door, and saw a cop standing on the porch with a middle-aged couple. My heart started pounding, but I kept my cool. I wiped my fingers casually against my jeans—I never used gloves when I bagged, so I had all this cocaine packed under my fingernails. Then I invited them into the house (I figured it would look suspicious if I didn't). Now I had a cop standing in the hall and two kilos of coke heaped on a table upstairs; my whole life was on the line, right there.

The couple turned out to be the parents of a fifteen-year-old girl George knew. They couldn't find their daughter and wanted to ask George about it. I said, "Well, I'd love to help, but he's not here. When he gets back, I'll ask him to call you . . ."

They accepted what I said and left. I rushed upstairs, frantic-nervous, gathered my stuff, and took off. That was the closest I came to going to jail. I was totally in the life, though, the whole nine yards. I was there when fights broke out because somebody was trying to take over our hot corner. I mean fists, guns—you could not believe what went on. When you're in that life, you lose perspective. You could kill someone, get killed, go to jail—you don't notice. It all seems normal. Guns are like some joke. You're living on some edge, but you don't even know it. I spent almost all my time out on those streets. I rarely went home, and when I did, I paid scant attention to the rest of my family. I had no idea what was going on with my siblings.

One day, right in the middle of that time of bling and coke and guns and money, I came home and saw a bunch of strangers in the house. I went upstairs and found my mother fixing my sister Parveen's hair and putting mascara on her eyes. Parveen must have had a pound of makeup on her face, but behind that mask of makeup she was wearing a devastated look. I knew something big was going on, but I didn't know what.

My father then came upstairs and spoke to Parveen and Mom in a voice too low for the guests downstairs to hear. "Do you want this marriage?" he said. "Now is the time to say something. Will you go through with this?"

Marriage? This was the first I had heard of any marriage. As it turned out, this was the first that any of us had heard of it, including Parveen! At eighteen, according to our Pushtoon traditions, Parveen was too old to be single. She was, however, barely out of high school. Yet my father had suddenly arranged a match for her.

He didn't know the man he wanted my sister to marry. He didn't even know much about him, except that he was Afghan—that was the only thing that mattered. The only other Afghan family we knew in Philadelphia had referred him to my father. I don't remember Parveen responding to my father, but Mom said, "Yes," with her eyes cast down. She was just telling him what he wanted to hear. I think my dad wanted to feel like he was giving the women an option, but there was no option, really. There was no way my sister or my mother could have told him, "Call the whole thing off. Send them home." Not at that point.

I went to my room, feeling very confused. I didn't know what to make of it all. I didn't want to be connected. My life was outside, hanging with my friends on the streets. A few minutes later, I went out to meet some of those friends. On the way out, I saw Parveen sitting downstairs with her head drooping, surrounded by strangers, all of whom were smiling at her. One of the strangers, a bald older man with a round belly, had a particularly big smile on his face. He was to be Parveen's husband.

A few days after the marriage announcement, my sister went out as if she was going on an errand, but she never came back—or rather she came back just once, very briefly, accompanied by a gigantic, intimidating African American guy. My father was out, but she told my mother that the marriage was off. Then she left again, and she was gone for good, just gone.

Eventually we found out she had run away to Puerto Rico with her boyfriend. My father didn't even know Parveen had a boyfriend. He didn't know a whole lot about any of us. For that matter, none of us knew much about each other, either. I had no inkling about the boyfriend, for example. I was too involved in my life outside the home.

None of us ever even saw the boyfriend. He wasn't the intimidating black guy, who was just a friend. The man Parveen ran away with was a

Puerto Rican fellow who lived up the street from us. My father reacted badly to Parveen's disappearance. Basically, he said he was going to kill her for this. Would he really have killed her? I don't think so. I don't think so, but he did have an intensity about him that she feared. We all did. No kid of his could talk to him without being scared. He wasn't a big guy, and outside the house, especially around other Afghans, he was unbelievably charming, friendly, courtly, and diplomatic, but he did not have a drop of emotional weakness in him. He was one of these proud Pushtoons who held his own, any time, any place.

God knows, I was afraid of him. He beat me mercilessly many times—many, many times. I don't even know how many times. He'd take the radio cord and hold my feet up. He'd take a broomstick and hit me on the back.

And yet, in that whole drama surrounding Parveen's engagement, I lined up with my father emotionally. I was angry at Parveen! I remember doing stupid things like cutting her picture out of a family album. I was ashamed of her on my father's behalf. He beat me, but I still identified with him. Only later, looking back, did I come to understand my feelings. I was an adolescent, still trying to discover my own identity, my manhood, and I couldn't stand any humiliation to my father. Shame on him was shame on me. Being the oldest boy, I felt like I had to uphold whatever was left of our family honor. Looking back, I can see that ignorance was a big part of it all, but this didn't soften what I felt at the time: painful, painful shame.

We never had much contact with the tiny Afghan community in Philadelphia, but after my sister broke her engagement and ran away with her boyfriend, even that slight connection was completely severed. My father felt his prestige had suffered with the community and that every time Afghans looked at him, they were thinking, "That man can't even control his own daughter." In his heart, the worst thing that could possibly happen to an Afghan man had happened to him.

And it was then—amid all that turmoil of my father's rage, my life on the streets, Parveen's disappearance—it was amid all that madness that my mom gave birth to her eighth and last child: Nicolle.

We didn't keep her. After what had happened with Parveen, my father announced that he didn't want another girl in the house, so we would give this one up for adoption. My mom had no say in it, nor did any of the rest of us. Nicolle was sent away at birth, and we didn't see her again for eighteen years.

My friends ask if all that abuse scarred me. I say, not at all, not at all. I'm not scarred because I've learned to let go of that kind of grudge. I know it does no good to hold onto hatred. Besides, I've always reasoned that my father suffered in his own way when he was young. His mother died when he was little: he never had a mother to love him. He got hit a lot when he was young, as a way of being disciplined. The fact is, he didn't know how to deal with any situation except to hit. He didn't know any other way to solve things. His communication skills just weren't there. The beatings? They were his way of communicating. His way of saying, "I love you."

My drug-dealing days didn't last long. Within one year George's cocaine business had gone down. He got locked up and lost most of his money and all of his cars. I never did get caught, and I broke away from the business then to look for a safer route through life. Parveen came back from Puerto Rico after a year, but I had little to do with her at first. I was still angry. I didn't really connect with her again until many years had passed and I had gone through my own changes.

The only Afghan whom Dad kept in touch with after that was his best friend, Ibrahim, in California. They had known each other since their teenage years, and Ibrahim had often urged Dad to come to California, telling him that he would have a better life there because the San Francisco Bay Area had a much bigger Afghan community.

I longed for us to make that move. I longed to live where I could find other people like me. The day my father told us we were moving to California, I felt so happy, I couldn't sleep. I just lay in bed all night thinking about that warm California sunshine. Dad and I got a fifteen-passenger van for our drive across the country and a small U-Haul trailer for our few possessions. When the day of our departure came at last, we packed quickly, much as we had done the day we left Afghanistan. Dad said, "Bismillah-i-rahman-i-rahim" (In the name of God, the bountiful and the merciful), and started the car. Once again we set off almost empty-handed with no idea of what new life we were heading toward, only that we were leaving Hope Street for a better future—we hoped.

AFIFA YUSUFI

Afifa Yusufi is the daughter of Imam Yusufi, who was the clergyman and community leader of the Sayed Jamaludin Masjid in Flushing, Queens, New York. He passed away in 2005. This is Yusufi's tribute to her father. Imam Yusufi, born in Kandahar, was one of the first men to send their daughters to the United States to study abroad. Afifa Yusufi's eulogy to her father is interwoven with stories of her own growing activism within the community to create bridges between the United States and Afghanistan.

Daughter of the Imam: From Kandahar to Queens

I once asked a bird,
"How is it that you fly in this gravity
Of darkness?"
She responded,
"Love lifts
Me."

—HAFIZ

As the youngest of ten children, I saw in my father a striking resemblance to Mother Theresa, who performed God's work through kindness and immediate action. No one person can be compared to our prophet Mohammad (peace be upon him), but in many ways I personally saw similarities between my father and our magnificent prophet (*pbuh*). I once asked my father how one could try to be the best Muslim one can be, since there are so many interpretations of the Hadiths, and he said to resemble the prophet as much as one can through character, actions, and so on. He was known to be a well-traveled, worldly man, part of the educated and elite class in Afghanistan. He was a pioneer in southern Afghanistan and served as the Afghan community leader in New York for nearly a quarter of a century, right until he passed away in 2005. I was told how many family members frowned upon his progressiveness for being the first from his conservative, strict family to permit his eldest daughter to go to school. He always stood firm for what he believed. In minimal and paramount ways, my father became an influential member of his society and a pioneer whom other community members soon looked to for advice and trust. He was known as a moderate imam in his conservative circles and broke barriers to empower the helpless and women.

Early on, I watched how my eldest sister, Latifah, struggled as a modern girl in a male-centered world. She kept a tough exterior and always carried her books by her side. She constantly, even to this day, quotes from the books she read and helps me relive my experience in a land where I lived for a very short period of my life, too young to develop memories of my own. In the late 1970s my sister Latifah came to the United States on a Fulbright scholarship. She later sponsored my family in 1980, shortly after the Russians invaded Afghanistan. We were the fortunate ones. Only very few family members who were left behind were kidnapped and tortured. My father wanted to take us to a place where we would not be harmed and could achieve a better life, and he referred to America as a second home. He always told us this country was special because it was place to worship freely without violating others, a place with abundant resources, a place where you are able to gain knowledge and become educated, and most of all a place where you have freedom.

New York was like a land filled with various types of sweet candy, each tasting unique and diverse. When I grew up in Queens, New York, my neighborhood was made up of kids from India, China, Korea, Afghanistan, Haiti, Jamaica, Israel, Russia, Colombia, El Salvador, and Mexico, among other countries. My father always welcomed every one of my friends. He supported me through my career decisions, reminding me to be righteous, to do good for others, and to have patience during times of turmoil. He was my teacher, my best friend, my role model, and my dad. He taught me about right and wrong; he helped me develop strong morals and values, to have faith, integrity, and an overall good character. This gave me strong foundation and a set of core values that in the end helped me in all the different types of situations that I have faced throughout my adolescent and adult life.

After the tragedy of September 11, while my father was still alive, the world changed in so many ways. I met a woman named Dr. Catherine (Katy) Papell. She had been a neighbor of ours for many years, but we had minimal contact prior to this tragedy. I was a Queens College student at the time and lived with both my parents above the mosque that was guarded for many months by police officers.

When we asked the two police officers who stood at the corners of the mosque what they were doing there, they would say that they were there to protect us. Katy was a social worker and a member of the Unitarian Universalist (UU) church. She was the only person who had the courage to knock on our door. She introduced herself and made us feel part of the community, as opposed to feeling victimized and abandoned. I answered the door and welcomed this warm woman in for tea with my family. After that Katy invited my father and me to her church to talk about Islam and increase interfaith dialogue. We attended several times. At the interfaith sessions, my father answered questions about Islam, since many people needed answers regarding the most talked-about faith after the tragic downfall of the Twin Towers. It was beautiful watching my father flourish in this kind of place, where he could explain our religion honestly and where he handled all questions with patience, leaving the church audience content and satisfied. I also had the chance to share my childhood memories of Afghan fables, the tales my grandmother had told me; the audience was quite eager to absorb the beauty of my country.

Education was very important to my family. My father always whispered, "My dearest Afifa, education is the key to end poverty, to end corrupt ignorance." He always told me education is part of our faith. During my undergraduate studies at Queens College, I took the opportunity to introduce my culture by becoming the president of the Afghan Student Association (ASA) and meeting a group of diverse women of different races and religious backgrounds all committed to empowering the women of Afghanistan, both in our community and in Afghanistan. I also was appointed to serve as a community outreach chair on the board of Women for Afghan Women (WAW). I introduced WAW to the Afghan community in New York and to the UU church members. I volunteered many hours a week for several years at WAW, establishing the organization's initial projects for the Afghan women of New York, which was my local community at the time.

I remember my father, who in the back of my mind kept whispering, Do good and your heart will be pure. With my father's support, I decided to aid WAW by setting up several programs: setting up English as a Second Language (ESL) classes, providing legal advice for women seeking asylum, providing a therapist to talk to the women with troubles in their families. We offered a safe haven for the women of the community and helped them formulate careers for themselves by helping them with job placement and moral support. I organized a Mother's Day event at my college where thousands of women from the community showed up to be honored as mothers; we celebrated their motherhood and woman-hood in an event organized to make them feel special and to help them learn about WAW and its services.

It has been a blessing to learn of all the people around me. Katy became a mentor to me, and during my college years as a teaching assistant, I got the chance to be inspired by a very kindhearted psychology professor, Dr. Arthur Witkin, who took the time to understand me as a human being rather than focusing on my background. These non-Muslim people have touched my life in special ways, inspiring me to do good for others. In 2006, I spoke at the United Nations on a panel that consisted of social workers, with Katy addressing the importance of social work to provide relief in regions struck by disaster. After that, Katy and I spoke regularly about the U.S. situation and how poorly most of the international community viewed us. We spoke about what we could do as citizens to create a peaceful world. Katy and I continued to organize interfaith events at the UU church, inviting Muslim speakers so that people would learn more about Islam and not fear Muslims. One exceptional speaker whom I remember introducing to Katy was a social worker named Robina Niaz, the director of the nonprofit organization Turning Point, which provides safety and support to victims of domestic violence and their families, as well as to survivors of domestic violence.

I have faced some people's preconceptions regarding my background, especially when they learn that I am an imam's daughter from Afghanistan, from a Pashtun family, from Kandahar. Kandahar was considered a Taliban stronghold; Pashtuns were considered some of Afghanistan's tribal people, who did not let their females out of their homes. Some people sometimes assumed I was raised under austere conditions, whereas others questioned me. I am taken aback at times at some of the questions I get from others, who may be curious about my background and upbringing but hold readymade preconceived ideas. However, I enjoy explaining to them the way I was raised, how I have always been quite satisfied with my upbringing and how I was allowed to make my own choices, although God always had a strong presence in our household. I do not wear a hijab unless I am in the mosque or during the time of prayer. Most of my decisions are made with regard to intention. I was taught that if my intentions are good, then God will see what is in my heart. It was often difficult to maintain an identity in America and at the same time obey a religion to the fullest. However, with the help of good people, I have been able to maintain my faith and feel accepted by this beautiful country.

My father was a dynamic speaker who encouraged questions and debate, searching for answers, for the truth, working to solve the complex problems that people were facing, offering solutions that were parallel to the teachings of Islam. To the outside world, he was an influential and well-respected religious leader. His teachings and lectures were progressive and enlightening. The public viewed him as a gifted and extraordinary individual, and most people felt this when they were in his presence. This is why they trusted him as their leader and continuously came to him for answers in difficult situations. Although my father was extremely well-versed in Islam and understood the Quran completely, I knew times had changed, and both Muslim and non-Muslim people came up with complex questions that he was able to answer with ease. His answers did not upset people: they made perfect sense, lifting listeners to a higher level of understanding. He told me once that he did not know where his answers came from, especially when he was questioned about Islam or the Quran, but he felt a natural flow in answering easily, without difficulty, as if divinely guided. It often surprised me how he was full of natural wisdom, able to address difficult questions and situations that he had not prepared or planned for.

During his last days, I was driving him to meet with someone who had invited him to discuss the issues facing Afghanistan. He had said that he wasn't feeling too well that morning, but he knew how much this visit meant to me, since the person who had invited him to this meeting called me consistently, pleading that I bring him to meet with her. This was the second day of Eid. I asked him whose side he was on, whom he supported, and he gave me an answer that stuck with me. He said, "I am on the side of Truth and Justice." He always told me I would never lose anything by doing good deeds and performing acts of kindness for everyone; he told me to always do well and to be kind even to those who are my enemies. I once asked him, "Father, what if the person is taking advantage of me? Do you still think I should be good to them?" He said that if a person does wrong to you, you must try to do good in return, until you realize that they continuously do wrong when you do good. Only then, he said, remove yourself from them, but continue to try to do as much good as you can. He was very selfless and desired love and goodness for others.

My father was not involved with WAW, but he knew I was, and he nurtured my passion to help Afghanistan and people in general. He allowed the diverse group of women from WAW to come into the mosque, although it was not common for non-Muslims or even women to enter the section of the mosque where men prayed. This was for educational purposes, and as long as they respected the mosque, he allowed their presence. Once I was interviewed on the radio by an international news station with regard to women's rights in Afghanistan. The next morning he heard the interview. He was regularly interviewed on the radio, but this was the first time he had heard me speak publicly. I remember it clearly. It was very early in the morning, right after he and my mom had completed their morning prayers, which is when he usually listened to the news. He was so excited that he made my mom listen. I had no idea they would hear it. I am sure he never expected that I had that kind of passion in me, speaking out for causes similar to those he championed. I was beginning to develop my community outreach and advocacy skills as well, and that made him proud. There were certain things about the organization where I volunteered that I did not entirely agree with, and I sought his advice about this. He told me to be honest and voice my concerns, and he supported my courage to speak out.

In the darkest time, my only rock, my best friend, my sole support . . . my father . . . suddenly had a heart attack, passing away in 2005. It was a tremendous loss and something I have not recovered from yet. Through his unconditional love, kind eyes, and great work, I have learned to follow in his steps, using available resources in the hope of helping the less fortunate. I wish my father had lived to see that I was accepted to the Columbia School of Social Work. It would have made him proud to see how much I had followed his example, helping those in need. I was first attracted to the field of social work when I spoke at a social workers' panel in 2006 and realized that I shared qualities that these social workers displayed: empathy, objectivity, acceptance of diversity, communications skills, and self-awareness.

I will be starting school this fall, and I am both excited and nervous, since I have been in the professional workforce for about five years now and will now have to adjust to the student lifestyle again. I am eager to learn and expand my knowledge. I consider myself a very curious person, and the jobs I have chosen and some other things I have done have often been very educational experiences for me; I am happy to have had these experiences. I helped deliver food, medicine, school supplies, and clothing to destitute Afghans in local villages in 2003. I risked my life in Baghdad in 2006 by traveling into the red zone to meet with Bpeace's Iraqi Business Women to assess whether Bpeace could help businesswomen in Iraq, as they were empowering women in Afghanistan. I have helped raise awareness about Afghan culture and people in my local community here in Schenectady, New York, where I have been involved with the organizing of an Afghan Cultural Festival for the local upstate community. I have done volunteer work for Bpeace and have helped revive the membership of Ariana Outreach as a board member. I have had my friends from Unitarian churches send clothes and school supplies to Afghanistan to give to poor children. I have served for four years on the board of Women for Afghan Women and helped launched their community outreach program, which I chaired and raised funds for. I try to help wherever I can.

I am extremely grateful to have had my father in my life for as long as I did and wish I could have had him longer, but I cannot. I do know that to a large extent he has helped shape the person I am today and formed my core values. Therefore, my father is in my heart, as my friend Katy told me on the phone when I gave her news of his death. Knowing he is in my heart comforts me. I am happy that he helped shape this much of me already. I miss his long talks, his friendship, his face, and his warm smile. I wish I were not always in such a rush whenever he would call me to check up on me because I thought he would always be there.

Since my father's death, I have tried to continue to replicate the things he taught me, continuing to spread awareness about peace and justice in whatever small ways I can. I have inherited his love for humanity. Even though he may not be physically present with me, he is always with me in my heart and present in the air brushing my face.

I have pretended to be tough and strong on the outside, as if his death did not affect me, but that is not true. I feel lonelier without him and at times lost. I wish he were still here to celebrate my successes with me and provide me guidance and comfort during times of turmoil. I wonder how the events I have experienced after his death might have been different if he were alive. I try to mask my loneliness by going on trips, spending time with family and friends, but nothing replaces having him in my life.

In addition, when things are very fuzzy, when I feel disconnected and lost, the two things that seem to help me most are praying to God and knowing that God is great above all and that he will take care of me, and visiting my dad's grave in Washington Memorial Cemetery, exit 63 on the Long Island Expressway. It is a shared Muslim and non- Muslim cemetery.

It looks like a beautiful big park. It does not resemble the gloomy, frightening cemeteries I have seen at all, and so I enjoy going there. My grandmother Sara Bebe, and my cousins' mother Nafus Gula, are buried at his side; therefore, I remember them and all the other distant family members and community members buried there when I visit. I recite my prayers/duas for him and all the others when I visit. It was in fact my dad who conducted the burial services for most of the Afghan Muslims buried in that cemetery. When I visit his gravesite, I talk to him as if he were alive and imagine the responses he would give me. Even though it is not as satisfying as having a real conversation with him, it still helps to clear things up for me. I remember being a young girl, when he would arrive for the long drive to the cemetery, wearing his bright white long Afghan dress and pants, with one of his many assorted *chapans*. A *chapan* is a kind of Afghan robe that comes in a variety of colors, materials, and designs. My sister-in-law Mariam, known as the Martha Stewart of our family, had sewn a few of the heavier ones for him; the majority of them were custom-made or had been bought in warmer countries such as Saudi Arabia. The brown and beige chapans were heavy, made of wool. They had woolen tassels and embroidery on the front and some more embroidery along the edges. The lighter ones were were off-white and gold, navy blue, taupe; others were black with golden edges. I was always fascinated by my father's style. He was tall, slender, and a sharp dresser. Whether he wore Western-made suits or Afghan chapans, his clothes were always made of high-quality fabrics, and he always wore them well.

During my entire life, I remember my father having silver hair and a silver beard with a mustache; he had an olive skin tone, almond-shaped eyes, and a tall noble nose with cherry red thin lips. He always smelled great. After he entered a room, his floral scent would carry on even after he had left. The scents that remind me most of my father are tea rose and sandalwood. I remember his favorite scent was tea rose.

A couple years after my father passed away, I was going to visit him at the cemetery, and I asked my friend Sabera if she wanted to go and visit her mom while I visited my dad. Sabera and I have been friends since the fifth grade. Her mother passed away when she was in sixth grade. Sabera had not had a chance to visit her mother's grave in many years, and I knew she would want to come with me, so we went together. Once we got there, I noticed Sabera walking around a great deal while I was reciting duas by my father's graveside. Sabera located her mother after a while and was very upset to see her mother did not have a gravestone. She immediately went into the office of the cemetery to order a gravestone. I followed her into the office several minutes after I had completed my duas.

As I walked into the office, a man was talking to Sabera about designs and prices for the gravestone for her mother. I asked if we could make my dad's gravestone bigger because the print on the stone was quite small. The man asked me which gravestone I was talking about, and when I told him, he immediately became very excited. He said that my father was a good friend of his and that he knew him very well. He said he had never met such a remarkable person as my father. As this man was telling me this, I began to get goose bumps and chills down my spine. The man could not stop saying enough great things about my father, and I knew his words were genuine. A part of me wanted to give this stranger whom I had never seen before a big hug and cry to him about how much I missed my father. But then I remembered that this was not the first time I had felt this way, and I remembered all the other times when people whom I had never met expressed their love or respect for my father, how I felt this way with them as well. I experienced an instant connection with that stranger and anyone else who loved my father. I did nothing but say, Thank you, I am sure my father would have been pleased to hear all the kind words you are saying right now, sir. In my heart I felt that my dad could hear and see everything that was happening but could not be here physically to respond, even though I know he would have wanted to.

That man happened to be in charge of the entire cemetery and slashed the price for Sabera's mother's gravestone in half the moment he found out I was related to Imam Yusufi. The man said, Well, if you knew her father, then you will not pay in full for this stone. I felt so proud to be his daughter, as I always do when I realize that even after his death he continues to help people.

MARIAM EBRAT

Mariam Ebrat documents the very surreal experience of acting as an Afghan "refugee" in the Hollywood film Charlie Wilson's War, with Afghan Americans acting the parts of the refugees some may have been during the 1980s. Ebrat's biting wit has its own charm in this essay that gives voice to marginal characters, "the Afghans," in a film about Afghanistan. This was originally published in Snapshots: This Afghan American Life, *edited by Mir Tamim Ansary and Yalda Asmatey (2008).*

The Critic

April 11, 2007

Bright and early Wednesday morning, approximately ninety other Afghans from Fremont, aside from myself, met in the parking lot of Flamingo Palace, ready to board two blue passenger buses en route to Mystery Mesa Ranch, nestled high amid the mountains in Santa Clarita Valley, the site for the movie *Charlie Wilson's War.* I had bought a copy of the book *Charlie Wilson's War,* by George Crile, to read on the ride. I knew the book was about a rogue CIA operative and Congressman Charlie Wilson and the funding of Afghan rebels to fight the Soviet Union, but it also told the story of the Afghan people.

Despite the harsh wind, the dust, and the heat of the southern California sun, despite the warnings to watch out for baby rattlers, we had shown up. Of course L.A. Casting had thrown its net far and wide; many faces, young and old, mothers, children, fathers and grandfathers, even infants, had been picked as background extras for this picture, yet we still felt we had been "chosen" for the part. Let the Afghans descend upon Hollywood ... was the thought that crossed my mind on the early-morning bus ride to Santa Clarita. A typical filming day ran close to eighteen hours, with breakfast, breaks, and an hour lunch. It started at four o'clock in the morning and ended about eight-thirty at night. We were hauled in buses to the movie set from our hotels; we went into costume, hair, and makeup to get dirtied up, ate breakfast, and were then given directions to go on set. The set of *Charlie Wilson's War* was a windy, dusty campsite where a village of cloth tents had been set up. As the hot white rays of the early-morning beat down on this dry, rocky area, and a thousand extras in full costume, wearing worn-out, stained, dirty Afghan clothes and shoes, were situated, the refugee-camp scene came to life.

My overwhelming passion for theater and film had seduced me into trying out for the part of a background extra in the refugee-camp scene. My motive and hope was that my face would stand out and speak to a character befitting the director's artistic vision, and bring awareness about the lives of forgotten Afghan refugees. Auditions were held at the Caravan Restaurant in Hayward. As I drove up to the restaurant, I saw an entire family of Afghans in bright, colorful traditional Afghan dresses, hair, and makeup done to perfection. I wondered if they knew they were auditioning for the part of background refugees.

I had what used to be my mother's simple black empire-waist Afghan dress crumpled up in a bag, along with a black chadar and bright leggings. It was a dress that had been passed down and worn by every girl in our family at least once. It didn't have fancy decorations like other dresses I had seen; only red embroidery panels marked the neckline and the cuffs. I walked into the restaurant, dodging the curious glances and stares. I took a contact information card from a casting crew member and went to the bathroom to change. I looked in the mirror at my clean face and thought I could pass for a refugee with no makeup on! I smoothed down my undone hair and wrapped the black chadar around and walked out to the photographer. I handed him the card with my contact info; he quickly took two head shots in the outdoor area of the restaurant and told me I would get a call if I was chosen. As I drove back home, I wondered if my picture could be chosen so that I would audition for a speaking part.

I got the call to be an extra on March 25, 2007. The speaking parts had already been taken, but I could be a background extra. I was to be ready to leave for filming April 11–20. I felt excited, impassioned, and hopeful.

My overwhelming passion also blinded me to the reality of what diverse motives would do to my "hopes." The reality of the movie experience was a disappointment. Rumor has it that a woman somehow hurt her arm on set and got it in her head that suing the production company might prove to be lucrative. Whether this was true or not, she had left behind a vague misrepresentation of Afghans who were new to acting and their opportunity to work in film. The scene directors wanted every single detail of the film and campsite to reflect reality. They had a film crew member adjusting women's chadars to make sure they were wrapped around the face. A group of Afghan women extras would readjust the chadars after the scene director left, each wrapping her chadar around her head, with the rest hanging in the back like a long bandana. I was five years old when I saw a refugee camp; I have a vague recollection of what I saw. I thought, I don't remember refugees worrying about how they wore their chadar, but I do recall seeing the long bandana-style chadar in a few Afghan fashion shows. During the filming, one of these same women, perhaps attention deprived, with a rather long face that resembled a horse's face, stole opportunities to get in front of the camera at every angle possible, in every single scene. In one scene, the assistant director asked, "Okay, who wants to get in the mud? We need a few shots of people struggling through mud." My gallant, self-sacrificial response to film and art took over, and without thinking twice, I volunteered to sludge through the thick, gooey mud, only to be foolishly told to get out. The director thought the mud was too "gross" and had chosen to take a different direction, at which point the horse-face woman, who seemed to think she was in a fashion show, rather than representing a poor Afghan refugee woman, and had made sure to stay in direct view of the camera, was chosen to walk across the village during the lost child scene.

Sadly, most people were not there for artistic reasons; they were there because the job paid well, approximately $330 dollars per day, plus room and board. The narcissistic desire to be in the spotlight showed like a sharp flint in the eyes of the younger crowd, while the call for a quick couple hundred spoke to the elders. Those of us with actual experience in acting and theater had to sit back and watch our drive and passion be squandered away by "extras" with inferior/ulterior motives. In another scene, the director asked the woman with the long, skinny horse face, along with a group of others, to switch positions with others in front of them, so as to get a variation in the scene movement, yet no one would budge for fear of losing camera time. The director repeated himself and got blank stares back from the group of women. He then physically resituated them with the help of others. As the day wore on, I became angrier by the hour. Perhaps I was angry because I knew my hope to "stand out" was far-fetched among this mess of extras. I thought some of these people should have been debriefed about what their role was and whom they were representing before they had been allowed on set.

I was also angry because I couldn't bring myself to compete in the desperate attempts for camera time. I was happy to be there, and I thought of the extra work as a holy experience, a chance to express my passion for film and art. I thought of it as a chance to bring awareness about the harsh life of Afghan refugees and what they endure on daily basis. I had gone so far as to order DVDs from a charity organization called Children of War, whose president had made video footage of visits to these refugee camps. I wanted to bring them with me and show anyone who was interested, sharing my reasoning for being a refugee extra in this film. The DVD did not arrive in time for my departure, but it didn't matter, because my perception did not seem to match the views of those around me.

In another, quite important scene, a mob of hungry refugees were to run up to a food truck that they had been waiting for and beg for food; instead the mob hobbled toward the truck; with the exception of a few, they smiled, giggled, and laughed, waving their hands in the air as if they were at a live concert, vaguely calling out for food. At this point, I got my first glimpse of the director Mike Nichols, who stepped out of the director's area and yelled, "What the hell is this?" waving his hands in replication. "What the hell are you waving your hands for?! You're hungry! You're supposed to be begging and screaming for food!" He gestured with cupped hands toward the food truck. "Ask for it, don't wave your hands!" My heart ached to show them what he meant, and to show my passion for the film, but I stood sulking and embarrassed by our lack of focus.

The film site replicated the roughness of an entire village of refugees I had seen in Pakistan and the outskirts of Afghanistan, where Afghans struggle to live day in, day out. It was comprised of tattered tents held up by skinny wooden stakes; small boulders lined up around the tents served as walls. Tattered flaps of dirty, dusty cloth blew in the harsh wind, riling up the dirt from the bare floor. Dented, rusting pots and pans lay empty outside the tents as signature signs of hunger. Some tents had the luxury of a few sticks for firewood or a tattered mat on the dirt floor, while others were barren. The scene director had smoke circling up from strategic parts of the camp site, evoking the daily life of many people in the Third World. There were goats, sheep, donkeys, and trainers in costume treading across the village, perfectly replicating the sights and sounds of the background village.

At the beginning of each shooting day, extras stood in a line to check out props that they were to return at the end of the day. There were all sorts of light bundles tied with rope: baskets piled with blankets, a plastic sieve, dirty pots and pans, a bicycle with small bundles attached to the front and back, a rickety horse cart piled high with baskets, pots, and pans, a broken wheelbarrow piled with old blankets. The props helped depict the mass displacement of thousands of Afghans who flooded through the Pakistan border with nothing but the clothes on their backs and anything they could carry.

The first scene we worked on was the arrival scene. The shot was focused on capturing the flooding of Afghan refugees into Pakistan. Pakistani guards with rifles, guard posts, and wooden border posts were all a part of the scene. A broken-down car with its hood lifted, smoke rising, was placed strategically on the side of a dirt road a few steps away from the border; three women and their bundles were placed sitting near it. A thousand people and their props—carts, wheelbarrows, and bundles— were placed along either side of the dirt road. In the background was a cemetery marked by small gravestones and an open grave. The scene direction was to start walking toward the border patrol area as each section heard the words, "Background action!"

I was fortunate to have a scene partner for this shot who was as avid a theater lover as I was. We collaborated on the expression and relationship we were going to depict as we trudged to the border. We understood we could be mere specks in the camera's view but nonetheless wanted to live out the experience to the fullest. We decided our relationship was that of a brother and sister whose parents had been killed. We felt dogged about looking out for each other and decided to walk dazedly toward the border, exchanging concerned glances of anguish, thinking of what would happen to us.

This scene also included the arrival of actors Tom Hanks and Julia Roberts. Julia Roberts had a double for the scene. They were to be driven by guards in a Jeep, through the border, into the camp. What proved interesting was the crude behavior that erupted from a few of the background actors. The day of check-in, before filming started, everyone was given verbal and written warnings about bringing cameras to the movie set. Despite these warnings, people had camera phones and digital cameras hidden in their clothing and openly tried to snap pictures of Tom Hanks each time a take was done of him driving into the camp. He was kind enough to grant permission to them. More interesting yet was, again, the disregard of scene directions. The directors wanted everyone to pile onto the main road slowly, from different angles, yet when Tom Hank's Jeep came through, extras hastened their pace to get close to the Jeep, to get a glimpse of him and ensure their camera exposure. No one seemed to be discussing their relationship to the scene or the film, or to each other, before the take. Sadly, I believe my partner and I were the only ones.

Extras of other ethnicities were just as careless or carefree as the Afghan extras. During the takes of the food truck scene, two American girls casually conversed about their acting portfolios. One girl was describing how she was now into her "Afghan refugee" role and saying that after this she was ready to move on to other work. Another pair behind me, during a scene the director was shooting from afar to capture the top of the hill we were on, chatted about life in general. We formed a line down the hill toward the border post to represent the consistent flow of caravans of refugees into the border. This shot included a camel and its trainer dressed in costume. I don't think I had ever been that close to a camel. Meanwhile I was trying to be innovative and make the shot real by putting a small, flat, black metal pan with a broken handle on my head, placing within it some twigs I had randomly found on the ground. The scene director saw me and complimented my "great use of props." I smiled and said thanks.

When it comes time to edit the film, the cutting-room floor may see that shot, along with many others; I and everyone else may be mere specks in a bigger picture. My unrealistic expectation had been that all one thousand people would take as much pride in this opportunity as I did. No doubt my unrealistic yet impassioned vision saw my early departure from the filming. Filming ended on April 19th; I left on the 18th. I left because I was exhausted, sunburned, and disheartened. I am still glad I had the opportunity. I can't wait for the film to come out to see what was kept and what was discarded and, more importantly, to see the picture the world will see about the story of Afghan refuges.

FARHAD AHAD

Farhad Ahad (1970–2003) was an incredibly vibrant Afghan American with an MBA from the University of North Carolina. He was the founder of Afghan Solidarity, an Afghan American activist group, and the economic advisor to the minister of foreign affairs. Ahad was also one of the central advisors in the $3.2 billion gas pipeline deal involving Pakistan and Turkmenistan. He wrote these short responses in public forums and emailed them to his friends. Ahad was a charming gentleman with an easy smile, a generous spirit, and a sharp intellect, steadfast and committed to reconstructing Afghanistan. Farhad Ahad is sorely missed.

An Afghan American Perspective

From the roar of the collapsing towers to the silence in my home, I watched as New York grasped for life. First there was numbness; I was crippled from the shock. Then there was grief; I began to weep for the country. Finally, I was nauseous.

"Most evidence points to Osama Bin Laden. The Taliban is harboring Bin Laden," stated a reporter. Blood drained from my body and left me paralyzed. I was haunted by images of war and struggle in my birthplace, Afghanistan. Here, young and old fought not so much with weapons but with ammunition fueled by the desire to win the war against Communism. That is the Afghanistan I remember.

My family, along with many others, made the great escape from this war what seems like a lifetime ago. We were the lucky ones.

"Who could do such evil?" asked one man. Not those who fought the Russians. Comprised of different nationalities, the Taliban governs the country now. They did not take over by popular rule, but rather by brutal force. The people they govern are dying from drought and starvation. They are extremists governing in the name of God. If the accusations against Bin Laden are true, then God does not stand behind assassins.

Everyone is angered by Tuesday's events, and rightly so, but retaliations against those who are productive members of society and those have lived here all of their lives makes me sick. Guilt by association. I hear stories of backlash against the Muslim community. I hear about slurs of hatred and acts of violence. Don't they know we are Americans?

Last night, my family and I prayed for the victims. This morning, I'm not sure if I should leave my house. If America isn't united now, then the enemy has truly won.

Memories from Kabul's Playing Fields

The changing seasons in Kabul brought with them different social flavors for its youth. In my family of nine, my siblings, apart by about one year with me smack in the middle, would confirm the beginning of each new season with a saying: "Now, we can play this and that." This was never truer than at the very beginning of winter, when the school season was over, removing with it the endless tasks of arduous homework, not to mention the close scrutiny from both parents, ensuring we were good students.

We lived near Kohe Asmae mountain. Well, I should not say near because, like most dwellers in Afghanistan's central and northeastern provinces, we lived up in the foothills of the main mountain, high up from its steppe, which was marked by Asmae Street. The mountain and its plains made for a fantastic playground for my playmates and myself. It was a particularly advantageous setting in the winters, the season to be free!

I hardly recall ever being disappointed with Kabul's consistent, clear, and ample snowfalls. When very young, I was spared the task of shoveling snow from our rooftop. I would wake up in the early morning to the unique sound of my father moving the hand plow, *raash-bail,* scraping against the mud (*kah-gel*) rooftops, starting at one corner and slowly disappearing in the adjoining roofs. Shortly afterward, my father would appear at the door of the main room, getting ready to go to work. After a breakfast of mostly sweet tea and bread, I would put on my special "winter shoes" and be off and ready to enjoy the fresh snow.

The view from our house was spectacular. We had a panoramic view of much of Kabul, from the valley on the right, to Shir Darwaza mountain, to the countless dwellings against it, Cinema'e Pamir, all the way to Masjid'e Shah'e Du Shamshira—where I had earlier studied much of the Holy Quran. Squarely in front of our house sat the famous Balahe Saar, and far away to the left stood Maqbara'e Nadir Shah. Down below our house were the endless rooftops of our neighbors' dwellings, where men were clearing the snow. The rooftops were separated by occasional evergreens, *darakht'e sabr,* while slim streams of wood-fire smoke rose from cubical smokestacks. Once in a while a car, mostly the common Russian jeep type, would dare to drive in the snow of Asmae Street, clearing the path for other cars behind it.

Fresh snow cleared from rooftops found its way to the narrow alleys. I would almost choke from excitement at the mere sight of piles of fresh snow. It was going to make for another long, steep and curving, daring and thrilling *yakhmalaak,* or snow slide. It would take a bit of effort and thinking to make the right kind of slide—one with bumps, dips, and corners, and always with a sufficient speed. An hour later, many boys from the neighborhood would join in. We would slide down, walk up, and repeat until news came of an even better yakhmalaak in the next alley. I would return home only to warm up, since I always lost my gloves, and my hands would start turning purple from the cold. I will never forget the joyous spirit of the boys in those winters.

Back in the house all the concrete terraces would be covered with snow, thereby eliminating any chance of playing *joz baazi* or *rissman baazi,* jump rope, for my sisters. When they were outside, or doing housework or cooking, my sisters would resort to telling stories from behind a warm *sandali,* heated with a Siemens *manqal,* or playing with their hand-made dolls, or putting up a heated *sherjangi,* or playing a game of *karambol.* The karambol is a square board with four circular dips, one in each corner, and twenty total chips. The goal was to tip the larger serving chip and make it touch one of the other players' chips and cast the latter into one of the four voids. Karambol interested me because it drew on my interest in physics and dynamics. Hence, I would join a game of karambol myself. However, it was an indoor game, and in Afghanistan, there was nothing like being outside, enjoying its great outdoors.

At one point in his series of careers, my father was a teacher for twelve years. For that reason, when it was time to study, we took the form of his students. He was as unrelenting on us as he must have been on any of his regular students. Then, some of my father's teachings often skipped us, and that is when my mother stepped in, despite the fact that she had no formal schooling. While my father made for a teacher like no other I would come across in my years of primary schooling and college and graduate educations, my mother was a teaching assistant like no other. For the better—in hindsight, of course—a large part of our Fridays, our only day off, was spent doing homework and studying. Only when I reached my teens would I find a way to leave home and have my father's consent to pursue a much-coveted new hobby: flying kites, *goodi paraan baazi.*

I made my own special string, largely because of the inconsistency found in those sold in the market. I would buy my own raw string, powdered glass, and glue, mix them, and in the front yard make sharp string, *tar'e shisha,* after school. On rare occasions, I would be lucky to pick up a freed kite, *azadi,* sometimes with much string attached to it. However, often I would be out drumming up enough "loans" to purchase the smaller colorful kites. Then, on Fridays, it was time to join the masses flying kites from their respective rooftops. The ensuing kite matches required many skills—precision, timing, and perception, not to mention the ability to spot and dodge the cheap *chelak andaazes.* More often than not, probably nine out of ten times, the only way out of a match was after one kite was "lost," a rather dreadful experience. Hence, it took many dares to start one. Only over time, and with much experience, would one become a good *goodi paraan baaz.*

After the Saur Revolution, my father switched careers to the private sector, taking a job as a salesman for Hoechst AG, a German outfit supplying many of the over-the-counter and prescription drugs available in Afghanistan. His duties required him to manage the transporting of massive loads of pharmaceutical drugs to other provinces where Hoechst had depots, namely Jalalabaad and Kundoz. As such, he would be gone for weeks at a time.

His was an increasingly dangerous job, particularly when Hoechst was not able to secure an airplane to transport the loads and had to resort to ground transportation and hire trucks for the job. I recall each specific time when, returning from one of his numerous trips, my father would recount stories. He would tell of being stopped by the Mujahidin or the Shorawis, Soviets, yelled at for proceeding to direct the trucks to drive over mined roads, sometimes directly shot at, or often apprehended and taken for questioning by the local Mujahidin commanders, who took up positions up in the mountains. However, with God on his side, and his duty ultimately helping all Afghans, he never received as much as one scratch from any of these encounters.

Anyhow, when my father left for his business trips during the school season, I usually rushed my homework and went outside the confines of the study room to make new friends, some of whom I knew from high school. Then, I picked up new games. The first must have been *qotakaan*, or *shudumak*, a game not too different in objective from horseshoes, except that a stone replaces the stick, and coins or a flat stone replace the horseshoe. After all players have thrown their coins, the one closest to the stone wins. After excelling in shudumak, there were others to move on to, mainly marbles, *toshla baazi, danda kelak, top danda, tokhom jangi,* and *maishakaan.*

The game of maishakaan I had long forgotten, only to relearn it recently from another Afghan. It is like an advanced game of marbles, except that it involves placing upright one small flat stone called a *maish* for each player. The maish are placed evenly distanced for each player. A player tries to knock down other players' maish with his marble in exchange for winning the fallen player's marbles. The more knock-downs, the more winnings, but the game ends in a draw if a player knocks down his own maish.

Back at the house, my young sisters were busy playing *shahidakaan*, or hide and seek. Another was "Enni Minni Miney Moe," where they would take turns pronouncing, "Aalam delam spartaang. Aakaa keshe del-wazir. Wazirtang, pir pad-cha!" The one receiving the last word had to drop from the game, and the last one standing was the winner. Others played *dharmagz baazi, kamsaahe,* catching *bambeerak,* and *bojol baazi,* but as I grew older, I picked up a new hobby: playing soccer.

In the five years after the Saur Revolution, my playmates would escape from Afghanistan, ultimately heading to Germany, the U.S., or India, one by one. Of course, for their security, none would disclose their plans for departure, so "goodbyes" were out of the question. I would be a witness to Afghan games for the last time in March of 1985, when we joined the flood of escapees to Pakistan. Now, sixteen years later and thousands of miles away, I only dream about those moments and hope that with the Almighty's help I might someday return to Kabul, to the same vibrant alleys, and see children happily flying kites from their rooftops.

AWISTA AYUB

Awista Ayub is the author of However Tall the Mountain: A Dream,
Eight Girls, and a Journey Home *(2009). She founded the Afghan Youth
Sports Exchange, an organization dedicated to nurturing Afghan girls
through soccer. Fifteen teams now compete in an organized league,
with hundreds of girls participating through the Afghanistan Football
Federation. Her book tells her story and the stories of the eight original
girls who joined the country's first girls' soccer team.*

You Proved Me Wrong

I grew up in two worlds: the private Afghan world at home, and the public American world outside. We spoke Pashto at home, ate Afghan food every day, learned how to pray and read the Quran in Arabic. The Afghanistan my mother and father conjured for my siblings and me was simple, mischievous, saturated by the sweet taste of melons, juice squeezed from pomegranates, steaming rice, and, of course, the patient intimacy of Kandahari embroidery, the painstaking hours spent pricking a sliver of needle through thin white cloth again and again, the patterns slow to emerge.

While other kids enjoyed after-school programs, joined the local youth soccer team, or acted in school plays, we had our own activities. On weekends, my mother taught my sister and me *khamak dozi,* the Afghan embroidery endemic to Kandahar. At first, I put up a fight. When I started, at age five, I would poke my finger with the needle, hoping my mother would have pity on me and let me wander free of the needle and cloth. But she didn't buckle under the pressure, determined to pass on the skill her mother had taught her.

Over the years, my skills improved. I viewed my mother's embroidery with a different eye. I studied each of her patterns and stitches. Although I never achieved her mastery, I appreciated her knowledge and this art of the women of Afghanistan.

While my mother taught us embroidery, my father shared his life in Afghanistan.

On the weekends, my father would make us an Afghan breakfast of sautéed onions and tomatoes with eggs, served with milk *chay*. Sitting at the breakfast table, I was captivated by his stories about the trouble he and his brothers caused climbing trees, how he played in the beautiful gardens of Paghman, going to the *masjed* early in the morning to pray, pulling pranks on their teacher or on women on Alokozai Dana Street, outside their house in Kandahar—often with comical and unforeseen effects.

His tales of childhood in Afghanistan reminded me of stories from *Huckleberry Finn:* kids entertaining themselves through resourcefulness and simple, plucky pleasures.

I knew that without war, that would have been my life too. I would have spent my childhood running through the gardens of our home, snatching fresh fruit from the neighbor's yard, scrambling up our own trees. I often caught myself daydreaming about Afghanistan, wishing I could lie on the flat roof of our house, breathing in the fresh evening air, counting the stars that shone so clearly.

At least growing up I would have fit in. In America, sometimes I didn't. I always dreaded the first day of school, waiting for the teacher to go through roll call, knowing that when my name came up, they'd stare, puzzled. I'd speak up quickly, before the teacher butchered my name and embarrassed me in front on my classmates. "It's Awista," I would say, "but I go by Sara." In kindergarten I'd given myself a new name, and it stayed with me until my middle school years.

The desire to fit in is a standard immigrant experience as we straddle two sometimes opposing worlds. While I struggled throughout my adolescence to find my identity, it wasn't until I stumbled into the sports arena that I finally found my voice and a new passion in life. Sports would become my sanctuary, and I would do whatever was necessary in order to protect this aspect of my life, particularly from the Afghan community. I had always shielded it from one of my least favorite aspects of Afghan culture: judgment.

I learned this the hard way.

"You've gotten chubbier," some relatives would announce when I arrived at family gatherings. Or, "That's a really unattractive outfit."

They weren't saying it to be mean, just stating facts as they saw them. They were blunt, without feeling the need to protect my feelings. I wore jeans, no makeup, and learned not to care. But when it came to sports, I did not want to hear their judgment—it had come to mean too much to me. I fell in love with sports watching Olympic ice hockey during the 1994 Winter Games. I was transfixed as players flew across the ice with grace, speed, and toughness. I'd wake up early to watch ESPN's *SportsCenter,* often viewing repeats of the same half-hour show two, sometimes three, times in a row so that I could see my favorite highlights again. On days when I controlled the remote—once every three nights—I had the TV tuned into the hockey playoffs or the latest tennis tournament, much to the dismay of my two siblings.

Eventually, I stepped into the sports arena myself when I was twelve—relatively late by American standards. I'd become an avid tennis fan, watching Monica Seles and Andre Agassi win tournament titles throughout the 1990s. But watching wasn't enough; I wanted to play. In my freshman year of high school, I joined the tennis team, walking on the court with no tennis experience—and undeterred by the coach's name: Mr. Killer. He lived up to his name. He took every chance to remind me that I had to prove myself on the court. I dreaded when he drew us to the net with a drop shot, only to volley back so fast my arm would shake at the ball's impact on my racquet. If we weren't fast enough to react, the ball hit us right in the stomach. But it fired my competitiveness. I recruited my brother and my sister to play on the team, giving myself two extra hitting partners. I stayed two hours after practice each day, until my father picked us up from school. Over the years, the extra practice time paid off—as I moved up in the rankings to become the number-one singles player on the team and captain by my senior year.

Sports taught me there are no shortcuts in life. One day at practice, when Coach Killer wasn't looking, I cut through the grassy island during a dreaded running session, slicing my time in half. Then I heard his voice, yelling.

"Awista!" he roared, as everyone's heads swiveled toward me. "Four more laps!"

I was mortified. And I never took a shortcut again. Through sports, I learned that there is no substitute for hard work; in every game there will be a winner and a loser, and we can't always win—and in the moment of loss, you see what you're really made of. I continued playing sports in college, including founding the women's ice hockey team at the University of Rochester and playing the position of goalie for three seasons. Academically, I graduated with a B.S. degree in chemistry, and in September of 2003 I accepted a research chemist position in Niskayuna, New

York, at General Electric Global Research, much to my father's delight. I accepted the position reluctantly; my heart wasn't in it, but I wanted to do what was expected of me.

I'd fallen in love with chemistry my junior year in high school after being taught it by Mr. Purcaro. He opened my eyes to its beauty—the logic of its method, cooking reactions in the lab, learning by trial and error—and he'd taught me not to be afraid to make mistakes. I was hooked and knew then that I'd major in chemistry in college. By my senior year at Rochester, the passion had dimmed. I couldn't picture working in a lab all day, shut out from the world outside, without windows, without fresh air, feeling suffocated from the fumes, my head always congested.

Yet by the end of 2003, I was working forty hours a week beneath a lab hood, wearing goggles and latex gloves, repeating reaction after reaction. The bridge of my nose throbbed at the end of the day from the weight of the goggles, as my father's expectations weighed on my head. I felt numb as I walked GE's halls. The days dragged, and I had to force myself to get to work at eight a.m. each morning. I had convinced myself that I could be a research chemist, at least for the sake of making my father proud. But this was not the life I'd dreamed about. I had reached a crossroads—continue with research or break away and work in Afghanistan. I chose Afghanistan.

I believed that sports could become a vehicle to help young children in Afghanistan find themselves in their new world in the same way that it had helped me. I decided to create a sports camp for young female athletes and sponsor their trip from Afghanistan. I wanted them to have a chance to discover their own strength and character, to feel ownership and control over their experience, instead of living lives dictated by war.

Although my father expressed initial support, he was more proud of my position at GE, and I didn't dare tell him that I planned to leave the company as soon as the program was pulled together.

"How many B.S.-degree chemists are organizing soccer camps for Afghan girls?" he would ask me over the next few months, knowing the answer to the question before I answered it.

"None."

"Then why are you doing it?"

"Because I know that this is what I should be doing with my life."

"It doesn't make any sense, Awista."

But it made sense to me, and I became more determined than ever to make this project a reality and do what little I could to help heal the country we both loved.

Thinking it through, I could understand my father's resistance. He had left his homeland to bring us to safety; he had worked hard to make sure we had opportunities. He and my mother had lived the struggle for all of us. He was proud of me, and the security of a position at GE. Why would I voluntarily put that security at risk? Only his struggle wasn't my struggle.

Sometimes our culture can be too sheltering; we worry about what our people will say about almost everything we do. I'd seen this firsthand within the Afghan-American community. Parents were afraid to let their children find themselves through travel, career exploration, sports, "because others will talk." Activities outside a path of academic study, professional achievement in medicine or science, and traditional Afghan culture could be stopped with the question, "What will they think of you, of me, of our family? They will say we let our daughters run wild— that they misbehave."

My parents faced this judgment in 1997 when I moved three hundred miles away from home to start my chemistry degree at the University of Rochester. I know that some Afghans in the community disapproved of my parents' decision to let me go. Later my father told me, "I didn't care what they had to say. I trusted you. This was your education—and I won't let anyone get in the way of that."

Until my decision to devote myself to supporting sports programs for Afghan girls, my father could always justify my decisions because they were about education. But this time, I was challenging the community, and most importantly him, for the sake of sports. This he couldn't justify. But even though my choice forced him out of his comfort zone as my father, my protector, he wouldn't hold me back.

Years later, after the success of my work bringing a girls' soccer team from Afghanistan to the States, and then my work in Kabul, bringing a delegation of Afghan American coaches to assist local female soccer and basketball teams, my father realized that the work I had been doing was meaningful.

"You proved me wrong, Awista," he said.

BLOGS

♦♦♦

MASOOD KAMANDY

This blog is an account of Masood Kamandy's project to experience the country of his heritage, Afghanistan, and build the beginnings of a Department of Photography at Kabul University's Faculty of Fine Arts. The project lasted from September of 2002 until July of 2005. This archive is a testament to an experience that changed Kamandy forever. His hope is that it inspires others to engage with the world around them and pursue their own projects.

Dispatches from Kabul

SEPTEMBER 24, 2004

Welcome to the Dispatch

On October 1, 2004, I will begin my long journey to Kabul, Afghanistan. This blog is meant as a travelogue to document the experience as it happens. An introduction to me: I'm a twenty-three-year-old Afghan American photographer, recently graduated from the School of Visual Arts in New York City. I live and work in New York. On September 11, 2001, I was near the courthouse in Lower Manhattan. As soon as I understood that this was a terrorist attack, I also knew that I had to go to Afghanistan, and one year later I spent two weeks in Kabul photographing family members I'd never met, the plastics factory that my family abandoned, and the aftermath of twenty-three years of war.

Now it's 2004, and Afghanistan's first national elections are on the horizon. I am extremely excited to be able to capture this period of time in Kabul and to share it with you. Media coverage of Afghanistan from here is very sparse, so I'm interested in feeling the sociopolitical climate of Kabul.

Blogging is a new experience for me, but I'm attracted to its organic nature. I look forward to being in contact with you from Kabul and hope to update it as often as possible.

Thanks for reading, and enjoy.

SEPTEMBER 25, 2002

Where Do You Come From?

This is an email I wrote to friends upon returning from my first trip to Afghanistan in September of 2002.

From: Masood Kamandy
Date: September 25, 2002, 6:41:54 p.m. EDT
Subject: Where do you come from?

As most of you know and some of you are now finding out, I spent the last two weeks in Afghanistan. While it is fresh in my mind, I wanted share it with you all.

I woke up a couple of hours ago, at ten a.m. [Tuesday morning], after sleeping for fourteen hours straight due to exhaustion from jet lag. They say that you don't get jet lag on your way back from Asia, only going there; alas, for some reason that was not the case for me. Actually, I spent the whole flight next to a Bollywood cinematographer who was taking his first trip to America. He was in awe at the idea of America and couldn't help but share his excitement, which felt ironic considering what my feelings were at that moment about my trip to Afghanistan.

I spent all day Monday in a daze, trying to explain, in my drunken tiredness, to my friends and family what my trip was all about and how it felt. By the end of the night I was telling everyone that I would get back to them in a week.

Intellectually, I've always known where I come from. I had heard stories and knew, vicariously through my parents and other family members, what it was like to be Afghan, but I didn't really know. My life has always been about knowing what to say; having the right words to describe my heritage, where I come from, who I am: "I was born in Colorado, but my parents are from Afghanistan." But words and intellectual understanding are never enough. Now when I think about where I come from it's not a collection of words anymore. It's visceral.

I thought that going to Afghanistan would be a clarifying experience, and it did add to my understanding of my family's heritage, as I said above. But in some ways it had just the opposite effect. I realized that because the diaspora of Afghans across the world lasted for twenty-three years, even Afghans born and raised in Kabul who are now returning are and will always be foreigners. If I felt split, drawn in two directions before, I feel shattered to bits now.

I've never been a mystic, but so many of my experiences in Afghanistan seemed to be so coincidental and meaningful. Everything about the last two weeks has been magical in a way:

1. The weather was perfect in Afghanistan the entire time. There were so few clouds, but the day before we left for America it rained, and the well for our house simultaneously ran dry.

2. The moon went through a full cycle while I was in Afghanistan, going from new moon to full moon. When an Afghan sees the first crescent moon, he or she always stops, closes his or her eyes, and says a prayer for good luck.

3. There was a painting in our guesthouse above our dining table depicting Kabul thirty years ago. We would share breakfast and dinner there every day. It was a huge painting of the Kabul River, with the sun setting in the background. The river was full of water, the sky full of clouds, and the buildings exuded the grandeur of the Italian-influenced architecture that was once very popular in Kabul. Now the river is dry, there are seldom clouds in the sky, and those buildings are ruined. What was once the river has become an open-air bazaar the local people call the "Titanic" market, seemingly unaware of the word's dire implications.

4. On my first day in Afghanistan I went to a place called Chicken Street. In front of a bookstore I began taking photos

of some children in front of a big painting of Ahmad Shah Masood (the Northern Alliance leader who was assassinated on September 9, 2001). A boy about my age approached me. He asked me where I was from, and we started to talk. He worked as a janitor for the United Nations Mine Clearing Agency. He started talking about how important it was for educated Afghans to come back because all people know in Afghanistan now are guns. He said, in his simple and straight-forward words, "Your heads are better than our heads right now." His words are a testament to the people's desperation. After our conversation he gave me his phone number and told me to come have tea with him and his family sometime. He walked off but after a few minutes came back, having decided to give me something to remember him by: a ring. He took it off his hand and put it on my right middle finger, where it still is as I write this.

5. After visiting the Kabul University Faculty of Fine Arts, I was walking out of the building, and a man stopped me to ask if I recognized him. I'm not sure if he was plainly mistaken or if he truly saw someone from my family in my face, but he swore that he knew me. He said that I used to drive a white car and attend school at the Faculty of Engineering thirty or forty years ago (my father?). I was in such shock at the time that I didn't take his picture. When I realized this, I ran halfway back across the campus back to the building, but he was gone.

What does it mean to know where you come from? I was just listening to a *This American Life* show about the Trail of Tears, where two girls, part Cherokee Native American blood, retrace the Trail of Tears on a road trip and record their experiences. It's similar to what I did in Afghanistan, retracing and photographing the important landmarks in my parents' lives and things that were important to my extended family. I saw the French school that my father went to until tenth grade, which has now been rebuilt by the French. I saw the flour mill that my father said was near their house, which supplied all of Afghanistan with bread before it was destroyed. It's a huge yellow building of twelve or thirteen stories, with no windows but huge craters in its walls from shelling. I saw the place where my parents had their engagement party. It used to be an upscale restaurant and banquet hall on top of a hill. It had an Olympic-sized swimming pool behind it and a garden, complete with vineyard. The road leading up to the hill was once lined with large pine trees. Now the pool is empty. Part of the building has big black stains on it, evidence of a fire. The windows are shattered. The pool is empty. The restaurant was replaced with a teahouse. The trees, which lined the road, are dried skeletons, stripped completely of their bark and any branches. And the gardens that once lined the hills are now just dirt. As for the vineyards . . . the Taliban systematically destroyed all vineyards in certain areas of the country. Some said that they would first rip out the plant and then melt rubber tires over the soil so that nothing would ever grow again. I'm not sure if that's true, but it wouldn't surprise me.

Parts of this trip were terrifying. Understanding the depth of the loss in Afghanistan was a hard pill to swallow, but on the other hand roads are being rebuilt. The country's highways are supposed to be done in five years, and people are out on the streets living their lives. Returning refugees are swelling the population of Kabul and other areas of Afghanistan, opening up new businesses and helping with the rebuilding process and in government ministries. It was amazing seeing people walking on the street, just observing the way that they interact. It's hard not to notice the way people treat each other with such respect and kindness. Everyone you meet offers you tea, and sometimes food. Sometimes you'll see three men riding on one bicycle, completely comfortable . . . or a man carrying huge amounts of produce tied to his bike. They all seem to make it work. There's a determination that I've never seen anywhere else in my life that was incredible to witness.

Everyone I spoke to said that I had chosen an exciting time to be in Kabul and to see the country. Also, while much of the destruction I witnessed centered around Kabul, I did get a first-hand taste of what it used to be like in Kabul. When you drive north into Parvan Province, many of the vineyards, farms, and fields of wheat grow as far as the eye can see, irrigated by rivers

of water, which are fighting the drought and apparently winning.
Cows graze. Little boys and girls play in the fields while their
mothers and fathers work in them. It was beautiful, and I know
that in time it will be like that again, as long as enough trained
people go back to help and as long as money keeps flowing into
the government and into projects.

Everywhere I went, I had to see everything twice: once in
today's reality, and once in my family's past, in Afghanistan's
glory days. The climax of that split experience was visiting my
grandfather's factory, a place that had once fed my mother and
her family.

Once upon a time my family owned a factory in Afghanistan,
which produced plastic products. I never really understood the
depth of their loss before my trip. One man I spoke to said that
all the plastic plates he ate off of when he was growing up said
Kabul Plastic on the bottom. They made socks, shoes, slippers,
plastic bags, rolls of plastic, polyester fiber, and other products.

It was because of this factory that my grandfather and his eldest
son were killed by the Communists in 1980, a year after the
Soviet invasion. My understanding, although it is hazy, is that
they systematically killed all industry leaders, people who were
considered a threat to the new government. It was weird meeting people who worked there, men who knew my grandfather,
and seeing their reactions when they found out I was his grandson. Their eyes would open wide, and they would list names of
people they wanted me to say hello to. They were proud of the
way they had maintained the factory, and in fact, it looked amazing, considering that it was one of the only buildings in this
industrial neighborhood still standing and not looted. Around it
was all rubble and dust, but the logo on the gate was still there,
though faded, and the same groundskeeper still opened and
closed those doors. To rest in, he took a wooden bed frame and
tied dried thistles to the bottom of it to protect him from snakes.
I have a photograph of him on it. It's pretty amazing how ingen-
ious people can be and the lengths they will go to just to survive.

My guide, we called him Mama (maternal uncle) Majid, opened
all of the doors for me and showed me how they had preserved

all of the machinery. Yards and yards of white fabric had been put on the machines to protect them from the city's incredible amount of dust (unlike anywhere I've seen or been). In one building, in addition to the fabric on the machines, they had also built scaffolding from wood, on top of which they had draped more white fabric. It was a surreal and pretty ghostly sight, all of that dusty fabric hanging over endless rows of machines. Everywhere there were piles and piles of dusty plastic shoes, waiting for over a decade to be remelted and made into new shoes. On the walls there were black handprints made decades ago, perhaps the marks of a person painting shoes. In addition to the shoes, there were shoe molds everywhere. In the largest factory room there was an entire wall of shoe molds of different sizes and shapes.

Mama Majid also showed me things that my family had put together. He showed me a giant wheelbarrow that my grandmother had bought in Kandahar and put together specifically for the factory. He told me I should photograph it and show it to my grandmother. Apparently she was once quite proud of it.

I've always been envious of my American and European friends who had family trees going back eons. What is it like to know with such accuracy who you are descended from? Maybe it gives a person a sense of history, a sense of lineage, and helps in the creation of a mental image of what/who one comes from. For me, my family started with the present. I had a vague idea of what my family's story was, but no real personal attachment to any of it, because it came from a different culture and a different time, and the facts about it never really seemed straight to me. I couldn't really relate to it. I always felt like an outsider, and maybe part of that is my fault, but now things have changed.

Now I've experienced my past in such a visceral way that it puts into question every aspect of my own life and future. I now know firsthand where much of my family lived, worked, died, and escaped from, and I felt a connection with it that has affected me profoundly and placed a big question mark on my future. Am I going to return to Afghanistan? What preparations am I going to have to make?

The light in Kabul is unbelievable. In the afternoons as the sun was setting, and workers began going home, the activity created a cloud of dust. Light filtering through the dust shined a hazy warmth on everyone and everything that was almost celestial. My goal was to see Afghanistan only as I could, but I still think I need more time. Could I ever have enough? I hope my pictures will reflect some of the simultaneous anguish and joy that I had from visiting these places of the past, but I know I must go back at some point. I feel like I need more time to explore what being Afghan means to me. In the process maybe I can help.

One possibility is to help rebuild the Photography Department at Kabul University (which was destroyed by the war) and teach photography there someday. I kept on trying to tell the dean of the Faculty of Fine Arts and others at the university how important it was for Afghans to keep expressing what it is like to be Afghan using photography, to maintain our cultural heritage through art. They kept mentioning that Kabul University already had a journalism department, and that's important, but entirely different. Journalism is focused on current events, not exploring the identity of the people. In my opinion, the nature of photojournalism is to isolate certain ideas about a place and take photographs that illustrate those ideas. It is not true always; at times photojournalists transcend those traps, but it is difficult. It is very important for Steve McCurry, Sebastiao Salgado, or James Nachtwey to go into a perilous situation and photograph atrocity, and the downtrodden people of certain nations, but I wonder if that sort of photography ignores culture, and can't help but remain focused on the differences between the First World and the rest of the world. Doesn't it focus on situation and environment rather than identity?

The best example of what I would like to see being taught in Afghanistan is/was done by Manuel Bravo. I kept on thinking about him no matter where I went. He's Mexican (I think he just turned one hundred, maybe more, this summer), and he was beloved by the Surrealists, but didn't consider himself one. He was asked repeatedly to leave Mexico and photograph elsewhere (Paris in particular), but he always refused. He relished his personal cultural experience in his homeland. I consider him to be the photographer's equivalent of Gabriel García Márquez in his magical realism. When you look at his photographs you sense the profundity of his attachment to his culture and not his distance from it, like a photojournalist or a tourist.

What are the things in an Afghan's life that make him or her truly feel Afghan? What little things are missed when an Afghan leaves his country? These are the questions I have, and honestly, I might never be able to answer them because I was raised as an American, but I wish I could, and that wish, I hope, will drive me to further explore the country.

To end this letter I wanted to give you a list of the most important words that I learned in Dari while I was there. I won't forget these:

Watan—homeland
Watandar—people from the same country, compatriots
Ghazi—someone who has fought invaders successfully, a champion
Khaarijee—foreigner
Khaarij—foreign land
Waaqiat—truth
Pul—bridge
Gharb—West

I thought those words would speak for themselves.

Oh yeah, on my first day back, Monday, I had lunch at a restaurant on Spring Street in New York, and who walked in but James Nachtwey!

I hope you all are well, and I can't wait to see each and every one of you soon.

Love,

Masood Kamandy

FRIDAY, OCTOBER 22, 2004
Panjshir Valley

Today we took our first trip outside of Kabul. My goal was to see the gravesite and memorial to Ahmad Shah Massoud, the leader of the Northern Alliance, who was slain on September 9, 2001, by two members of the Taliban pretending to be journalists. He was killed when a bomb in the light above the video camera exploded.

I didn't know what to expect. Some whom I'd asked had said it would not be anything special, but I insisted that I wanted to see this key battle-ground in the battle for Afghanistan during the time of the Taliban.

The Panjshir Valley was the last frontier that the Taliban were unable to capture. It was the stronghold of the people who now control much of the government here in Kabul.

Driving up about halfway, everything is flat. You can see for miles around, and the farther north you drive, the greener it gets. Oddly shaped plots of farmland go as far as the eye can see, before towering mountains shoot up, as if out of nowhere. For about an hour and a half the road is newly paved, but then it ends. The road into Panjshir is a treacherous one.

When we hit the valley, the mountains became extremely vertical. They are dry rocky mountains, and in the distance, the highest and most jagged of the Hindu Kush are visible with snow scattered on top. The road is a slow one that skirts along the west side of the valley, with the emerald green Panjshir River to the right, rushing with water. It's a spectacular sight to see, the color of this water. I've never seen anything like it.

The road is narrow, but at the same time, meant to accomodate two lanes of traffic. When cars came from the opposite direction, sometimes it was within inches that we passed eachother, and the drop to the river was, at times, hundreds of feet.

But we made it through. At first the valley is extremely tight and rocky, with a small amount of sky visible on top. Then you reach a gate that has two lions painted on it and a checkpoint where you are supposed to "register." It's for security, and the guards were nice enough. About a half an hour out of the gate the valley begins to open up, and as you drive along the side of the mountain there are constantly these moments when the view is just breathtaking. There are small villages all along the Panjshir, and as we drove by people would stare, or wave. With Massoud's grave so far into the valley, they are now accustomed to the sight of foreigners, especially those from France, who are obsessed with Massoud and are constantly visiting.

The colors of fall were everywhere, with beautiful oranges and yellows in the valley and in the rocky, dry mountains above. There were several moments when the beauty of the land drove me to tears. I can't say that's happened often in my life, but it does happen here.

Massoud's grave was about three hours' drive into the valley, and we were glad to finally see its green-domed building from a distance. It is located at the top of a hill that they have named "Massoud Hill." The walls are brand-new, and it is guarded by some of his former bodyguards/commandos, who turned out to be extremely welcoming fellows, although his army is notorious for their dislike of Americans.

I don't know very much about Massoud. I know the basics, and I know his reputation, so I was not expecting to be moved by his grave. We took off our shoes before we walked into the small, circular, green-domed building. There were four men sitting in front of the grave in the center of the room. One was reading an excerpt from the Quran, and the rest were sitting with their legs crossed and their heads down before the grave.

I sat as well. Thoughts began to flood my mind of the time when he died. I had just started school. It was two days before September 11, and both events combined were the tidal wave that reintroduced me to Afghanistan and made me determined to reclaim the past. The connection, and the fact that I was now sitting in front of his grave, moved me greatly. I sat there, and everyone else left. There was one guard in there, and he saw me crying. It's so odd when my emotions hit me. It's like a tidal wave, and I can never be sure when it's going to happen. The events of the last few years have led to positive change, but the irony and tragedy involved never cease to amaze me. The guard stayed in there with me, standing at the door in his military fatigues and his traditional pakul hat from the Panjshir valley.

Finally I got up to leave, and as I was walking through the door he stood right in front of me and blocked my way. He said, "Take as many pictures as you want to, don't worry about it." I hadn't taken one picture yet, but my camera was strapped to my back, and he knew that I wanted to. So I took pictures of his grave. The guard even asked me if I wanted to rearrange the flowers or anything to make it more beautiful, and I said it was fine.

I stayed for about an hour and a half, part of it inside of the tomb and some sitting on the grass beside it, looking out into the valley. The view from his tomb was the best view that we had come across so far. Finally it came to me that I would love to sit with this guard and listen to his story. We asked him if we could take his portrait and write down some anecdote of his about Massoud. We all sat on the grass, and as he spoke to me in his Panjshiri accent, he would look deep into my eyes as if the story he was telling me was a story passed down for centuries. It's a way that Afghans have about them when they tell stories: the ability to evoke time-lessness. He had tanned skin and dark wavy hair coming out from under his pakul. Listening to him, I felt like I had known him for ages, and I was happy to hear stories about a man who was such a good leader.

One of the stories he told was about guarding Massoud's home while he slept. He was a teenager at the time, and his assignment was to guard the door in the middle of the night. Terrified that he was going to fall asleep, he put his chair in front of the door, so that if he did fall asleep the door would awaken him. Sure enough, the door awoke him when it was time for morning prayers. He moved his chair, and as Massoud came out and asked, "Did you get enough sleep last night?" the guard responded, "I wasn't asleep." "No, you did get your sleep." Massoud went back into his room and came out with a note scrawled onto a piece of paper. He told the young guard to go and give it to one of the higher commandos and he would know what to do. Terrified of what the note entailed, the boy went to give the note to the commando, wondering what his punishment would be. After reading the note, the commando smiled, went into his room, and came out with eight thousand afghanis, which he handed to the boy.

Regardless of whom he killed, these people love this man. Righteousness and morality in times of war are often very hazy, and that keeps me from worshipping this man as many Afghans do. But I understand what they appreciate about this religious and supposedly benevolent man.

MONDAY, OCTOBER 18, 2004

Iftaar in the Seventh District

Fasting here has been an amazing experience. It's incredible to know that the vast majority of the people in this country, and in the Muslim world, participate in this tradition. The first day was rough. The most difficult aspect of fasting was the fact that I could not drink any water in this arid environment. I feared that this would affect my ability to work.

It's now been four full days that I've fasted, and my body has adjusted. Not only that, but I find myself giddy when it's time to eat.

At sundown, all of the mosques in the area have either a recording or a person with an amplifier reading verses of the Quran in Arabic. You can hear it across the city, and it's the sign everyone waits for to eat their first bites. We all take our first bites together.

To settle a stomach that has not had food for at least fifteen hours, we eat dates and drink tea. Then the full-scale dinner is served. People here eat on the floor on top of a mat. Although many traditionally eat with their hands, silverware has now become commonplace in the household. This meal at sundown is called "Iftaar."

Tonight's "Iftaar" was special. An employee of the guesthouse invited us to his house to visit his mother and grandmother, whom he lives with in Nayha-i-Aftom, or the "Seventh District" of Kabul. It was about a twenty-minute drive from the guesthouse. I bought biscuits and cookies from a local bakery as a gift to give to them.

Afghans have a long tradition of hospitality. My suspicion is that this has a lot to do with the amount of trade that has gone on historically, but that's just conjecture. We arrived at this neighborhood, which is on the side of a large hill on the outskirts of Kabul, and parked our car. The mud-brick houses in this area here are built very close together, and to get to the right one you have to walk through small alleys. This is highly representative of "old" Kabul.

The house was a small two-story structure. The mother, grandmother, and son live in the lower level, and the landlord lives above with his wife and children.

As soon as we arrived the preparations for "Iftaar" began. The mother came in and greeted us quickly and went back into the kitchen to work away. Slowly plate after plate was revealed of the most delicious Afghan food I've had while I've been here. There was *qabeli,* which is rice cooked in onion broth and served over lamb with carrots, raisins, and almonds on top. There was *mantu,* which are meat dumplings with yogurt, tomato sauce, and lentils drizzled on top. They had French fries, grapes, melons, and cauliflower. All of this is eaten with a piece of freshly baked Afghan bread, which is bought at the local bread-baker. There is one around every corner.

We ate by the light of a kerosene lantern, which spread a warm yellow glow about the entire room. Our host made constant appeals for us to eat more. This is a very Afghan tradition that they call *salaa.* It means "invite," and it's something every host does. It's taken me a while (my whole life) to learn how to respond, because sometimes these appeals can be very aggressive.

Being at his home, I understood a little of the devotion this boy has for his mother. He is the only man in the family, and as such, is the only breadwinner. His mother is getting on in years, probably around fifty, and he estimated his grandmother, who also lives with them, to be ninety-five. He is a twenty-eight-year-old guy paying the rent for his home, and feeding his family. That is not at all an uncommon circumstance in Afghanistan.

But he's such a mellow and relaxed guy. He's always cheerful and always has something funny to say. It's one of the things I enjoy most about seeing him every day.

After his mother was done in the kitchen, she came out to talk to us for a while. Dinner was done, and it was time for a few stories. She spoke the entire time about how much she wants her son to get married. He's a shy guy, and I could tell he was a bit embarrassed by the entire conversation. He looked at me once and said to everyone in Dari, "Masood and I have both decided to wait a few years before we get married."

After saying thank you and leaving, we stepped outside, and the crescent moon was there to greet us. I realized it was the first time I had seen it since I'd been in Kabul. Using our wandering flashlight we found our way back to our car, but I was somewhere else. Kabul at night is a sight to see.

There's a glow above the mountains, revealing their jagged silhoette and the lights scattered about them. There is the dust that's in the air, and the light of oncoming traffic that bounces on the rocks and lights up the dust flying through the air. The small stores that line the streets glow in various different colors and reveal the activity within. People are very active at night these days because of Ramadan, and it's interesting to see them riding their bikes in total darkness, and greeting one another in front of stores.

I did not want the drive home to end.

MARCH 26, 2005

To Remember What It Feels Like

Being here I've really had to think a lot about what it means for me to be Afghan. Arriving in Kabul many things happened that I could never have foreseen. It was not smooth for me, but more and more I'm beginning to understand where I fit into it all, and truly how I feel about being here.

More and more I feel like I'm home. I feel comfortable and happy.

Some people come to a country because they are fascinated by the history, or the culture. It's a desire to satisfy a curiosity about something outside of themselves. However interested they might be, they will never truly feel what is like to be an Afghan, or what it is like to have a part of your soul invested in this land.

Some in Kabul have high-paying jobs. Many people working with the United Nations or USAID or nongovernmental organizations have very high salaries that they would not be able to get if they were living in their respective countries.

I am here without a true salary (but well-funded nonetheless), but with the opportunity to experience what it's like to simply exist here. And it's just that, existence, that's my goal. Perhaps it's simple, but at the heart of this idea is the very thing that I believe makes me most Afghan.

Some might come and discuss their knowledge of Afghan history with others, or talk about some quantity of information they have about this country. I claim none of this, because it seems, so transparently, an exercise of insecurity. I know a fair bit about the history. It's something people fight about, and differing interpretations abound, especially among Afghans.

More than the quantity of knowledge that I'm gaining from this experience, the importance of being here lies in the everyday experiences I have.

Every day at 8:30 a.m. I get in the car with my driver, we shake hands, and we kiss each other on the cheek. I've taken to calling him *watandaar,* which means, "fellow countryman."

Our hello is thus:

> *Salaam*—"Peace, or hello"
> *Khub asten*—"Are you well?"
> *Che hal daren*—"How are you?"
> *Sahat-i-tan khub ast?*—"Is your health good?"
> *Khair-i-khairat?*—"Everything's good?"
> *Khana khairat ast?*—"How are things at home?"
> *Shao-i-tan khub gezasht?*—"Your night went well?"

It's a ritual that happens in the space of fifteen seconds, and yet embodied within these simple phrases is a kind of love that I've never felt before. It's not lust, or romantic love, or familial love. It's knowing that he cares about me and thinks about me, at times intensely. It's a love that is expressed possibly about fifty times a day to different people, and yet it feels the same. One would think that this would cheapen the phrases, but somehow the ritual retains its meaning.

Saying hello is such an intricate ritual here, and embodied within it is the knowledge that people care about what you think of them. They want you to like them, and they want you to feel loved.

While the ritual goes on, sometimes men will hold your hand in a strong and sometimes tender way. Men are not afraid of showing affection here, and will touch one another as a sign of brotherly intimacy.

To an American that's odd, and perhaps that's a testament to how alienated we are from one another in the States, and perhaps in the West in
general.

Some expats I've met are highly interested in how I feel about being an
Afghan American here: whether Afghans see me differently. They want to
know how Afghan I am and how American I am, as if I can quantify my
nationality or ethnicity. They want to know how well I speak Dari, and
will jump to judgment upon hearing me speak. They ask about my ethnic
background and whether I'm Muslim or not.

What I've learned from Afghans is that once I say hello, and they know
that my blood is Afghan, they never ask questions, or try to make distinc-
tions. They accept me and are happy to know me. They sit down with
me, and sometimes there is silence, but it's never uncomfortable. They
look me straight in the eyes and smile. Sometimes they ask questions
about Afghans abroad, or what it's like to be in America. They have questions about Western culture as well.

To the Westerner everything is about quantity. It's about distinguishing
one characteristic from another in order to ultimately pass judgment, or
analyze. In contrast with my experience with Afghans, it can seem cold
and calculating. Many Afghans say that the West seems "loveless." I
understand what they are saying.

Just existing here is my goal. It's not about being able to say how many
places in Afghanistan I've been to, and what historical fact I know about
this place or that place. It's not about some statistic I've calculated, or read
somewhere, or some piece of specific information that I have. It's also not
about proving how Afghan or how American I am to anyone because in
many ways I am an anomaly in both cultures.

No one will ever truly understand my connection to this land because I
have no twin, and that's a good thing. The fact that I am Afghan
American is just a statement of geography and does not say anything
about my emotions. Just being able to touch this land in my garden, plant
seeds in this earth that my mother and father took their first steps on, is
enough for me.

My driver tells me Afghan sayings every day. Hearing him tell them you begin to understand the importance of the oral tradition in Afghan culture. Things are just remembered as a part of a collective memory. Any experience I might be having will inevitably have already been described by an age-old axiom, which offers insight into the everyday.

This is what being Afghan is to me. It's just existing and not worrying about the details. It's looking across at a person, smiling, and asking how things at home are going. It's watching the leaves on the apple tree outside my window grow and seeing the yellow sun fade away in a moody Kabul sky. It's holding a man's hand as he tells you about his son's marriage. It's remembering a person you briefly met three years ago and remembering their name, and who they are.

Perhaps being a first-generation son of immigrants I do not fit neatly into categories listed on the standardized exam. I cannot buy my name on a mini–license plate in the States. And some real estate agents will always be rude to me after hearing my name. It's tough being somewhere where I am forever different, but I will say that I feel more different in America than I ever feel here in Kabul. In America we cling to the barriers we put between each other. We relish our private property and take pride in our blackness or whiteness. We gather in separate communities and define ourselves by our heritage, our religion, our skin color, our political affiliation, our class, our jobs, our sexuality, or the coast we live on.

We like to be able to define ourselves, and distinguish ourselves from everyone else.

Here I'm just an Afghan from Kabul sitting quietly in the backseat of a taxi cab, watching the city pass me by and hoping that I'll remember what it feels like to be beyond definition.

JUNE 20, 2005

Mullah Omar / Eleven Giggling Women

Ah yes, our old friend Mullah Omar, the ousted leader of the Taliban, reared his ugly head on a Kabul weekly recently as some in the government of Afghanistan considered giving him and Gulbadin Hekmatyar an amnesty agreement. It was an ill-fated consideration that was smartly and swiftly squashed by Karzai and his backers at the U.S. embassy.

The photograph of him is striking. It's a very direct image, clearly from a record of some sort. It looks like a passport photograph of the type that many Afghans carry around with them in case bureaucracy calls for it. He's blind in one mutilated eye, with a thick bushy beard, which makes for an interesting face.

It occurred to me that this photograph could prove to be very useful, so I scanned it.

Segue to giggling girls—

A few weeks back the women in charge of the new women's computer lab at Kabul University approached me. They asked me if it would be possible to teach them Photoshop so that they could teach it to their students.

I said of course, and waited for my host, the head of the Cultural Council at the university, to arrange it. He never did, despite my repeated requests, so I decided to take it into my own hands. In Afghanistan nothing gets done unless you do it yourself, and everyone will criticize you, and think that you're arrogant for taking things into your own hands. That's one thing that makes it so tough working here.

Two examples—

The administrators criticize me for sweeping and mopping my classroom, saying that there are people here with that job, and that I'm a guest. They say it will look bad that I'm mopping. It's a combination of hospitality, and making sure they don't look bad for not helping me. The building is filthy, and dust is a huge problem here. If I don't do it, no one will. It's a photographic laboratory. Dust and photography don't mix well. I've taken to coming after hours to clean so that they are not offended.

The electricity for the darkroom is supplied by a generator, the keys for which only two people had. Rather than just teaching me how to turn on the generator (a very easy affair), the professors kept the keys and had me asking them to turn it on before every class. On five separate days the two people just didn't show up, and we were left without electricity, so I gathered a bunch of my students in a mini-strike, and we all went to ask for the keys and learn how to turn it on. They resisted, but in the end gave it over and now I can turn on the electricity myself.

Back to the girls—

My girls' Photoshop class started on Saturday. We're going to be having class two days a week in their beautiful new computer laboratory. I asked for at least five women, and ten came, including a very sensitive young man from my photo classes that I invited who is an amazing photographer.

It's wonderful being around women. Growing up in America we take it for granted that we have social access to the other gender on a regular basis. In Afghanistan I've found it very frustrating always being around males. As much as I love my male students, and many are very talented, the boys are very privileged here. I can feel it in the way that they treat each other and talk to me. The women are polite, ask questions that make sense, and listen to what I say. I never have to repeat myself, which is such a wonderful change.

When I first came to Kabul I requested that there be a proportion of girls in my classes that reflected the proportion of girls in the School of Fine Arts. My offer was rejected because it "would somehow look bad if we specifically targeted girls."

Out of my first forty-five students I had one girl.

Well, "looking bad" aside, I decided to go after them myself. My time here is coming to an end, and I have about five weeks left to really make as much of a difference as I can. Every woman that I've seen in the building, I've asked to be a part of my classes, and as a result, rather than one, I now have seventeen. This has also resulted in constant dirty jokes about my new female students from some professors, but I think the professors whom I really respect are happy to see the change in attitude. Since I'm leaving, I'm in a privileged position where I can jeopardize my social standing by demanding more, and I'm taking advantage of it.

I've increased my course load by adding shorter workshops and decided to buy as many chemicals as I need to teach them all photography, or Photoshop. I've added one girls-only darkroom class, one girls-only Photoshop course, and one course for the talented male and female students that my hosts, the professors here, told me could not be a part of my class for their own political reasons. I have about seventy students total, and it seems to be growing as I invite more to attend.

I'm doing it on my own, and it feels great. It's the youth who want to get going, and learn more, and unfortunately a lot of stuffy old men are in charge who move very, very slowly and always prioritize territory before education.

I'm not sure if that's just a Kabul University thing, or more of a problem with bureaucratic academia in general, since this is my first time working at a large university. My sense is that it's a combination of both, and I feel very privileged to be able to work outside the system a bit.

The first Photoshop class—

Packed into the administrative offices of the girls' computer lab, we all sat around two computers as I introduced Photoshop to my new students.

Our first project was transforming a scanned image in order to better understand screen resolution versus print resolution, layers, levels, and curves.

You guessed it: our subject was my scan of Mullah Omar, in many ways the arch-nemesis of these educated women in positions of power at this new lab. When his picture came up on the screen, they giggled, and a hand went up:

"Professor Masood, is there any way in Photoshop that we can remove his beard? I think that would be a very useful skill."

By the end of class, we had made him pink, cloned in a good eye over his bad one, and lightened his beard a bit. He was beginning to look a bit more friendly, and I feel like the girls were enjoying seeing this transformation!

It was fun and weird, and I think they'll come back for more.

In the meantime, I've realized how useful this little image of Mullah Omar truly is, and how wonderful it is not relying on anyone but myself to get things done.

JULY 4, 2005

An Eden of That Dim Lake

Yesterday, I woke up and got ready to go to work. I drank some coffee, had some granola, and listened to music. One song that I listened to was an adaptation of an Edgar Allen Poe poem, "To the Lake," by Antony and the Johnsons:

> In youth's spring, it was my lot
> To haunt of the wide earth a spot
> To which I could not love the less
> So lovely was the loneliness
> Of a wild lake, with black rock bound
> And the tall trees that towered around
> But when the night had thrown her pall
> Upon that spot as upon all
> And the wind would pass me by
> In its stilly melody
> My infant spirit would awake
> To the terror of the lone lake
> Yet that terror was not fright
> But a tremulous delight
> And a feeling undefined
> Springing from a darkened mind
> Death was in that poisoned wave
> And in its gulf a fitting grave
> For him who thence could solace bring
> To his dark imagining
> Whose wildering thought could even make
> An Eden of that dim lake

My dim lake has been Kabul, and at times it did feel like an Eden. There were moments here that I would sit on our balcony and think to myself how it would be fitting for me to die here someday and be buried in this soil.

The thought of letting go of everything that I love in New York flooded my mind when I first came because of how much of a sense of purpose I felt here. One of the more remarkable aspects of this journey has been going from that extreme to where I am now. Somewhere in my mind I always knew that I'd eventually have to make a choice between New York and Kabul, and that certain opportunities would present themselves that would make either a viable option.

In the end, I know now more than ever that I'm a New Yorker. And as much as this test of altruism, and question of identity, has been a necessary part of my life, I realize that this path here in Kabul is not the one I want my life to take. Perhaps all questions of identity raise more questions than they answer, and perhaps ultimately the quest leaves us with nothing but an understanding of how important our humanity is over anything else.

Last night, I sat with the employees of the house next door. One of them is very fond of me and constantly brags about me in a way that makes me blush. He was also telling me jokes to make me laugh. He says he tries to laugh at least once every two weeks. We also talked for a few hours about the differences between Afghanistan and the West, a common conversation topic.

The conversation, and my own oddities, my answers to their cultural questions about the West, made me realize something . . . and perhaps this has been the biggest and best realization I've had so far:

I'm just as much of an eccentric here as I've always been everywhere that I've lived, and there's no way I can suppress that, nor would I ever want to. But I've had to try here in Kabul. That's the major reason I moved to New York in the first place, and that's why I'm going back. Eccentricity is embraced there, and I feel like exploring that is how I'm going to grow as a human being and learn to really express myself in the way that I was meant to.

These months have made me more sure about who I am than I've ever been in my life, and that, along with all the memories, is what I'll take back with me.

Going back to yesterday morning. After I listened to the song over and over again, I got into my bed and stared at the ceiling. A housemate knocked on the door, opened it, saw me, and asked me what I was doing:

It just came out, surfacing like the instinct of a whale determined to beach itself but not fully understanding why. I told him I would be leaving Kabul on Friday and that I had come to this decision this morning while lying in bed.

Classes officially end on Thursday, and finals begin. All of my students have expressed an inability to attend during finals, so it doesn't make sense for me to stay any longer. I miss my home and the people I love very dearly in New York. My project has been successful, and my usefulness has plateaued. This darkroom and my students have been a gift for these months, but it wasn't a gift solely meant for me. It was a gift for the university, and at some point it needs to be handed over. It's a difficult but necessary final step in this project.

I've been training professors on how to use the facilities for the last five weeks, so my hope is that they know enough to carry on my duties. My feelings about the future of the photography courses are guarded. Several professors have told me that they will not be able to teach the number of students that I've taught. I was not able to secure a budget from the university. The professional photographers I tried to get hired to be part of the Department of Photography were not hired for one reason or another (I believe ethnicity played a role in at least one of their cases). The official Department of Photography was never created, even though it was planned for by all parties. I tried so hard to diplomatically convince them that it was possible and necessary to create a department, and it was, but there was no one on my side. I was alone. For now photography is a part of the Department of Graphic Design, and as much as I disagree with that, I have to remind myself that this is a gift. It has no conditions. If it had conditions, perhaps we'd be crossing the line into colonialism.

Besides the bureaucratic pitfalls I ran into, the actual work we did in that darkroom made a huge impact on the lives of about seventy students. It is absolutely the most beautiful and best-equipped darkroom in Afghanistan. The construction employed fifteen people for about forty-five days. I was able to recruit female students on my own, and I think I was able to get a lot of people very excited about photography. Seeing and talking to them every day renewed and strengthened my faith in art and in the talent here in Afghanistan. It also makes me feel very good about the future.

Perhaps I've stepped on a few toes in trying my best to encourage bureaucratic changes at the Faculty of Fine Arts, but in the end I think the seeds have been planted for very radical changes in the future, and perhaps, from my position, that's the best I could hope for.

Many in the older generation of Afghans in the arts don't consider photography an art form at all, and that was definitely a factor in their dismissal of our goal to start a department. Many just use photographs as source material for their drawings, but don't see the value in photographs in and of themselves. That said, I have many students who really get it, who were with me every week and saw the possibilities. People can spend their lives guarding their bureaucratic territory, but in the end it's the will of the students that will shape how things change, and my humble hope is that I influenced that will, if even just a little bit.

So this is my last week here. It's an abrupt end to a project that has taken almost three years to finish, and hopefully it will go on in some form, but for now my current job is done, and it all feels wonderful.

If you're in New York, please tell her I'll be back soon.

GAZELLE SAMIZAY

In this blog about her trip back to Kabul with her family, Samizay explores the ways an Afghan woman must negotiate her journey through Afghanistan. Gender issues are addressed with light, grace, and humor.

Gazelle Speaks

TUESDAY, SEPTEMBER 26, 2006

In Two days I'll Be Halfway around the World!

Wow. In less than twenty-four hours I will be on a plane to India and then Afghanistan. I'm not sure what to think or do, so I'm just going to go with the flow! No use stressing! I'll be in each country for one week between September 28th and October 14th, and I'll do my best to update this blog so you know what's going on.

You may ask WHY!? Aside from the adventure of it, I'm going to start on a project called *Resonance,* which will include the stories and photos of Afghan women and women around the world. I'll keep you posted on the progress of this on *Resonance* and I welcome any suggestions/participation anyone may have to offer!

I'm excited, scared, and curious all at once. Part of me expects my trip to be like my last one in March 2005, while part of me knows it's going to be different. Incidentally, this will be the twenty-five-year anniversary since my family originally left the country during the Soviet invasion. Funny how things work out like that. My sister and dad will be going with me on this trip, and this will be Wazhma's first time back to Afghanistan since we left when she was seven. I'm definitely anxious to see her reactions and how her old memories come to terms with this "new" country.

TUESDAY, OCTOBER 03, 2006

Afghan Gardens

Yesterday we went to the Immigration Office to take care of Wazhma's letter that would give her permission to be in Afghanistan. It was a small cramped office filled with a lot of sweaty men all trying to crowd to the front window. As my dad squeezed a shoulder in to get to the front, I noticed how tight his pants were in comparison to all the other men, who were wearing the traditional *paron-e tomban* (loose pants and long loose top). Wazhma and I were going to pass out from the smell of B.O., and she kept her eyes safely focused on the design of my top.

We got shifted from one line to another, and my dad started to get impatient. I remembered John and me returning our cheap IKEA stools, which were impossible to put together correctly despite their cute diagrams with the bubble man. IKEA had a number system. You took a number, then sat down and waited for your number to be called. I thought, wow, how that simple number machine would revolutionize the Immigration Office and other such offices over here. I wondered how a number system would be received here. Would people use it? Like it? Or just keep crowding forward?

My dad finally made it to the front of the line and was given a piece of paper that would give us permission to go to another building in the same complex. However, they only allowed two people in—my dad and my sister. Mustafa (our driver/cousin; he is my half cousin's half brother) and I had to wait behind. I thought, "That's fine, I don't want to wait in a crowded line anyway. The weather is nice out here." But they wouldn't let us wait outside for security reasons. So back into the sweaty man sandwich we went. The smell was killing me, and I made my way toward the entrance, where I could see the light of day and get a breath of fresh air. After some time the security man took some pity on me and told me to stand on the other side of the door—man free.

Bored, I watched security search all the people coming in. They had an x-ray machine, but they didn't use it. Maybe it was broken. Instead they searched the bags. Well sometimes they did, and sometimes they didn't. That made me a bit nervous. We were standing in an official building (higher chance of being targeted), and the security was so-so. I was anxious for Wazhma and my dad to return as my overactive imagination went wild with dreams of bombs and crazies. My imagination is not doing me any good on this trip.

To my surprise, they returned after a half hour. I thought the process might take all day given the way things work here. Even in the U.S. you would wait months to get a letter like that with all the bureaucracy. It was good my dad went with her (he originally wasn't going to come) because apparently only your husband or father can give you legitimacy. Hurrah! Wazhma is now officially Afghan ;).

After the Immigration Office we did a little shopping near Chicken Street, but ended up staying in the first shop we entered, which had colorful rugs and dresses hanging in the window. There were two young guys running the shop—probably teenagers. I wondered if they went to school and kicked myself later for not asking. We ended up buying all sorts of colorful shirts, and I got two really incredible dresses. It was a fun experience, mainly because the boys were really cute, and they were definitely lying. It was easy to tell they were lying because they were so young. We called them out on it a few times but didn't bargain too much because we wanted to give them the money. At the end the older boy gave my sister and me an embroidered wallet as a gift. I think he felt guilty because he knew he had made a killing.

After shopping we headed back home, and our driver talked about the suicide bombing that I mentioned before. It's really not fair because the people here want security, but it's just a few cuckoos that are ruining it for everyone else. I understand these suicide bombers are frustrated with the way things are going here, and they have every reason to be. But I don't believe violence solves anything. no matter what side you're on.

Later that day my uncle took us on a tour, and we went to Babur's Gardens, which I had visited a year and a half ago. They had made much more progress in renovating the place. There were rosebushes, grass, and the walls had been fixed with beautiful rock work. It was beautiful and peaceful there. The sun was bright and the atmosphere a hazy blue. Behind the gardens you could see all the houses climbing up the steep mountain. I was sad to see that the old tree that had been here since Babur's time (thirteenth or fourteenth century) that I had photographed last time had been cut down or "severely pruned." But I guess releasing the old makes way for the new.

On our way to Chehel Setun (Forty Pillars) I saw many signs for boxing gyms featuring Arnold Swarzenegger and other buff men. I have a totally different association with Arnold now that he's the governor of California. (By the way, did you know that a Republican that murdered someone is now running for office in Arizona? GROSS!). Anywho, my favorite painting depicted a black man with a pirate's eye patch on. This was the first image of a black person I had seen here.

My uncle's wife and Mustafa were commenting on how so many more people live in this area, but how it still didn't have electricity. The park hadn't been renovated; the garden was dry and the castle in shambles. Unlike Babur's Gardens, which had an entrance fee of twenty afghanis, there were lots of men and children here hanging out and playing. I saw one old man in the corner doing some sort of exercises. Our SUV barely made it up the steep windy road that led to the castle.

There were all sorts of little kids, dirty and covered in dust, playing among the rubble of the castle, which concerned me a little. It was nice to hear their laughter, but it seemed like they could easily get hurt. From this vantage point we could see across the gardens and across Kabul. Next to the castle was an old restaurant riddled with bullet holes. I could see a person through one of the bombed-out walls.

As we drove away from Chehel Setun, I saw a group of men and boys swarming together like a hive of bees. In the center were two men fighting, and everyone came to watch—sad. In my daydreams I imagined myself the only woman walking through the crowd and breaking up the fight. Funny, huh?! Our driver stopped so I could take a picture, when the car behind us hit us. No one was hurt—just a love tap. Our driver got out and talked to the guy. He said he was watching the fight, he hit us, and then hit the brakes. There wasn't any damage, and we all went on our way. I like this system much better than our silly insurance system in the States.

After that we went home, and Wazhma and I discussed the state of this place. The fact that the area around Babur's Gardens still didn't have electricity put its renovation into question. Yes, it's a beautiful place, and a piece of history, but I wonder if it's a good idea to put all this money into the past rather than into the present: water, electricity, security . . . It would be nice if Babur's Gardens didn't have an entrance fee so that all Afghans could go there and enjoy the peace and quiet. Seeing as how full the free and unrenovated Chehel Setun space was, Babur's Gardens would serve as an important refuge from the chaos of Kabul.

Wazhma and I are thinking of raising money and finding grants to make a school with solar panels here. My dad said the technology is very expensive, but we thought once implemented, it could be very useful as it would provide electricity not just for the school but the whole community. I think in the U.S. there are laws prohibiting the sharing of electricity (dumb), but here that wouldn't be a problem. I'm going to ask my friends Tom and Mark and other architect friends about the possibility of green architecture and renewable energy in Afghanistan. Who knows, maybe this could serve as a prototype for the U.S. (What a concept! The U.S. learning from other models?!)

WEDNESDAY, OCTOBER 04, 2006

Gazelle the Tomboy

The night before last my cousins came over with their kids. It's a good form of birth control to see a room full of wandering, crying children. It was a little bit awkward in the beginning because I hadn't seen them in a year and a half. I brought some pictures of my aunts and uncles in the U.S. and showed them to them. I also had some pictures of John, which I was reluctant to bring, but I knew I had to be honest about what my life was like. They were like, who's that "khorijee" (foreigner)? You're engaged to a khorijee? There weren't enough Afghans for you to choose from?

The next day we went to Salang with a few of my cousins, my aunt, and my uncle's wife, Salma. As we drove through the north end of Kabul, Salma showed me the area where she and her family lived before selling their house and fleeing to Iran in '96. She said it was such a wonderful area—lots of shops and things to do.

As we exited Kabul I saw tons of small houses climbing up the mountains like small little matchboxes staggering up the hill. Apparently this is where all the poor live. Kabul is surrounded by mountains, and most of the country seems like a series of various mountain chains. My uncle's wife imagined how difficult it must be for these people to go back and forth to their houses during the winter when the mountains are full of snow. Just two minutes further down the road were huge mansions, built in the style of Pakistani houses—some were completed, and some were just being built. I asked who lived in these, and apparently they are all owned by one person. My cousin, Mustafa, explained that the owner may have four wives who then have five children that marry and have five kids themselves . . . the point is that all these houses belong to one family. These houses are large and luxurious by U.S. standards, so you can imagine what a contrast it is to see these in Afghanistan where people live in tents, bombed-out buildings, or worn-down mud-walled dwellings.

As we continued on, my aunt described how green this area is during the spring. She loves greenery and misses it tremendously. She kept after us about how we came during the month of Ramadan during winter. If we had come during the summer we could have gone to the river and had a picnic and eaten melon.

We passed some schools, and my aunt explained that all the buildings are new. The Taliban burned everything that was here before. They even burned cows and sheep alive, and their skeletons remain as proof. Apparently they have burned 150 schools, and Karzai says for each school they burn they will build another one.

As we drove along, the sun started to bake me, and I wished I hadn't worn my mom's green silk "paron" that was from the old days. It was very windy in the countryside, and I saw girls walking around the road with scarves wrapped around their mouths to block dirt out.

Driving in Afghanistan is like driving in *The Italian Job*. Here I was worried about suicide bombers, when really driving in a car is probably a higher threat to my life. There are no set rules, it seems. For the most part people drive on the right side of the road, but there is an imaginary middle lane that people use to pass other cars whenever they can. There is always a race to pass the next car, and the game of chicken is the norm, not an exception. This was especially nervewracking as we made it closer to Salang, where the road winds around the mountains. First there is the fear of getting hit by a car (or bus) winding around the corner, and then there is the fear that your car won't make it up the hill.

Once we neared the river we stopped alongside the road. There were houses built upon the hill overlooking the river and tons of goats running around. My aunt and Salma sat by the river to chat while the boys and I went exploring. We crossed the river by traversing a bridge that was made with scrap pieces of metal, wood, and other materials. I tried not to look down too much. The river was beautiful. The crisp air was a nice reprise from the diesel- and dust-filled drive. I started to get excited as we explored the area, and my tomboy side started to come out again. It was me and the boys, as it always had been when I was a kid. We came across another bridge, and my cousin turned to me and asked if I could cross it. "Of course!" I said. I'm a bit competitive when it comes to men. I always have to prove I can do whatever they can, if not more. When we got to the bridge I started to regret my need to prove myself as a more than capable woman, as this bridge was not as complete as the last. It was very narrow, and at the end there was as HUGE gap—a gap much bigger than I was comfortable with. My cousin went before me, and though I had denied his hand of help walking down the mountain (I could walk down the mountain just fine, thank you very much!), I had to give in this time. I did not want to cross that bridge! But I took his hand and made it across. Phew!

I saw some goats walking up the steep rock face, wondering how they could do it. One of my cousins jumped on a rock and started washing his face in the water. It looked nice, but the word "giardia" kept me from doing the same. It felt good enclosed between the rock walls, the water, and the mountains. I felt like I could breathe and just be. No worries about suicide bombers, no overactive imagination of what does so-and-so think of me, is my scarf on properly, etc., etc. Just a few minutes of being me. Tomboy Gazelle. Screw the scarf. Though I must say it's much more liberal here than when I went to Iran in 2001. After a few minutes of enjoying the atmosphere we decided to head back. Who knows where the others were. We passed by some more goats chillin' in the shade of the trees and ran into some shy schoolgirls. They stood there and stared at us as we walked back. It was particularly hard not to return the stare of the girl with the blue eyes. I tried taking their picture, they were so cute, but they ran.

After that we went farther up the river and stopped. This time Wazhma and I followed our cousins' lead and took our socks off and put our feet in the cold water. We couldn't stay long, but it was really nice to see a different part of Afghanistan.

Mustafa played "chicken" all the way home, so it was an interesting ride. By the time we got home I was feeling pretty sick from the diesel, dust, and bumpiness of the road, but there wasn't much time to rest as we headed to a school that my dad's cousin is running. They teach English and computer skills. They were having a ceremony of sorts, and we walked in while one of the students was giving a speech in English about the importance of learning English and computer skills in the twenty-first century. It was nice to hear the kids talk, and I was very proud of them for being in school. We also watched a little video about my dad's cousin's relief work. Apparently he had come to deliver food and clothing when all the other aid organizations pulled out. He had to come as a "journalist" because they weren't allowing aid workers in because it was dangerous. He himself had some very close calls with the Taliban. He founded a nonprofit by the name of Afghan Relief Organization based out of Los Angeles: www.afghanrelief.com. I'm thinking about setting up some kind of online communication between this school and a school in the U.S.

After going to the school we headed to my aunt's house for dinner. We were a little bit late, and on the way there I saw some soldiers breaking their fast at a food stand. We turned off the main road down a bumpy dirt alley. Their home consisted of a walled courtyard made of mud. In the front were some propane stoves boiling water for tea.

They held a propane lamp to shine the way to the living room, which had red rugs across the floor and floor cushions. It's not typical for Afghan homes to have chairs and tables. Instead we all sat around the floor on the cushions. I sat next to my cousin's mother-in-law, who had bright red hair (probably from henna) and twinkling eyes. She was spunky with a good sense of humor.

They turned the generator on and screwed a lightbulb in to provide light. They made tons of food and kept feeding us until we were stuffed. The melon was particularly sweet. Mustafa's fiance's family lives in the adjacent room. If you saw her family, you would think they were Brittish or Swedish. They have blond hair, super-fair skin (John, they make you look tan ;), rosy cheeks, and blue eyes. Mustafa's sister's child is also blond and blue-eyed. It was funny because I was always surprised when they spoke Dari. I half expected some European language to come out of their mouths since they were so fair.

It was nice seeing all my cousins together, telling stories. Though they don't have much in the way of money, they are all together and take care of each other, which is very endearing to see.

Unfortunately we didn't stay too long because my dad was tired from his trip to Jalalabad. I was sad to leave. I was having a good time and enjoying the company. I think I was finally starting to get used to things here and getting comfortable. On our way home we drove past a few mosques that were basically one mud room. There were men outside praying in the dark. On the opposite side was a small stand that was plastered with colorful images of women. They almost looked like baseball trading cards. I wonder if they trade cards of women.

THURSDAY, OCTOBER 05, 2006

Bargaining

We decided to go shopping in Chicken Street, which is where all the antiques are sold. Well . . . supposedly they are antiques. Sometimes they purposely make things look old so they can yield antique prices. A "fifty-year-old carpet" can easily be a five-week-old carpet run under the tires of a car fifty times.

Bargaining is a necessity here, especially if you're a foreigner, which made things interesting considering that neither Wazhma nor I like to bargain. We first went into a shop run by a friend of my uncle's. As my uncle's niece, I felt obligated to buy something, but there wasn't anything that caught my eye, and we quickly left the awkwardness. We walked further down the street through pairs of men with sideways glances and furtive stares. I had my protective bubble turned on, so I didn't notice rude comments such as the "have you no shame" my sister later mentioned to me. Ignorance is bliss, right?

I was drawn to one particular shop that had bright blue lapis pieces lined along the window. Inside was an old man with a white cap and light brown eyes—clear like tea. Even in the waning light (the electricity was out of course) his jewelry glittered, and the strong colors were drawing me in. I felt myself retract into my shy six-year-old self. "Damn it!" I thought. "Not again!" I couldn't even ask the prices, I was so shy, and remembered my mom prodding me: "Just ask!" I glanced at my sister, hoping she would start, but my otherwise chatty sister was conveniently silent. After ten minutes of circling the store, knowing exactly what I wanted, I started the negotiations. I'm sure the old man made a killing, but somehow I could tell from his eyes that he had a hard time ripping me off. After all, he himself had two daughters.

A beggar child came to the door, dirty, with hair tousled about. The shopkeeper told him to go away and lamented about all the beggar kids in this area.

"It's hard for people like us not to feel bad and give money, but it teaches them the wrong thing. They should be in school or learning skills for work, not begging," he said.

I liked this man. He had a sweet face and good philosophy. I took his picture as he told me both his parents and grandparents were jewelers and he had learned his trade from a very young age.

The next shop we went into was run by a handsome man about my age. By this point I had gotten warmed up, and the shy six-year-old went to bed. I remembered my mom and her bargaining skills and wished she was here to charm the shopkeepers with her infectious laugh and beautiful eyes. I knew I had to up the ante and make my momma proud :).

A few stone pendants etched with gazelles caught my eye. Wazh wanted one with a lion on it, but the shopkeeper said he was all out. Still he tried looking for one, trying to pass a horse off as a lion and a camel for a gazelle! We had some good laughs about that. In the end I was able to bargain with him for a good price. The poor guy was outnumbered by female strength and had difficulties combating our bargaining. He would tell my sister the price, and I would ask for less. Meanwhile my uncle's wife was clamoring in the background about good prices in her sweet and high-pitched voice. We finally set on a price, and I gave him a one-hundred-dollar bill. He said, "Ohhhh this is so old . . . and the corner is torn!"

Apparently Afghanis are deducted for each blemish on a bill. This torn corner would cost him about twenty afghanis. Wazhma managed to find a cleaner Benjamin, and the shopkeeper was happy but looked somewhat dumbstruck by our recent transaction.

Satisfied by our shopping, we decided it was time to go home, and we called someone to pick us up. The problem was we'd have to wait another fifteen or twenty minutes before the driver came. I wanted to go into more shops rather than waiting on the street, but Wazh felt guilty because it was almost time for the shopkeepers to break their fast, so we waited on the corner. Bad idea.

An old beggar man on crutches asked for money with his raspy voice, but I didn't have any small bills to give him. Plus when you give to one they all come out of the woodwork and swarm you. I stood there uncomfortably, and a small boy selling mini-Qurans approached me. I wasn't quick enough, and the bastard slipped one into my hand. This is the game they play. I tried giving it back, and he backed away, giving me the most mournful look—his eyes were like a black hole sucking my energy. Finally I convinced Wazhma and Salma to go into the shop and escape. The boy lingered by the doorway, and I saw some new boys sitting a few feet away. I found some money and called the boy in, trying not to call the attention of the others. What had started as a happy shopping day ended in us feeling drained. It is emotionally draining seeing the poor and not knowing what to do about it. So you give them money one day. Will that really solve anything or keep them in a cycle of begging?

After we got home, my dad decided he wanted to have a party and invited friends over and some musicians. One was a tabla player, and one played harmunia, which looks like an accordion but sits on the floor like a piano. Many of these friends were expats working in Afghanistan. They represented Los Angeles, Virginia, and Germany, and a generation lost, finding its way. They didn't belong to the West, and they didn't belong to the East. They certainly don't belong in the new generation of Kabulites who are not familiar with the education, cleanliness, and openness of Kabul's yesteryear. Old Ahmed Zahir tunes filled the house as they chimed in and danced one by one. Meanwhile my dad was snoozing on the chair—still recovering from jetlag. But the man sitting next to him made sure my dad's tea did not go to waste. I was reminded of an old black and white picture my dad has hanging in his office at WSU in little ole Pullman. He is sitting cross-legged on rugs with his friend in a smoky haze. It looks like they're having a party, similar to this one. I felt like I was being warped back into that time—a time that no longer exists, but somehow does among all the "Afghans" of that generation.

FRIDAY, OCTOBER 06, 2006

Caged Birds

The next day was Friday—a holiday in Afghanistan. They only have one day off here. My dad wanted to buy some curtains and take us to "bird street." "You should wear some conservative clothes, 'cause we're going to Old Town," he said. Wazh and I looked at the clothes we were wearing and then at each other. We were wearing our conservative clothes! Did he want us to wear a burqa or something?!

Old Town was an interesting experience, mainly because we were the center of attention. Everywhere we went men were staring at us, and you could hear people talking about the "foreigners." I was so tired of hearing the whispering I almost wanted to shout out and formally announce ourselves to put an end to the curious stares and questions:

"My name is Gazelle Samizay. Yes, we are foreigners, but we are not dumb, and we can understand what you're saying. We live in the U.S. I am a woman—have you ever seen one before? I don't wear a burqa 'cause I don't want to. I am educated, and I could kick your ass if I wanted to, so bug off!" That was the soliloquy going on in my head. But the shy six-year-old didn't think unleashing her older feminist "I'm going to kick your ass" sister was appropriate.

On the corner was a stall full of white fluffy cotton being used to stuff cushions. It was early morning, and the sun was glowing. It was perfect picture-taking time, but I was so afraid that if I stopped to take pictures I'd lose my dad that I passed up the opportunity.

We continued walking through the alley and entered a rundown concrete building that housed several fabric shops. The only light available was that which was coming through the courtyard. We stopped at one fabric seller who was busy with two burqa-clad women requesting that he give them more change back. Unfortunately my dad was being indecisive about his fabrics, and we continued out of the building onto the street, where there were more eyes to peel the skin off my body. It is interesting how you can feel someone's stare. Now imagine one hundred pairs of eyes staring at you! And they're not subtle about it either. At one point I almost burst out laughing because this fat man saw us, and he seemed to particularly notice Wazhma. He slowed down and tried to make himself as big as he could so that he would run into us, but we managed to pass him without any contact.

My dad finally went back to the original fabric seller to buy his fabrics, and the fabric seller carried the large roll of fabric to our small white Toyota. As we walked I noticed how dirty and smelly Old Town was. It smelled like a toilet. After dropping off the fabric we walked toward "bird street." Bird street was a tight alleyway packed to the brim with men, even though today was a holiday. I shuddered, imagining it on a weekday. It reminded me a lot of the souks in Morocco, which are easy to lose yourself in without a guide. Too bad I was too busy keeping my eyes to myself and my invisible walls of protection up to really take in the sights around me. Here the men sandwich was worse than in the Immigration Office, and these men were having a heyday at the sight of Wazhma and me. Teasing, staring, laughing. I wanted to get out of there as soon as possible.

On either side of me, past the crowds of jeering men, were hundreds of birds caged in small spaces. I saw about ten pigeons trapped in a 1'x 2' cage. They could barely crawl over each other, let alone spread their wings—not unlike how I was feeling at that moment. I wanted to take the birds and run away. Further down the alley was a large owl cowering in a cage while small boys poked their fingers through the cage in awe. I don't believe in caged animals. I think they should be enjoyed in their natural habitat. If we cage animals, is caging women such a long shot?

We finally got to the end of bird street, and my sister said, "Let's get out of here!" My dad said, "You know, I didn't think about it, but do you think we could get bird flu here?" "Yes!" my sister exclaimed angrily. "I was thinking that the whole way!" "Great," I thought. I wish someone had clued me into the bird-flu warning earlier so I could have at least covered my mouth or something. With the way these animals are caged, it seems very likely that any disease could manifest itself here.

After getting out of bird street, we headed to an old run-down tomb overlooking Kabul. The space, quiet, and kite flying put me at ease. Small squares dotted the sky as little boys chased runaway kites. It's funny the things that stick with you. Whenever I see a kite I'm transported to the beach along the Oregon coast. I was seven, and my family went to the Oregon coast with the Bartuskas, some family friends (whom, incidentally, my parents met in Afghanistan when they were on a Fulbright). They had a nice blue kite, and they were so nice they said I could fly it. One of them held the spool and told me to take the head of the kite to let out the spool of string. I was so excited I went running, but I ran too far, and the head of the kite broke from its string. I was devastated. The Bartuskas were very nice about it and said it was no problem, but I felt SO bad that I broke these wonderful people's kite and that I couldn't play with the kite anymore. Now that I think of it, I don't think I've ever flown a kite. I should buy one when I go home.

My uncle tried to shoo away the circle of boys staring at us in awe like animals at the zoo. I guess my name is Gazelle. No amount of shooing worked, and we hopped in the car to head home. As we headed back down the road a guy alongside the road stared hard at Wazhma. "It's as if they've never seen a woman before!" exclaimed Wazhma, at her wits' end. My uncle and dad chuckled in their signature Samizay laugh. I wondered if they really get what it's like to be a woman. My sister said, "Well, I guess they haven't seen a woman, considering the ratio of men to women on the street is fifty to one." I think it's more like three hundred to one.

When we got home, I read my *Lonely Planet India*. It was saying that in India one woman is raped every thirty minutes, but that in the U.S. a woman is raped every TWO minutes! I can see that women have a long way to go.

Appendix: Themes Index

ARRIVAL

"The Irony of Life and the Survival of the American Dream,"
Asadulla Abubakr   106

"A Penny," Ariana Delawari   154

"Awaiting My Return," Naheed Elyasi   32

"Hope Street," Bismillah Iqbal   174

"The Odyssey of Coming to America," Rameen Javid Moshref   116

"Neptune Avenue," Zohra Saed   28

"Coming to America, 1966," Maliha Zulfacar   85

DISPLACEMENT

"The Irony of Life and the Survival of the American Dream"
Asadulla Abubakr   106

"Dreaming in Dari," Mir Tamim Ansary   43

"Demystified Calamity," Qais Arsala   17

"Horns of the Tiger," Qais Arsala   17

"Placebo," Qais Arsala   18

"A Penny," Ariana Delawari   154

"As I Watch," Donia Gobar   9

"Time Passes in Colorado", Masood Kamandy   7

"The Enemy," Nadia Maiwandi   128

"Journey to Afghanistan, Septemember 2002," Tareq Mirza   145

"Home," Aman Mojadidi   93

"What Can One Say about Living in Kabul?" Aman Mojadidi   36

"Marriage to Azim," Sedika Mojadidi   3

"The Odyssey of Coming to America," Rameen Javid Moshref   116

"The Things They Wait For," Sahar Muradi   125

"Voting in Afghanistan," Homira Nassery   161

"Family Album," Zohra Saed   29

"Identity Card," Wali Shaaker   50

"Coming to America, 1966," Maliha Zulfacar   85

FAMILY

"The Irony of Life and the Survival of the American Dream,"
    Asadulla Abubakr   106
"My Earliest Memories," Wajma Ahmady   73
"What? You Never . . . ," Wajma Ahmady   39
"age three at grandpa's funeral," Jessamyn Ansary   15
"Dreaming in Dari," Mir Tamim Ansary   43
"Stand-Up Comedy," Fahim Anwar   140
"You Proved Me Wrong," Awista Ayub   201
"An Old Garden," Farhad Azad   56
"A Penny," Ariana Delawari   154
"The Girl with the Green Eyes," Yasmine Delawari Johnson   103
"Living on a Prayer," Naheed Elyasi   66
"Pick Me, Please!" Nahid Fattahi   13
"Aya," Donia Gobar   59
"Hope Street," Bismillah Iqbal   174
"Dispatch from Kabul," Masood Kamandy   209
"Time Passes in Colorado," Masood Kamandy   7
"Journey to Afghanistan, September 2002," Tareq Mirza   145
"Marriage to Azim," Sedika Mojadidi   3
"The Odyssey of Coming to America," Rameen Javid Moshref   116
"Exile, or My Father's Elbow," Sahar Muradi   21
"Of My Mother," Sahar Muradi   19
"The Things They Wait for," Sahar Muradi   125
"Family Album," Zohra Saed   29
"Neptune Avenue," Zohra Saed   28
"A Week Later," Zohra Saed   135
"The Cab Driver's Daughter," Waheeda Samady   171
"Gazelle Speaks," Gazelle Samizay   234
"My Mother," Khalida Sethi   113
"Daughter of the Imam: From Kandahar to Queens," Afifa Yusufi   181
"Coming to America, 1966," Maliha Zulfacar   85

HYBRIDITY

"What? You Never . . . ," Wajma Ahmady   39
"Stand-Up Comedy," Fahim Anwar   140
"Cheshme Siah Daree," Ariana Delawari   26
"Oh la Lo," Ariana Delawari   25

"Awaiting My Return," Naheed Elyasi 32
"Hope Street," Bismillah Iqbal 174
"Dispatch from Kabul," Masood Kamandy 209
"The Enemy," Nadia Maiwandi 128
"Journey to Afghanistan, Sептember 2002," Tareq Mirza 145
"The Things They Wait For," Sahar Muradi 125
"Voting in Afghanistan," Homira Nassery 161
"Neptune Avenue," Zohra Saed 28
"Gazelle Speaks," Gazelle Samizay 234
"My Mother," Khalida Sethi 113

IDENTITY AND SELF-MAKING

"The Irony of Life and the Survival of the American Dream,"
 Asadulla Abubakr 106
"My Earliest Memories," Wajma Ahmady 73
"What? You Never . . . ," Wajma Ahmady 39
"The Invention," Jessamyn Ansary 16
"Dreaming in Dari," Mir Tamim Ansary 43
"Stand-Up Comedy," Fahim Anwar 140
"Like a Rabbit Caught in the Spotlight," Nushin Arbabzadah 70
"Horns of the Tiger," Qais Arsala 17
"My Thoughts . . . If You Don't Mind," Yalda Asmatey 34
"You Proved Me Wrong," Awista Ayub 201
"A Penny," Ariana Delawari 154
"The Girl with the Green Eyes," Yasmine Delawari Johnson 103
"The Critic," Mariam Ebrat 190
"Awaiting My Return," Naheed Elyasi 32
"Living on a Prayer," Naheed Elyasi 66
"Hope Street," Bismillah Iqbal 174
"Dispatch from Kabul," Masood Kamandy 209
"Afghan Awakening," Halima Kazem 165
"The Enemy," Nadia Maiwandi 128
"Journey to Afghanistan, Sептember 2002," Tareq Mirza 145
"What Can One Say about Living in Kabul?" Aman Mojadidi 36
"Marriage to Azim," Sedika Mojadidi 3
"The Odyssey of Coming to America," Rameen Javid Moshref 116
"Who the Hell is the Foreigner?!" Rameen Javid Moshref 121
"Exile, or My Father's Elbow," Sahar Muradi 21

"Of My Mother," Sahar Muradi   19
"The Things They Wait For," Sahar Muradi   125
"Voting in Afghanistan," Homira Nassery   161
"Neptune Avenue," Zohra Saed   28
"A Week Later," Zohra Saed   135
"The Cab Driver's Daughter," Waheeda Samady   171
"Gazelle Speaks," Gazelle Samizay   234
"*Astagfurillah* (God Forbid!)" Khalida Sethi   23
"My Mother," Khalida Sethi   113
"Identity Card," Wali Shaaker   50
"Daughter of the Imam: From Kandahar to Queens," Afifa Yusufi   181
"Coming to America, 1966," Maliha Zulfacar   85

MEMORY

"The Irony of Life and the Survival of the American Dream,"
    Asadulla Abubakr   106
"Memories from Kabul's Playing Fields," Farhad Ahad   197
"My Earliest Memories," Wajma Ahmady   73
"What? You Never . . . ," Wajma Ahmady   39
"An Old Garden," Farhad Azad   56
"A Penny," Ariana Delawari   154
"Marriage to Azim," Sedika Mojadidi   3
"The Odyssey of Coming to America," Rameen Javid Moshref   116
"Exile, or My Father's Elbow," Sahar Muradi   21
"Of My Mother," Sahar Muradi   19
"Family Album," Zohra Saed   28
"My Mother," Khalida Sethi   113
"Daughter of the Imam: From Kandahar to Queens," Afifa Yusufi   181

POST–9/11

"An Afghan American Perspective," Farhad Ahad   196
"Notes on the Disappeared," Mariam Ghani   10
"The Enemy," Nadia Maiwandi   128
"A Week Later," Zohra Saed   135

RETURN

"Dreaming in Dari," Mir Tamim Ansary   43
"Like a Rabbit Caught in the Spotlight," Nushin Arbabzadah   70
"You Proved Me Wrong," Awista Ayub   201
"A Penny," Ariana Delawari   154
"Dispatch from Kabul," Masood Kamandy   209
"Time Passes in Colorado," Masood Kamandy   7
"Afghan Awakening," Halima Kazem   165
"Journey to Afghanistan, Septemember 2002," Tareq Mirza   145
"Home," Aman Mojadidi   93
"What Can One Say about Living in Kabul?" Aman Mojadidi   36
"Who the Hell is the Foreigner?!" Rameen Javid Moshref   121
"Voting in Afghanistan," Homira Nassery   161
"Gazelle Speaks," Gazelle Samizay   234

WAR

"The Irony of Life and the Survival of the American Dream,"
    Asadulla Abubakr   106
"My Earliest Memories," Wajma Ahmady   73
"Like a Rabbit Caught in the Spotlight," Nushin Arbabzadah   70
"Demystified Calamity," Qais Arsala   17
"Horns of the Tiger," Qais Arsala   17
"Placebo," Qais Arsala   18
"You Proved Me Wrong," Awista Ayub   201
"The Girl with the Green Eyes," Yasmine Delawari Johnson   103
"The Critic," Mariam Ebrat   190
"Pick Me, Please!" Nahid Fattahi   13
"Aya," Donia Gobar   59
"Dispatch from Kabul," Masood Kamandy   209
"What Can One Say about Living in Kabul?" Aman Mojadidi   36
"The Odyssey of Coming to America," Rameen Javid Moshref   116
"Who the Hell is the Foreigner?!" Rameen Javid Moshref   121
"Family Album," Zohra Saed   29

WOMEN'S VOICES

"My Earliest Memories," Wajma Ahmady   73
"What? You Never . . . ," Wajma Ahmady   39

"age three at grandpa's funeral," Jessamyn Ansary   15
"The Invention," Jessamyn Ansary   16
"Like a Rabbit Caught in the Spotlight," Nushin Arbabzadah   70
"My Thoughts . . . If You Don't Mind," Yalda Asmatey   34
"You Proved Me Wrong," Awista Ayub   201
"Cheshme Siah Daree," Ariana Delawari   26
"Oh la Lo," Ariana Delawari   25
"A Penny," Ariana Delawari   154
"The Girl with the Green Eyes," Yasmine Delawari Johnson   103
"The Critic," Mariam Ebrat   190
"Awaiting My Return," Naheed Elyasi   32
"Living on a Prayer," Naheed Elyasi   66
"Pick Me, Please!" Nahid Fattahi   13
"As I Watch," Donia Gobar   9
"Aya," Donia Gobar   59
"Afghan Awakening," Halima Kazem   165
"The Enemy," Nadia Maiwandi   128
"Exile, or My Father's Elbow," Sahar Muradi   21
"Of My Mother," Sahar Muradi   19
"The Things They Wait For," Sahar Muradi   125
"Voting in Afghanistan," Homira Nassery   161
"Family Album," Zohra Saed   29
"Neptune Avenue," Zohra Saed   28
"A Week Later," Zohra Saed   135
"The Cab Driver's Daughter," Waheeda Samady   171
"Gazelle Speaks," Gazelle Samizay   234
"Astagfurillah (God Forbid!)" Khalida Sethi   23
"My Mother," Khalida Sethi   113
"Daughter of the Imam: From Kandahar to Queens," Afifa Yusufi   181
"Coming to America, 1966," Maliha Zulfacar   85

Chronology of Afghan American History

1916   Aurang Shah and Daulat Khan, two cousins, slip onto a freight ship at Karachi, British India (now Pakistan), and come to Seattle. A chili company, perhaps Hormel, buys their chili, most likely a *lubia qorma* recipe. These two pioneer Afghans in America are the father and uncle of the famous dance choreographer Robert Joffrey.

1919   Anglo-Afghan War: Afghanistan gains independence from England. Amanullah Khan, known as the modernizing king, reforms Afghanistan.

1925   Mirza Beg smuggles himself onto a freight ship in Karachi. At nineteen years old, he finds himself in Boston, where he marries an Italian woman. Their granddaughters Yasmin Delawari Johnson and Ariana Delawari are contributors to this collection. Mirza Beg's story is documented in "A Penny."

1928   Feroz Din, an immigrant from Afghanistan, petitions for U.S. citizenship. He is denied U.S. citizenship because he is not Caucasian. Under the 1917 Asiatic Barred Zone Act and the 1924 Immigration Act, immigrants from Asia are not allowed to become American citizens.

1928   Robert Joffrey, founder of the Joffrey Ballet, is born on December 24 to an Afghan father, Daulat Khan, later renamed Joseph Joffrey, and an Italian mother. He is born Anver Bey Abdullah Jaffa Khan.

1929   Amanullah Khan is overthrown for attempting to Westernize Afghanistan too quickly. Turmoil in Afghanistan brings on a bandit king, Habibullah Kalakani, who is also overthrown by Nadir Khan. Nadir Khan becomes king and reverses all of Amanullah Khan's reforms.

1932   Wahdat Shah Khan, born in Jalalabad, Afghanistan, is approved for a five-year visa granted by the U.S. Labor Department. This brown-haired, blue-eyed young man landed in New York City and was on his way to Cornell University. He is the first Afghan student on record in the United States. There is

	no record of whether he remained in the United States or returned.

1933 Nadir Khan is assassinated. His son Zahir Shah becomes king of Afghanistan at a young age. His era is marked as the Golden Age of Afghanistan.

1934 Amanuddin Ansary, along with four other Afghans, receives a scholarship from the king to study in the United States. After earning his undergraduate and graduate degrees, he marries a Finnish woman in 1944 and returns to Afghanistan to work at Kabul University. His son is the renowned Afghan American writer Mir Tamim Ansary.

1941 Ataullah Ozai Durrani comes to the United States to study. He invents a method with which rice can be cooked in a minute. General Mills buys the patent and calls it "Minute Rice." Durrani becomes a millionaire and settles in Colorado.

1952–59 The Immigration Nationality Act allows more immigrants from Asia. Immigrants from Asia are also allowed to own property. Seventy-eight Afghans become naturalized U.S. citizens.

1960 Three hundred Afghan students come to study in the United States with government scholarships.

1963 Mary Aziz, the first Afghan woman to study abroad on scholarship, begins her studies in economics at Bryn Mawr College. She ends up settling in Virginia.

196 Ataullah Ozai Durrani, the inventor of Minute Rice, passes away in Colorado, alone. Durrani donates half of his estate to Harvard University to develop an institute to study the works of Mughal poets. The university creates the Indo-Muslim Culture Program with the funds. The first works translated into English are the poems of Ghalib.

1966 Maliha Zulfacar becomes the second Afghan woman to study abroad on scholarship. She attends Western College in Oxford, Ohio, for her bachelor's degree and also completes her master's degree in the United States. She is the only Afghan female student to return to Afghanistan in 1973 to teach at Kabul University.

1973 A bloodless coup removes Zahir Shah. Mohammad Daoud Khan proclaims Afghanistan a republic and declares himself president.

1970–77 Three hundred Afghans become naturalized U.S. citizens. After 1973, 110 Afghans become permanent residents.

1978 The Communist revolution overthrows President Daoud Khan on April 27. Thousands are massacred for being royalists.

1979 The U.S. ambassador to Afghanistan, Adolph Dubbs, is killed in a botched kidnapping orchestrated by Afghan Maoists.

On December 25, the Soviet Union invades Afghanistan. Thousands of Afghans flee the country. This invasion creates the largest wave of Afghans to the United States.

1983 The United States becomes openly involved in supporting the mujahideen, the nationalist Freedom Fighters.

1985 President Ronald Reagan designates March 21 as National Afghanistan Day in the United States to commemorate the Afghan "Champions of the Free World."

1989 The Soviets are defeated and withdraw in December.

Two to four thousand Afghan refugees enter the United States this year. Afghan families are airlifted from villages. These families settle in New York, New Jersey, Connecticut, Virginia, Texas, and California. The U.S. Census (1989) reports that seventy-five thousand Afghan refugees have settled here.

1990–92 Even though the Soviets have withdrawn from Afghanistan, it is still under the Communist government of President Najibullah. Many Afghans in the United States cannot return; thousands take up U.S. citizenship.

1992–94 The Islamic Government of Afghanistan is established under President Burhanuddin Rabbani.

1994–96 A civil war rages in Kabul, with different mujahideen factions fighting for power. Kabul, once known as the Paris of Asia, is completely destroyed.

1996 The Taliban takes advantage of the civil war and takes over Kabul, then the rest of the country. It gains control of 95 percent of the country. The last anti-Taliban stronghold is under the leadership of Commander Ahmad Shah Masood.

Farooka Gauhari, a biologist at the University of Nebraska, publishes the first memoir by an Afghan woman in English: *Searching for Saleem: An Afghan Woman's Odyssey*, published by the University of Nebraska Press.

1997   Afghan American youth begin self-publishing their own publications to build community and discuss their identity as Afghans in America. *The Afghan Communicator*'s (New York) editorial board includes Rameen Javied Moshref, Jawied Nawabi, Abdulwahid Azizi, Shaima Ramin, and Zohra Saed; *Lemar-Aftaab: Online Afghan Journal*'s (California) editor is Farhad Azad; and *Afghan Mosaic*'s (Pennsylvania) editorial board includes Fareda Ahmadi, Fareshta Ahmadi, and Katrin Fakiri.

1999   The first national Inter Afghan Young Professional Summit (IAYPS) is held in Flushing, New York (August 14–15), hosted by the *Afghan Communicator*. The IAYPS is held from 1999 through 2006 in various states across the United States, hosted by organizations such as the Society of Afghan Professionals (SAP/California), Afghan Canadian Professionals of Ontario (ACPO), the Afghan Canadian Youth Organization (ACYO), and the American Society of Afghan Professionals (ASAP/DC).

Afghans 4 Tomorrow (A4T), an Afghan American professional organization geared toward rebuilding Afghanistan, is established by Najib Mojadidi.

2000   The Society of Afghan Professionals (SAP) is established in the San Francisco Bay Area. Katrin Fakir is the cofounder and president of this organization until 2003. This inspires the establishment of other chapters of the Society of Afghan Professionals in Virginia, Texas, Chicago, and New York.

2001   On September 9, Commander Ahmad Shah Masood is assassinated in a suicide bombing.

On September 11, the World Trade Center and the Pentagon are attacked by members of Al Qaeda headquartered in Afghanistan.

On October 3, the Afghan American filmmaker Jawed Wassel is murdered in Long Island City by his American producer,

Nathan Chandler Powell, over a financial dispute over the film *Firedancer.* The very morning of his death, the *New York Times* runs an article announcing the genius of this new Afghan American filmmaker.

On October 7, the U.S. military launches war in Afghanistan, under the moniker "Operation Enduring Freedom."

On December 22, the Taliban are defeated, and a new interim government is sworn in under the leadership of Hamid Karzai.

2002   In January, the U.S.-Afghanistan Reconstruction Council (US-ARC) is established in Virginia by Dr. Abdullah Sherzai, Omar Hadi, and a group of Afghan American professionals. This organization connects Afghan American professionals with reconstruction projects in Afghanistan.

In April, Mir Tamim Ansary publishes his memoir of growing up in Afghanistan and the United States in *West of Kabul, East of New York* (Farrar, Straus and Giroux). Ansary's email sent out on September 12, 2001, reached millions of readers and sparked interest in the life of this Afghan-Finnish-American writer.

In Afghanistan, Hamid Karzai is elected by the Loya Jirga (Traditonal Parliament) as the president of Afghanistan.

In September, *Firedancer,* the first Afghan American film directed by slain filmmaker Jawed Wassel, premieres at the Ghazi Stadium in Kabul. Veda Zaher Khadem, Wassel's directorial associate, stepped up to complete the editing of the film.

2003   *The Kite Runner,* by Khaled Hosseini (Riverhead Books), is published in January. It is the first work of fiction by an Afghan American. It becomes an immediate commercial success and is the most widely read book written by an Afghan, besides Rumi.

On February 24, the Mines and Industry minister, Juma Mohammad Mohammadi, the advisor Ahmed Rateb Olumi, and the Foreign Ministry's acting economic director, Farhad Ahad, also the founder of the Afghan American organization Afghan Solidarity, are killed along with four others in a suspicious crash off the coast of Karachi, Pakistan. These Afghan Americans had returned to Afghanistan to serve in the reconstruction and work on the Trans-Afghan Gas Pipeline Project.

Torn between Two Cultures: An Afghan American Woman Speaks Out, by Maryam Qudrat Aseel (Capital Books), is published in May.

Firedancer, a film by Jawed Wassel (completed by Veda Zahir Khadem), premiers in New York at the Tribeca Film Festival.

2004   First democratic presidential elections: Hamid Karzai wins.

Zalmai Khalilzad, an Afghan American, becomes the U.S. ambassador to Afghanistan.

2005   *Comeback to Afghanistan: A California Teenager's Story,* by Said Hyder Akbar and Susan Burton (Bloomsbury Publishing), is published after a successful show based on Akbar's return to Afghanistan and recordings for public radio's *This American Life.*

The Afghan government begins the destruction of poppy fields. Meanwhile, there is a resurgence of the Taliban.

Masood Kamandy establishes the Department of Photography at Kabul University.

2006   *My War at Home,* a memoir by Afghan American Masuda Sultan, is published (Washington Square Press). The memoir documents her conservative childhood in Queens and her later activism for women's rights.

2007   *The Kite Runner,* directed by Michael Forster, is released. The movie is based on the bestselling novel by Khaled Hosseini.

2008   *Snapshots: This Afghan American Life,* edited by Mir Tamim Ansary and Yalda Asmatey (Kajakai Press), is released. It is the first collection of writings by Afghan Americans in California.

2009   In August's Afghan presidential election, Hamid Karzai wins the vote. However, his opponent, Abdullah Abdullah, accuses Karzai of electoral fraud. A second runoff election between Karzai and Abdullah is announced, but Abdulla walks off. Karzai is declared president for another five-year term.

However Tall the Mountain: A Dream, Eight Girls and a Journey Home, by Awista Ayub (Hyperion), is published, a book based on the author's experience of starting the first girls' soccer team in Kabul.

In December, President Barack Obama announces that thirty thousand more troops will be sent into Afghanistan.

WORKS CITED

Anawalt, Sasha. *The Joffrey Ballet: Robert Joffrey and the Making of an American Dance Company.* Chicago: University of Chicago Press, 1997.

Ansary, Mir Tamim. *West of Kabul, East of New York: An Afghan American Story.* New York: Farrar Straus and Giroux, 2002.

Azad Pakhtunistan Association of America. "Pakhtunistan Day." Pamphlet. Sacramento, California: 9th of Sunbola, 1328 A.H. (1949).

Champagne, David. "Afghan Americans." In *Harvard Encyclopedia of American Ethnic Groups,* ed. Stephen Thernstrom. Cambridge: Friends and President of Harvard College, 1990.

Eigo, Tim. "Afghan Americans." In *Gale Encyclopedia of Multicultural America,* 2nd ed., ed. Jeffrey Lehman. Detroit. Gale, 2000.

Embassy of Afghanistan. "Planting Afghan Sahebi Grapes in Napa Valley." April 17, 2006. http://www.embassyofafghanistan.org/04.17ambjawadcopiaevent.html.

Encyclopaedia Iranica. "Ataullah Ozai Durrani." http://www.iranica.com/articles/ozai-durrani.

Poullada, Leon B., and D. J. Leila. *The Kingdom of Afghanistan and the United States 1828–1973.* Center for Afghanistan Studies/Dageforde Publishing, 1995.

Saed, Zohra. "Afghan American Filmmaker Leaves Eloquent Legacy." *New America Media,* February 11, 2003.

Index of Authors and Titles

Abubakr, Asadulla	106
"An Afghan American Perspective"	196
"Afghan Awakening"	165
"age three at grandpa's funeral"	15
Ahad, Farhad	196
Ahmady, Wajma	39, 73
Ansary, Jessamyn	15
Ansary, Mir Tamim	43
Anwar, Fahim	140
Arbabzadah, Nushin	70
Arsala, Qais	17
"As I Watch"	9
Asmatey, Yalda	34
"Astagfurillah (God Forbid!)"	23
"Awaiting My Return"	32
"Aya"	59
Ayub, Awista	201
Azad, Farhad	54
"The Broken Window"	54
"The Cab Driver's Daughter"	171
"Cheshme Siah Daree"	26
"Coming to America, 1966"	85
"The Critic"	190
"Daughter of the Imam: From Kandahar to Queens"	181
Delawari, Ariana	25, 154
Delawari Johnson, Yasmine	103
"Demystified Calamity"	17
"Dispatches from Kabul"	209
"Dreaming in Dari"	43
Ebrat, Mariam	190
Elyasi, Naheed	32, 66
"The Enemy"	128
"Exile, or My Father's Elbow"	21
"Family Album"	29
Fattahi, Nahid	13
"Gazelle Speaks"	234

Ghani, Mariam   10
"The Girl with the Green Eyes"   103
Gobar, Donia   9, 59
"Home"   93
"Hope Street"   174
"Horns of the Tiger"   17
"Identity Card"   50
"The Invention"   16
Iqbal, Bismillah   174
"The Irony of Life and the Survival of the American Dream"   106
"Journey to Afghanistan, September 2002"   145
Kamandy, Masood   7, 209
Kazem, Halima   165
"Like a Rabbit Caught in the Spotlight"   70
"Living on a Prayer"   66
Maiwandi, Nadia   128
"Marriage to Azim"   3
"Memories from Kabul's Playing Fields"   197
Mirza, Tareq   145
Mojadidi, Aman   36, 93
Mojadidi, Sedika   3
Moshref, Rameen Javid   116
Muradi, Sahar   19, 125
"My Earliest Memories"   73
"My Mother"   113
"My Thoughts . . . If You Don't Mind"   34
Nassery, Homira   161
"Neptune Avenue"   28
"Notes on the Disappeared"   10
"The Odyssey of Coming to America"   116
"Of My Mother"   19
"Oh la Lo"   25
"An Old Garden"   56
"A Penny"   154
"Pick Me, Please!"   13
"Placebo"   18
Saed, Zohra   28, 135
Samady, Waheeda   171
Samizay, Gazelle   234

Sethi, Khalida	23, 113
Shaaker, Wali	50
"Stand-Up Comedy"	140
"The Things They Wait For"	125
"Time Passes in Colorado"	7
"Voting in Afghanistan"	161
"A Week Later"	135
"What Can One Say about Living in Kabul?"	36
"What? You Never . . ."	39
"Who the Hell is the Foreigner?!"	121
"You Proved Me Wrong"	201
Yusufi, Afifa	181
Zulfacar, Maliha	85

Contributors

Asadulla Abubakr is a physician and part-time chemistry lecturer at California State University, East Bay. He was born in Kabul, Afghanistan, in 1969. He moved to the United States on May 3, 1980. He attended the University of California, Davis, where he earned a B.S. in biochemistry in 1991. Continuing upon his path of acquiring knowledge, he earned a master's degree in chemistry from California State University in 1992. Determining that he had found his passion, he became a student of medicine at St. George's University School of Medicine, where he completed his education in 1996. In 1998 he completed his first year of residency at New York Hospital Queens; in August 2000 he completed the rest of his residency at Kern Medical Center in Bakersfield, California. From 2000 to 2008, he worked as a senior physician in the Department of Medicine at the Permanente Medical Group in Union City, California, where he still works part-time. In 2009, he published his first book, entitled *Islam vs. West: Fact or Fiction?* In 2008, he joined Student Health Services of California State University, East Bay.

Farhad Ahad (1970–2003) was born in Kabul. His family migrated to the United States on December 4, 1986, and settled in Flushing, Queens. Ahad left New York to attend the University of Massachusetts at Amherst and graduated with a B.S. in mechanical engineering in 1993. A year later he received his master's degree in mechanical engineering, and in 1999, he earned his M.B.A. from the Kenan-Flagler Business School at the University of North Carolina. On June 4, 2001, Ahad founded an Afghan expatriate organization called Afghan Solidarity. After September 11, 2001, he became a prominent spokesperson for young Afghan Americans, consistently vocal about issues in support of the Afghan people and their cause. In July 2002, Ahad was appointed director of business and economic affairs for the Afghan Ministry of Foreign Affairs. After delivering a superb speech at the World Bank meetings in Washington, D.C., in February 2003, Ahad left for Pakistan to participate in talks concerning a proposed pipeline. Afterward, he and the rest of the Afghan delegation chartered a Cessna plane to visit a copper field in Baluchistan, but their plane, under suspicious circumstances, crashed into the Arabian Sea upon takeoff from

Karachi Airport. His positive spirit, call to action, and boundless hope for his country serve as inspiration for all Afghans. He worked endlessly on behalf of Afghanistan, fighting his war through scholarly and critical writings, activism, and ceaseless service. In his short life on this earth, he touched the lives of many. His legacy and memories will live on.

Wajma Ahmady, a native of Afghanistan, was raised in Germany and the United States. She has studied comparative literature and creative writing at the University of California, San Diego (UCSD), and the New School. In her spare time, she enjoys reading novels by Jane Austen and spending time with her nieces.

Jessamyn Ansary is a writer living in New York City. Her work has been published in the *Subway Chronicles* and *Improvisation News* and produced by Nick Entertainment, Everest Productions, and Magical Elves, Inc., among others. She evaluates screenplays for NYC Midnight and also works in film and television production.

Mir Tamim Ansary, an Afghan American writer, lecturer, and teacher, directs the San Francisco Writer's Workshop; teaches sporadically at the Osher Institute of Lifelong Learning; and writes fiction and nonfiction about Afghanistan, Islam and the West, democracy, education, current events, social issues, and other topics as they occur to him. Ansary is the author of *West of Kabul, East of New York* (2002) and *Destiny Disrupted: A History of the World through Islamic Eyes* (2009).

Fahim Anwar started his comedy career in Seattle shortly after graduating from high school, when he began performing stand-up. Anwar is now a regular on the LA comedy circuit, doing spots at the Improv, the Laugh Factory, the Comedy Union, the Ice House, and the Comedy Store, among others. Fahim was recently a finalist in NBC-Universal's Standup for Diversity showcase, where he was chosen to perform on the NBC stage at the annual convention of the National Association of Campus Activities in February 2010. Anwar also made his television debut in February 2010, with a guest-starring role on NBC's *Chuck*. He's also a regular on MTV's *Disaster Date* and recently filmed a small role on Showtime's *Californication*. Anwar can also be seen on Comedy Central's *Russell Simmons Presents: Stand Up from the El Rey Theatre*. Anwar also writes and stars in his own series of short Internet videos, and the viral video gods smiled upon him with the success of "Afghan Wedding," which amassed over half a million views on YouTube and was featured on Break.com and Digg.com. His YouTube channel videos have now been viewed over a million times.

Nushin Arbabzadah is an Afghan author, journalist, analyst, and translator. Arbabzadah grew up in Afghanistan during the Soviet occupation before fleeing to Germany with her family. She completed high school in Germany, later concentrating on European languages and Middle Eastern studies. She has earned graduate degrees from Hamburg University and Cambridge University, where she was a William H. Gates Scholar. She is currently a visiting scholar at the Center for India and South Asia at the University of California, Los Angeles (UCLA). Arbabzadah has worked for the British Council, running literary and journalistic projects on intercultural communication, with a focus on dialogue with the Muslim world. In 2005, she joined the BBC, where she specialized in media, politics, and society in contemporary Afghanistan. Her first book, *From Outside In: Refugees and British Society,* was published in London by Arcadia in 2007. Arbabzadah has also edited an anthology of writings by young journalists of different religious backgrounds living in Muslim-majority countries. Entitled *No Ordinary Life: Being Young in the Worlds of Islam,* it was published by the British Council in 2007. Her first literary translation is of the memoir of an imprisoned Iranian journalist, Houshang Assadie. Provisionally entitled *Letters to My Torturer,* it is due to be published in June 2010 by OneWorld. She has also edited a collection of short stories by the celebrated Iranian writer Sadeq Hedayat. Arbabzadah also regularly writes on contemporary Afghanistan for the *Guardian* online.

Qais Arsala was born in Kabul and immigrated to the United States (California) in 1984. He graduated from California State University with a degree in anthropology and currently resides in Northern California with his wife and three kids. His days are filled with dad daycare/diapers/milk/kindergarten, as the three-foot crumb snatchers are keeping him extremely occupied.

Yalda Asmatey was born in Kabul and raised in California. She is currently working on her doctorate degree in anthropology. She is the coeditor of the anthology *Snapshots: This Afghan-American Life.*

Awista Ayub was born in Afghanistan and immigrated to the United States in 1981. Ayub received her B.S. in chemistry from the University of Rochester in New York and her M.P.A. from the University of Delaware. She founded the Afghan Youth Sports Exchange in 2003, and from February 2005 to January 2007, she served as the education and health officer at the Afghan embassy in Washington, D.C. Ayub has been featured in a number of national news publications and programs, including ABC News (Person of the Week), ESPN, *Glamour Magazine* (Hero of the Month), *CNN American Morning,* the *New York Daily News,* Sports Illustrated.com, the *San Francisco Chronicle,* the *Washingtonian,* and *USA Today.* Ayub is the author of *However Tall the Mountain: A Dream, Eight Girls and a Journey Home.*

Farhad Azad, born in Kabul in 1976, moved with his family to the United States in 1983. In 1997, Azad established the first progressive online Afghan digest, afghanmagazine.com, to bring awareness to the arts and culture of Afghanistan. Along with the online magazine, he promotes the work of Afghan artists, writers, and musicians. From 2000 through 2004, Azad chaired the Art and Humanities Committee for the Society of Afghan Professionals, based in the San Francisco Bay Area. In 2002, he led the organization's first Art and Culture Trip from the United States to Afghanistan.

Ariana Delawari is a multimedia artist—a musician, actress, photographer, and filmmaker. Delawari has been traveling to Afghanistan since 2002, when her parents moved there to be part of the reconstruction of the country, making her first trip to Kabul after graduating from the University of Southern California (USC) School of Cinematic Arts. As a musician, she most recently worked with filmmaker/artist David Lynch on her debut album, *Lion of Panjshir.* Her debut album was partially recorded in Afghanistan with three Afghan elder master musicians (or Ustads) and was finished in Los Angeles with several guest musicians. Lynch produced a few tracks on the album and released it on his own music label.

Yasmine Delawari Johnson is an Afghan American actor who earned her political science degree at UCLA and then attended New York's Circle in the Square Drama School. Some of Delawari Johnson's television and film credits include *Backyards & Bullets, NUMB3RS, The*

Shield, The E-Ring (with Benjamin Bratt and Dennis Hopper), *American Family* (starring Edward James Olmos), *The Ode,* and *Mr. Brooks* (starring Kevin Costner and William Hurt). She lives in Los Angeles with her husband, Matt, and her three children, Kailey, Nicolas, and Maverick.

Mariam Ebrat Lives in Fremont, California. She graduated from San Francisco State University with a B.A. in social science. Currently she is a candidate for an M.A. in communication studies at California State University, East Bay. Mariam enjoys spending time with her huge family, cooking, reading, analyzing classic literature, and, of course, writing. She hopes to write and publish many more critical exegeses. Her work was published in *Snapshots: This Afghan American Life.*

Naheed Elyasi fled Afghanistan in 1982, three years after the Soviet invasion. Her family walked across the mountains into Pakistan, where they lived for one year before being accepted as refugees to the United States. Elyasi grew up in North Carolina, where she studied communications and public relations. After completing her degree at East Carolina University, she moved to Atlanta, where she studied fashion design. Her love for fashion brought her in 1999 to New York, where she worked as an assistant designer at Maggy London and in the production department at Marc Jacobs. She eventually left fashion to pursue a career in the nonprofit sector, joining School of Hope, an organization that raised funds for schools in Afghanistan. Elyasi is currently the director of communications at the Council for Economic Education and a contributing writer for *Zeba Magazine.*

Nahid Fattahi, born in Herat, Afghanistan, in November 1980, now lives in Fremont, California, with her husband and two kids. She has been writing poetry and short stories since childhood. She used to write in Farsi, but she has been writing in English in recent years. She is working on her bachelor's degree in Middle Eastern studies. Literature has always been a big part of her life.

Mariam Ghani is a Brooklyn-based artist whose work explores the private and public narratives that construct and reconstruct histories, places, identities, and communities. Her texts, videos, installations, and public and interactive projects have been presented and published internationally, and she has been awarded fellowships and residencies by the New York Foundation for the Arts, the Lower Manhattan Cultural Council, ETC, Soros, Eyebeam, Smack Mellon, and Schloss Solitude. Since 2004, she has collaborated with Chitra Ganesh on the project Index of the Disappeared, which is both a physical archive of post–9/11 disappearances—detentions, deportations, renditions, redactions—and a mobile platform for public dialogue on related issues and ideas. Ghani has a B.A. in comparative literature from New York University (NYU) and an M.F.A. from the School of Visual Arts. She teaches at Parsons, NYU, and Cooper Union.

Donia Gobar is the daughter of Salia Gobar and Mir Gholam Mohamad Gobar, one of Afghanistan's most distinguished scholars and the author of *Afghanistan in the Course of History*. Donia Gobar is a physician, educator, poet, artist, and international speaker. She is the author of *The Invisibles* and, among other published works, the short story "Aya." Her work has been published in *Speaking for Myself: Asian Women's Literature*. She is also the author of "Women the Human Beings vs. Women the Victims," presented at International Women's Day in Stockholm, Sweden.

Bismillah Iqbal and his family moved to America right after the Soviet invasion. They lived on the East Coast for ten years where they rarely had any connection to culture or community. In 1991 they moved to the San Francisco Bay Area to find a welcoming and thriving Afghan community. There he attended the Academy of Art University in San Francisco. His work was published in *Snapshots: This Afghan American Life*.

Masood Kamandy is an image maker and an aspiring sufi who splits his time between Brooklyn and Khorasan. He is currently studying the relationship between word and image through a collaborative series of photographs, videos, and found objects on his Web site, wordsbecomeimages.com.

Halima Kazem is a researcher and journalist with more than eight years of experience working in Afghanistan and the surrounding region. Kazem has worked as a human rights researcher for Amnesty International and Human Rights Watch. Her journalistic work has appeared in the *Los Angeles Times,* the *Christian Science Monitor,* and the *San Francisco Chronicle.* She has taught journalism and media courses for the Institute of War and Peace Reporting and the World Bank. Kazem is a coauthor of the Afghanistan National Human Development Report for the United Nations Development Program and a coproducer of *Frontrunner,* a documentary that follows the campaign of the first woman to run for president in Afghanistan.

Nadia Maiwandi is an Afghan American writer, editor, and activist whose work has been published in *Willamette Week,* the *Oregonian, Newsday,* and the anthologies *Another World Is Possible* and *Shattering Stereotypes: Muslim Women Speak Out,* among others. Maiwandi traveled to Afghanistan in 2003 and 2006 with a nonprofit organization, and her Afghanistan photos have been publicly exhibited in Southern California. She currently lives in San Jose, California. Contact Nadia Maiwandi at afghanactivism@yahoo.com.

Tareq Mirza has been creating since his parents bought him his first Legos set at the age of three. For hours each day throughout his child-hood, he would build whatever came to his mind and create a story to go with it. Legos were eventually replaced by comic books and a desire to create his own characters and content. He received his B.F.A. from George Mason University in studio art and computer graphics and went on to work in the visual effects industry. After several years in Los Angeles, working on television effects and animation, Mirza relocated to the San Francisco Bay Area to work on *Star Wars: Attack of the Clones* for Industrial Light & Magic. His other credits include *Matrix Reloaded, Matrix Revolutions, Pirates of the Caribbean,* and *Van Helsing.* In recent years Mirza has turned his attention back to his original passion for drawing and writing, and he currently attends the San Francisco Writers Workshop. His first essay was published in the anthology *Snapshots: This Afghan-American Life.*

Aman Mojadidi has studied and trained in cultural anthropology, with a B.A.-Honors degree focused on Third World development issues and an M.A.-Honors degree emphasizing Central Asia and Afghanistan, conflict, and the cultural politics of identity. As a writer and visual artist, Mojadidi creates work concentrated on the human experience as understood through interactions and confrontations, both internal and external, with personal, social, political, and cultural conflict. Through and across his different works run threads of cultural tradition (real, imagined, invented), identity, politics, diasporas, humanitarianism, war, and reconstruction, all weaving reflections, often contradictory, of humanity—a humanity that finds itself in a postmodern world that is simultaneously globalizing and fracturing, forcing us to confront each other and ourselves in ways we have yet to understand. Mojadidi is currently the director of culture and heritage at Turquoise Mountain, a nongovernmental organization dedicated to the promotion and development of arts and culture in Afghanistan.

Sedika Mojadidi is a documentary filmmaker who has produced both independent films and television projects. Her film work includes two experimental documentary shorts on Afghanistan, *Kabul, Kabul* and *Zulaikha,* both distributed by Third World Newsreel. Her feature-length documentary, *Motherland Afghanistan,* about her father's struggle to make a difference as an ob-gyn working in Afghanistan, aired as part of the Independent Lens Documentary Series and screened at the American Film Institute's film festival. The United Nations Populations Fund (UNFPA) hosted national screenings of *Motherland Afghanistan* to raise awareness about the maternal fistulas health crisis in Afghanistan and globally. Mojadidi has lectured extensively throughout the country on issues of Afghan identity, maternal health, and filming in Afghanistan. Currently, she is a supervising producer for ABC News on a medical series in the long-form documentary unit (*Boston Med*).

Rameen Moshref is an activist and expert on Afghanistan who earned his M.S. degree in Near Eastern studies from New York University, also spending a year at Princeton University. Moshref has published numerous pieces in books, magazines, newspapers, television, and radio on Afghanistan, Islam, and Afghan communities. Having witnessed the harsh realities of Afghanistan, Moshref now seeks to raise awareness about the true condition of Afghans and Afghanistan. He has been an active member of the Afghan community in North America since 1991 and has devoted his career to Afghanistan. In 1997 he founded Afghan Communicator, one of the most active Afghan organizations in North America from 2002 through 2007. In 2002 Moshref was honored with the prestigious Union Square Award as an Emerging Immigrant Leader by Funds for the City of New York. Having accomplished a great deal in the Afghan community in the United States, Moshref eventually felt the need to bring his knowledge and experience to Afghanistan, returning there in 2007 to help in the reconstruction and healing process. After working with the Afghan government and other international organizations, Moshref is now managing an independent consulting company. He is most proud of having established an arts and crafts gallery, the second largest in Afghanistan after the National Gallery. The gallery employs and supports hundreds of artists and craftsmen and - women to develop Afghan-inspired designs and products for domestic and foreign markets.

Sahar Muradi was born in Kabul and raised in New York and Florida. She received her M.P.A. in international development from New York University and her B.A. in literature from Hampshire College. She is cofounder of the Association of Afghan American Writers.

Homira Nassery was born in Kabul in 1961. She was five years old when her family immigrated to the United States, where she acquired a B.S. in biology and chemistry and a master's degree in international development. Nassery won the Myra E. Barrer Award for Journalism in 1992 for "The Forgotten Population of Refugees: Afghan Women and Children" and was one of the authors of Afghanistan's first National Human Development Report. Author of "The Reverse Brain Drain: The Role of the Afghan-American Diaspora in Post-Conflict Reconstruction and Peace-Building," she has a keen interest in diaspora contributions to postconflict states. Recently returned from a four-year leave of absence from the World Bank to live in Afghanistan—where she worked in all regions of the country for Save the Children/U.S., UNDP, NATO, the Government of Afghanistan, and Chemonics/USAID—she is currently the health, nutrition, and population coordinator for Fragile States, most recently in Southern Sudan. Her last year in Afghanistan was spent living and working in Lashkargah for the Alternative Livelihoods Project South (ALP/S), covering the three provinces of Helmand, Kandahar, and Uruzgan. This role provided broad exposure to the constraints of working in an active combat zone and the relationships between civilian and military reconstruction activities. In the ten years that she worked for the World Bank prior to moving to Afghanistan, she worked on postconflict situations, specifically in Rwanda, Eritrea, Mozambique, and Sri Lanka.

Zohra Saed was born in Jalalabad and raised in Brooklyn. She received her M.F.A. in poetry at Brooklyn College. She is a doctoral candidate in English literature at the City University of New York Graduate Center. She is cofounder of the Association of Afghan American Writers.

Waheeda Samady was born in Kabul but escaped the country with her family during the height of the Afghan-Soviet war. Her family lived in a refugee community in Islamabad, Pakistan, for several years before eventually resettling in San Diego, California, where she was raised. She completed her undergraduate degree at the University of California, Berkeley, where she majored in international area studies and molecular and cell biology, and then went on to obtain her medical degree from the UCSD School of Medicine. She is now completing her residency in pediatrics at UCSD, currently working on obesity and family violence prevention projects with the Community Pediatrics Department. She is also an active executive committee member of the San Diego branch of the Council on American Islamic Relations.

Gazelle Samizay is an artist who works predominantly in video and photography. Born in Kabul and now residing in the United States, Samizay creates work that explores the intersection of her Afghan heritage and her American upbringing, touching on both the personal and the sociopolitical. Her photographs and videos have been exhibited across the United States and internationally, in countries including Brazil, Colombia, Indonesia, Pakistan, Peru, and the United Kingdom. In addition to her studio practice, she has taught courses in Afghanistan, Jordan, and the United States. Samizay is a recipient of the Princess Grace Experimental Film Honoraria, the 1885 Graduate Fellowship in Arts and Humanities, and the Northern Trust Enrichment Award, among others. She received her M.F.A. in photography from the University of Arizona.

Khalida Sethi, a graduate student at Widener University, has been writing for as long as she's known how. She lives in Philadelphia with her husband and her daughter.

Afghan American **Wali Shaaker** is a political analyst and poet who earned his M.A. in political science from San Francisco State University. Author of *Democracy's Dilemma: The Challenges to State Legitimacy in Afghanistan* (2009), Shaaker has published numerous analytic essays, poems, and short stories in various English and Dari publications. His first collection of Dari poetry, entitled *Sham e Feraaq,* was published in 1997. To read his Dari poems online, visit Dari-poems.blogspot.com. His professional experience includes teaching American politics at San Francisco State University. As assistant professor at the Defense Language Institute (DLI), he has also taught Dari, as well as courses on Afghan politics, culture, and history. He has served as a political analyst at the Naval Postgraduate School and in 2001 was the president of the Society of Afghan Professionals in California. Having traveled widely, to Iran, Pakistan, and India, Shaaker is fluent in Dari, Pashto, and Urdu. He is currently employed at the RAND Corporation and is writing a novel, *The River Village,* in his spare time.

Afifa Yusufi, born in Kandahar, Afghanistan, came with her family to the United States as an infant, soon after the Russian invasion of Afghanistan. She grew up in Queens, New York, where she graduated from the City University of New York at Queens College. She attended the Columbia University School of Social Work for a year in 2009 and is currently completing her M.S.W. at the University of Albany. In 2002 Yusufi went to Kandahar, working with civil affairs units delivering medicine, food, and clothes to destitute Afghans and linking U.S. medical personnel with women and children in the local villages who desperately needed medical attention. Yusufi also served on the board of Women for Afghan Women (WAW) from 2002 to 2005 and was the initial member of WAW to serve as the chair director of WAW s community outreach work within New York. Yusufi has volunteered countless hours with such organizations, dedicated to humanitarian efforts in both local U.S. communities and Afghanistan. She is also a member of the Business Council for Peace (Bpeace). In 2006, while she was working as a strategic consultant for senior U.S. government officials in Baghdad, Iraq, Yusufi risked her life, traveling into the Red Zone to assess the feasibility of launching Bpeace's work in Iraq, to help Iraqi business women, her work there winning her the Volunteer and Excellence Recognition Award (VERA) in 2006. She is currently serving on the board and as vice president of Ariana Outreach, a nonprofit based in Washington, D.C., and is involved with advocacy work for Afghans in both Afghanistan and the United States.

Maliha Zulfacar is a professor of sociology at California Polytechnic State University and Kabul University.